WITHDRAWN

D1569890

European Union and the EFTA Countries

European Union and the EFTA Countries

Enlargement and Integration

Thomas Pedersen

PINTER
PUBLISHERS
LONDON, NEW YORK

Distributed in the United States and
Canada by St. Martin's Press

Pinter Publishers Ltd.
25 Floral Street, London WC2E 9DS, United Kingdom

First published in 1994

Distributed exclusively in the USA and Canada by St. Martin's Press, Inc., Room 400, 175 Fifth Avenue, New York, NY 10010, USA

British Library Cataloguing in Publication Data

A CIP catalogue record for this book is available from the British Library

ISBN 1 85567 148 4

Library of Congress Cataloging-in-Publication Data

Pedersen, Thomas.
    European union and the EFTA countries : enlargement and integration / Thomas Pedersen.
        p.   cm.
    Includes bibliographical references and index.
    ISBN 1–85567–148–4
    1. European Economic Community.   2. European Free Trade Association.   3. European Economic Area.   4. Europe—Economic integration.   I. Title.
HC241.2.P383   1994
337.1'4—dc20

94–1947
CIP

Typeset by Koinonia Ltd, Manchester
Printed and bound in Great Britain by
Biddles Ltd. Guildford and King's Lynn

Contents

To Ida Sophie and Simon Emil

Foreword

My interest in EC enlargement and the European Community's relations with the EFTA countries dates back to the late 1980s. In 1988 I had the fortune of being able to spend six lively and rewarding months at Chatham House under the inspiring guidance of Dr Helen Wallace, now professor at the University of Sussex. It was Helen Wallace who set me on the track which led to a deepening interest in the many aspects of EC–EFTA relations. This book thus summarizes five years of intermittent work on the subject. Helen Wallace deserves my sincere thanks but is of course absolved from any responsibility for this text. I also want to thank Per Wijkman, Head of the Research Department of the EFTA Secretariat in Geneva and Professor Finn Laursen of the European Institute of Public Administration in Maastricht for many an inspiring text and exposé.

The negotiations between the EC and EFTA are not the easiest to analyse, especially for an academic with no first-hand knowledge of international economic diplomacy. Fortunately, I have been able to rely on generous assistance from a number of officials in the European Commission, the permanent representatives of several member states and, not least, the Danish Ministry of Foreign Affairs. I am grateful that these persons – none mentioned, none forgotten – were willing to set aside precious time for interviews. Without this access to practitioners, this analysis would have been even more detached from reality.

I also want to thank the Danish Social Science Research Council for general financial assistance during the period 1990–3 which allowed me to undertake various study trips to relevant capitals. The Council deserves credit for its considerable patience in awaiting the results of its investment. Finally, Ms Riber has been of great help in preparing this text and helping me meet the basic requirements of customer friendliness.

Aarhus, 11 October 1993

1 Introduction

It may well be true as argued by William Wallace that Europe has never had clear boundaries but only shifting core areas (Wallace, 1989, p. 13). Certainly, informal integration follows its own laws: different from those of formal integration. Yet, with the rapid expansion of formal integration since 1986 and the new pressure from 'outsiders', whether through refugees or immigration or through formal applications for membership of the European Union, the question of 'Europe's' borders has acquired a new political saliency.

The European Community has expanded considerably since the mid-1980s. It has witnessed two system transformations involving expansion both in scope and institutional capacity (Pedersen, 1992c). But the Community which has now transformed itself into a Union has also grown in size, its membership having doubled in the course of only 15 years. At the same time a vast European economic system is emerging. Geographical expansion is thus the third and, we would argue, somewhat neglected dimension of the Community's expansion and one that looks set to receive growing attention in the coming years given the long queue of membership candidates. The slowdown in monetary and economic unification may also paradoxically pave the way for more rapid geographical enlargement: partly because some of the economies which come closest to fulfilling the EMU criteria are at present not members of the Union; and partly because leading members of the Union may opt for accelerated enlargement as a *fuite en avant* if the Maastricht Treaty proves difficult to implement.

One aspect of the geographical expansion of the Community is the inclusion of most EFTA countries in the internal market through the negotiation of the European Economic Area (EEA) agreement, creating an extended free-trade area and the preparations for membership of the Union underway in most of these countries. There are at least three reasons why the recent evolution in EC–EFTA relations merits closer attention. First, EC–EFTA relations form part of a global trend towards the formation of regional economic blocs. In North America, NAFTA has been set up as a response to the Community's internal market. The NAFTA agreement, signed by the United States, Canada and Mexico, aims at eliminating within 15 years for some products all tariff and non-tariff barriers (with some exceptions) to the free movement of goods, services and people. In Asia one sees various attempts at regional bloc formation although the level of ambition is lower than in Europe and the United States. More worrying, from a European point of view, America and Asia are threatening to join forces in the newly created Pacific Basin Council. The GATT negotiations may still be rescued, but if they do break down, a new process of economic rearmament between regional blocs is a realistic possibility. Seen from this perspective, it is of some importance that the adhesion of four EFTA countries, Austria, Sweden, Finland and Norway, would add around 10 per cent to the Union's GDP and increase its territory by 53 per cent.

Second, the European Economic Area regime linking the Union to the EFTA area is an interesting example of the flexible method of variable geometry integration which is gaining in importance as organized Europe becomes more heterogeneous (Pedersen, 1993a). What at first sight looks like bureaucratic complexity may, seen from another angle, be regarded as a flexible way of sidestepping the dilemma between marginalization and full integration or as a way of gaining precious time for domestic political adaptation to supranational integration. The EEA arrangement may thus be of direct or indirect relevance to other European states. Third, EC–EFTA relations are important because with several EFTA countries and a number of other European states headed for membership of the Union, its structure and identity will invariably be affected if not in the short- then in the medium-term future. This raises the intricate question of the relationship between the size and the institutional capacity of an integration system, a problem that will become more acute in a 'Continental Union' of between 20 and 30 member states.

EC–EFTA relations are part of a wider *problématique* having to do with the EC's external links. The relationship is part of an extensive and hierarchical network of external links established by the EC over the years. This invites us to study EC–EFTA relations from a comparative negotiation perspective. EC–EFTA relations furthermore constitute an example of the group-to-group approach in the Union's external relations (Regelsberger and Edwards, 1990). The group-to-group approach is essentially a way of economizing with scarce administrative resources, but in many areas of the world it has the additional political objective of fostering stability through regional cooperation. The EFTA countries are not the only European states seeking a closer relationship with the EC. Turkey, Morocco, Malta and Cyprus have all applied for EC membership. Eastern European states have concluded association agreements with the EC as a step on the way to EC membership and initiated a multilateral political dialogue with the Union. And the former Soviet Republics are involved in negotiations with the Union on various kinds of advanced cooperation agreements. The negotiations between the EC and EFTA may thus be seen as an example of EC negotiating behaviour towards European 'peripheral' states – peripheral in the sense that they are not part of Europe's economic core but heavily dependent upon this core.

EC–EFTA relations also reveal some rather unique features. EC–EFTA links have a longer pedigree than EC links with other third countries. What is more, formal links are underpinned by structural similarities between the values and political regimes of the member states in the two groupings and by an exceptionally high degree of economic interconnectedness. The economic map of Europe is thus very different from the political map of Europe and the West European area is clearly a 'Security Community' in which there are stable expectations of peaceful conflict solution (Deutsch, 1957). There are extensive transnational links connecting the two groupings, and the very closeness of the relationship and the prospect of full membership means that developments in the EC–EFTA relationship interact with internal developments in the Union. Unlike in most other third country relations there is thus both an external and an internal 'constitutional' aspect to the European Union's relationship with EFTA and EFTA countries.

The book is divided into three main sections. The first section offers an analysis of the negotiations on a European Economic Area (EEA) – a process which started in 1984 with the so-called 'Luxembourg declaration' signalling a willingness to heal the historical rifts in West European economic cooperation. Given the enormous complexity of the

EEA negotiations, any analysis of the EEA runs the risk of becoming either a technical maze or a superficial survey. The account offered here contains an analysis of the central phases in the EEA talks; an assessment of the EEA Treaty stressing the variable geometry element of the construction; and an attempt to explain the outcome of the negotiations using relevant political science theories.

The second section contains an analysis of the decision of a number of EFTA countries to apply for Union membership. It maps the debate on Union policy in these countries with special emphasis on the period following the finalization of the official EEA negotiations. It also includes a brief survey of public opinion in individual EFTA countries regarding membership of the European Union. The country analyses do not purport to present detailed accounts of the evolution in the EC debate of individual EFTA countries. They merely examine the major turning points in the evolution of elite attitudes which led to the decision to apply for membership of the Union and in each case seek to explain this decision. One of the propositions examined is whether there was some sort of policy linkage between the evolution in the multilateral EEA negotiations and the accelerated preparations for Union membership within the governments of Austria, Sweden, Finland, Norway and Switzerland. As microstates, Iceland and Liechtenstein are left out of this second part of the analysis.

The third and final section of the book deals with the relationship between enlargement and integration, often described in shorthand as the dilemma between widening and deepening. It first surveys the enlargement policy of the Union and the emerging policy debate on institutional responses to the challenge of enlargement. It goes on to examine more systematically the likely effects of enlargement on various dimensions of the EC integration system, focusing on the crucial issue of institutional adaptation.

The first major problem we want to address in the book is how to assess and explain the nature and outcome of the EC–EFTA negotiations. The literature on international negotiations is extensive and the theoretical approaches numerous. William Zartman identifies five approaches: structural analysis; strategic analysis; process analysis; behavioural analysis and integrative analysis (Zartman, 1988; Kremenyuk, 1991). In recent years, there has been a tendency to adopt a pluralistic or combinational approach in concrete analyses of international negotiations which is also the approach adopted here. From a structural perspective, EC–EFTA negotiations can be regarded as a case of asymmetrical negotiations, that is negotiations between parties with unequal power resources. Cases of asymmetrical negotiations raise the interesting question as to why and how the weak part manages to fulfil some of its aspirations. Previous studies of international negotiations between strong and weak parties indicate that the commitment of the weak party is a particularly important power resource. Baker Fox has made the point that small states (and by implication weak negotiating parties) are often able to concentrate their entire attention on the specific issue being negotiated, whereas large states must spread their attention over the entire international system. Fox concludes that this concentration can result in a more favourable outcome for the small actor (Fox, 1959 and 1964). Robert Rothstein, analysing the multilateral negotiations on the Integrated Programme for Commodities, emphasizes the desires and the needs of the actors. He concludes, perhaps not very surprisingly, that the more intense the interests of a negotiating party, the less willing that side will be to make concessions (Rothstein, 1979).

In a case study of a number of bilateral trade negotiations between the United States and Latin American states, John Odell concludes that the Latin Americans won some negotiations (Odell, 1982). He suggests three main explanations for the relatively high degree of success of the weak states: first of all, the Latin Americans often took advantage of the highly pluralist system in the United States and succeeded in creating domestic allies within it who were prepared to support their cause. Second, in cases where the Latin American states represented a market of significant size to US exporters, the threat of retaliation often resulted in an enhanced negotiation outcome. Third, Latin Americans were often technically very well prepared for the negotiations and used persuasive arguments.

There are certain structural similarities between the EC–EFTA and the US–Latin American relationships – particularly in the economic area – which would seem to make the observations regarding the US–Latin American negotiations applicable to EC–EFTA negotiations. Yet, it is possible to find other similar cases. In *Power and Interdependence*, Keohane and Nye thus undertake an interesting comparative analysis of US relations with Canada and Australia (Keohane and Nye, 1989, pp. 165ff.). They conclude that an aggregate structural perspective cannot account for the pattern of outcomes in US–Canadian and US–Australian negotiations. Both countries, though much weaker than the United States, were able to reap considerable gains in some bilateral negotiations with the latter.

Canada was more successful than Australia. The factors mentioned by Odell in his study of the United States and Latin America reappear in the case of the United States and Canada. An important reason for Canada's relative success was that the asymmetry of vulnerability and sensitivity was much less between Canada and the United States than between Australia and the United States. Mutual trade amounted to 11 per cent of Canadian GNP, but only 1 per cent of US GNP. Yet, US exports to Canada made up 25 per cent of total American exports which gave Canada an important (potential) weapon of retaliation. Transnational processes also appear to have modified the structural imbalance between the two parties. In a number of cases, transnational organizations in the United States proved to have interests of their own which did not always coincide with those of the US government. An additional factor is the intensity and coherence of the Canadian bargaining position. Interestingly, Keohane and Nye suggest that intensity and coherence of bargaining position is also related to politicization from below. The pressure of democratic politics is argued to favour the smaller party in the bargaining process because for this party politicization from below tends to lead to tough negotiating behaviour and coherent stands, whereas for a big actor like the United States (or the EU?) politicization tends to lead to fragmentation of policy (Keohane and Nye, 1989, p. 206).

William Mark Habeeb has suggested a useful comprehensive analytical framework focusing on power in asymmetrical negotiations. He defines power in broad terms as 'the way in which actor A uses its resources in a process with actor B so as to bring about changes that cause preferred outcomes in its relationship with B' (Habeeb, 1987). This enables us to add a behavioural concept of power to the structural concept. Habeeb further argues that structural power ought to be subdivided into aggregate and issue-specific power. Writing within the tradition of interdependence and regime theory, he proposes to study asymmetrical negotiations from three angles: aggregate structural power, issue-specific power and behavioural power.

The issue-specific power structure depends on the nature of interdependence between the negotiating parties. The interdependence paradigm is appropriate for analysing negotiation relationships, since in negotiation each actor depends on the other to the extent that each can unilaterally withhold agreements, prolong the process or even end it. Drawing on the twin perspectives of interdependence and social exchange, Habeeb argues that the power balance of an issue-specific relationship is determined by three variables: alternatives, commitment and control (Habeeb, 1987, p. 21). Alternatives denote each actor's ability to gain its preferred outcomes from a relationship other than that with the opposing actor. Alternatives may explain why an actor may be able to achieve much of its preferred outcome by not negotiating or by stalling the negotiations. This action is related to what negotiation theorists call the 'security point', the point at which the actor would prefer stalemate over negotiation. The side that has more alternatives at its security point has an advantage over its opponent. A lack of alternatives may, however, increase an actor's motivation and thereby commitment. Iceland's successful cold war with Britain in the 1970s is a case in point.

Commitment refers to the extent and degree to which an actor desires and/or needs its preferred outcome. Commitment is based on the values the parties attach to the various possible outcomes. However, there are two kinds of commitment: commitment based on aspiration is a source of issue-power strength, whereas commitment based on need – a form of dependency – is a source of issue-power weakness (Habeeb, 1987, p. 22). Control is defined as the degree to which one side can unilaterally achieve its preferred outcome despite the costs involved in doing so. In other words, an indicator of an actor's control is its ability to bear the costs of a failure to reach an agreement.

Neither the EC nor EFTA can be regarded as 'normal' unitary actors. This raises the question of how to study multilateral negotiations involving multinational negotiating parties. Are there special features of this kind of bargaining, and what are the consequences for the process and outcome of negotiations? Multinational bargaining falls outside the mainstream literature on bargaining. As pointed out by Zartman, the current notion of process has thus far worked to exclude effective consideration of multinational negotiation, and those multinational negotiations that have been studied have normally been reduced to bilateral analysis (Zartman, 1988, p. 40).

Underdal (1973) has made some useful deductive observations regarding the negotiating behaviour of multinational negotiating parties. His focus is on the EC, but Underdal expects his conclusions to apply to other organizations at a similar level of integration as well. We therefore expect at least some of the most general observations regarding multinational negotiating behaviour to apply to EFTA as well. Although he is careful to point out that no actor is entirely unitary and that consequently there are elements of bureaucratic politics in the wider sense in all negotiations involving more than one individual, Underdal nevertheless departs from the assumption that one of the keys to understanding Community negotiating behaviour and the outcome of negotiations is to be found in the logic of Community decision making.

In terms of its external behaviour, the Community can be considered a tight coalition of states. It does not have a strong executive in its external policy. The configuration of interests in the Council is a reflection of the considerable heterogeneity of the Community. The administrative capacity of the EC in its external economic policy is also limited though higher than its external political capacity. Altogether, the decision-making capacity of the EC is quite low, since the EC is a highly pluralistic international actor. This has a number of logical implications. Firstly, low decision-making capacity makes for a passive negotiating behaviour. Second, slow decision making may lead to inefficiency when it comes to making the most of integrative potential. Integrative negotiations in Walton and Mckersie's terms require an active and flexible approach (Walton and Mckersie, 1965). This approach may be difficult for a pluralistic actor to adopt: first of all because the more internal conflicts there are, the more the coalition will be likely to restrict the room for manoeuvre it gives to its negotiators and the more carefully their behaviour is likely to be supervised. This will restrict the coalition's opportunity to search actively for a solution. Second, the expected costs of trying to modify the mandate may discourage the negotiators from actively trying.

The effects of a low decision-making capacity for distributive bargaining are more ambiguous. In this case, pluralism may also lead to inefficiency. It may make it difficult to reach a compromise solution. Low decision-making capacity may also prevent successful exploitation of opportunities arising suddenly from unexpected changes in the negotiating situation. Yet, in some cases of distributive bargaining, low decision-making capacity may be an asset. One recalls Thomas Schelling's point that if two actors are to converge in an agreement, the one who will have to move is in fact the one able to do so (Schelling, 1963). If one side seriously believes that the other side is paralysed, then it may – if it wants an agreement – make the concession that brings the negotiations out of their deadlock (Underdal, 1973, p. 76). For example the Danish government's domestic political difficulties on the issue of European Union from 1972–86 and again in 1992 may be argued to have resulted in Denmark receiving 'extraordinary' concessions in negotiations on the future development of the Community.

8

Similarly, the need to obtain the support of strong sub-national actors like the Bundesbank, the German regions and in some cases the Constitutional Court whatever the negative effects on efficiency tends to strengthen Germany's position within the EU.

The Community's decision-making procedure also has an impact on the Community's external negotiating behaviour. The unanimity principle implies that decisions taken will often be close to the positions advocated by those members who feel that their vital interests are at stake on a particular issue. Indifference on the part of some members may also have the effect of leaving the matter in the hands of those particularly concerned. There may be a risk of 'veto rotation', that is that the role of negative member rotates among the members. But a countervailing factor is that members will generally have some overall view regarding the desirability of an agreement, and this overall view will sometimes be determined by issues or considerations not on the agenda. In the case of the EC and EFTA, such a general attitude could be, for example, a wish on the part of the EC to avoid a loss of credibility as a result of a failure to reach an agreement.

Given the principle of unanimity, one may ask how it is possible for a pluralistic actor like the EC to avoid continuing deadlocks. An explanation may be found in Robert Axelrod's concept of cooperation. In situations where each individual has an incentive to act selfishly it is possible for cooperation to emerge, Axelrod argues, because the parties may meet again (Axelrod, 1986). Man is not a mountain, as the Russian saying goes; nor are states. National representatives coping with a proposal are aware that more proposals, being dealt with by more or less the same set of actors, will follow. The future casts a shadow back upon the present and therefore affects the current behaviour of the actors. Especially in situations where one actor heavily depends on another in order to make binding decisions, for instance in situations where unanimity is the rule, reciprocity can be considered the main principle structuring the relationships among the various actors. Reciprocity, Axelrod holds, is one of the two key requisites for cooperation to thrive. For cooperation to prove stable, the shadow of the future must be large enough.

In multilateral negotiations, the unanimity rule often forces the parties to use various kinds of package deals. Package deals may be of two kinds: they may take the form of an agreement between the opponent and those members of a coalition who are particularly exposed. But it is also possible to envisage what Underdal calls 'two-step package

9

deals', in which coalition partners of the country most concerned in a negotiation make some concessions or render some favour to this country which equalizes the cost inflicted by the agreement with the opponent.

The unanimity principle may affect the behaviour of individual coalition members. There will be a temptation to 'free-load' if one member of the coalition is known to have a very negative attitude towards an agreement. In this situation, it will be tempting for other members to 'reap the benefits of good-will without having to pay the bill of extravagance', to use Underdal's succinct expression (Underdal, 1973, p. 178). It should be added, however, that there are likely to be internal consequences of 'parasitic' behaviour; besides the 'free-loaders' cannot be sure that the veto-country will not sooner or later change its position.

A pluralistic structure also tends to rigidify the negotiating position of the multinational actor. Once a pluralistic actor has reached a negotiating position, it will be loath to change that position. One of the members may already have reached the point where it considers it impossible to make more concessions. Besides, the complex network of package deals typical of negotiations involving the EC have a cementing effect. Rigidity will often be an unintended effect of structural pluralism. But it may also be a deliberate strategy aimed at avoiding fragmentation. For example, some types of negotiations with third countries – especially but not only accession negotiations – threaten to affect the political cohesion of the Union. In other words: the less internally cohesive an actor is, the less generous its international negotiating posture is likely to be. This explains for instance the EU's demand that new members accept the full 'acquis'.

The effects of the pluralist decision-making system described above may in principle be modified by two factors. First of all, one can imagine that the choice of procedure will affect the Community's negotiating posture. Thus, to the extent that responsibility for conducting the negotiations is centralized in the hands of the Commission, this should *ceteris paribus* tend to make the EC's negotiating position more flexible. One could imagine that the Commission, whose task it is to 'upgrade the common interest', might at least to some extent neutralize the factors weakening Community cohesion. To the extent that the Commission plays an important mediating and unifying role, the earlier description of the Community as a coalition is not correct. A central function of the Commission is to put together package deals which serve to overcome deadlocks. This is done *inter alia* by means of various kinds of issue linkages (Weber and Wiesmeth, 1992). Michael Taylor has argued that in principle there are three solutions to collective-action problems: (i) centralized solutions involving hegemonic coercion; (ii) decentralized solutions typical of a community with common norms, dense patterns of interaction and reciprocal exchanges; and (iii) intermediate solutions involving the activity of 'political entrepreneurs' who endeavour to change individual preferences, attitudes and expectations or to deliver new resources (knowledge, information or 'technology') (Taylor, 1987). The Union does not have a clear hegemon, although the Franco–German axis often acts as an informal leader, at times even as a semi-hegemonic force in Union politics. Socio-cultural integration is insufficient to make decentralized solutions the standard way of solving collective-action problems in the European Union. The Commission thus typically acts as a political entrepreneur, supplying information that gives the member states the confidence needed to engage in issue linkage (Weber and Wiesmeth, 1992, p. 255). It exerts leadership through activities such as initiation, consensus-building and the mobilization of support. One of the important differences between the EC and EFTA as negotiators is precisely the lack of an institutionalized mediator and bridge-builder in EFTA, a factor which must be expected to have seriously weakened its negotiating capacity.

The second major question which we want to address is why the EEA process was so quickly overtaken by the process of seeking full membership of the European Union. How do we explain the rapid changes in the attitudes and stated policies of EFTA decision makers and other relevant EFTA actors regarding European policy? Stated differently: how do we account for the transition from economics to politics in EC–EFTA cooperation? To the extent that we are dealing with a common pattern of behaviour in the EFTA countries, integration theories may be of some help in explaining this policy change. Integration theory offers explanations of growth in the level of integration which should in principle also apply to cases of 'asymmetrical integration', in which one side joins a going concern, that is an integration system essentially defined by the other side. Since participation is voluntary, it still seems possible to use the term 'integration' to describe the evolving EC–EFTA relationship.

Such explanations may focus on formal or informal patterns of integration. An explanation emphasizing cumulative informal integration through interaction is suggested by the transactionalist theory of integration (Deutsch, 1957). William Wallace used this theoretical perspective in his stimulating study to explain why the dynamic West European integration in the 1980s also included EFTA (Wallace, 1989). Wallace borrows from Deutsch the concept of a 'core area' around which expanding security communities are said to develop. Deutsch argued on the basis of a number of historical cases that the existence of core areas with superior economic growth and superior political and administrative capabilities was related to the success of integration schemes. But Deutsch also stressed the importance of similarity reflected in background factors such as compatibility of values and a distinctive way of life. Briefly, Deutsch made three observations regarding integration. First, similarity is an important precondition for integration. Second, social interaction understood as various forms of transnational communication is particularly important in promoting mutual trust and a sense of community. Third, superior economic growth leading to expectations of economic rewards is an important background condition facilitating integration. And the existence of a prosperous and superior core tends to create 'band-wagon' effects in adjacent countries. Transactionalism defines political integration in social terms, emphasizing shared values and mutual trust established through economic interchange and social contact. While stressing the relevance of the transactionalist approach to integration, Wallace is careful to avoid deterministic arguments: in his view there is no inevitability about the transition from intersocietal contact to the emergence of a political community. Transactions or informal integration, in Wallace's terms, only offer a partial explanation of modern European integration. European integration develops through the interplay between formal and informal integration set within the framework of a specific politico-security system. The growth of informal integration may be influenced by proactive formal integration as well as by the degree of stability provided by the prevailing security system. In Wallace's view, American protection and the East–West balance thus provided the climate of stability and predictability within which informal integration could flourish. However, at some point in the late 1970s or early 1980s, informal integration began to move ahead of formal structures creating strong incentives for responsive adjustments of institutions and rules in the wider Western Europe (Wallace, 1989, pp. 83 and 90).

The concept of informal integration seems helpful in trying to understand the dynamics of EC–EFTA relations in the last decade. The transactionalist emphasis on interaction and similarity has much to offer the analyst of current West European affairs. However, as recognized by Wallace it is also somewhat simplistic and only offers a partial explanation of current patterns of European integration. After all, not all kinds of similarity are conducive to integration. Economic theories of integration demonstrate that similarity in economic resources is a negative condition for integration. Conversely, complementarity of factor endowments favours integration. Another central problem is that the relationship between social interaction and political attitudes remains disputed. For example, social interaction between the West European states was very dense prior to World War I. This did not prevent hostilities from breaking out. The essense of the problem is that Deutsch and his pupils have not convincingly demonstrated that these socio-economic links between societies are all politically relevant. Moreover, the fact that there is a close correspondence between public and elite opinion does not necessarily mean that the first affects the second. It is possible that public opinion simply takes its cue from the elite (Pentland, 1973, pp. 63ff.). An additional problem is that developments in social interactions between societies are not related to exogenous factors such as technological changes or dramatic alterations in the structure of the international system. The growth of a European 'we-feeling' is unlikely to be as linear as suggested by the transactionalists.

This drawback is compounded by a problem of analytical focus: Deutsch's theory deals superficially with that part of transnational relations which is most likely to have affected political relations between the EC and EFTA: the relationship between firms and other economic interest groups. Interconnections between the EC and EFTA societies are known to be particularly strong in business and finance. While social and cultural links across borders may have indirect consequences for political processes in a long-term perspective, economic actors and organized interests are clearly of more immediate and direct relevance to political decision making. Pinpointing new forms of interdependence, Sundelius has thus drawn attention to the importance of what he calls 'transnational penetration strategies' in the EC–EFTA relationship (Sundelius, 1990). He argues *inter alia* that the European Commission was very successful in the late 1980s in penetrating the national political systems of the EFTA countries and that the Commission to some extent managed to shape the framework of reference of the EFTA debate on European integration. Precisely the interplay between interest groups, bureaucrats and political elites is of course the pivot of the neo-functionalist theory, which pays more attention to formal integration while claiming that expansion in integration is not always politically directed. The theory essentially claims that once a state has joined a sectoral integration scheme, transferring parts of its sovereignty to a supranational decision-making body, it may be drawn further into a binding cooperation structure as a result of pressure from societal and intra-governmental groups which gradually transfer their loyalty to the supranational centre. These groups may be interest groups, civil servants or, less often, currents within public opinion. Sometimes they exert their influence from the national level. But often they will organize at the transnational level in order to maximize their benefits from integration (cf. also Groom and Taylor, 1990). Bureaucratic interpenetration, which makes it difficult for governments to act as gatekeepers, facilitates this kind of spillover. Elite socialization is thus an important aspect of undirected integration.

Economic groups and bureaucrats are expected to call for an expansion of the community's tasks because they see functional linkages between problems arising out of the inherent technical characteristics of these problems. Supranational actors may act as midwives for an integration process, offering package deals that redefine a conflict and 'upgrade the common interest'. In most cases such compromise solutions will imply more integration, whether through expansion in scope or expansion in the capacity of supranational institutions (Tranholm-Mikkelsen, 1990). It is well known from the literature on negotiations that if a subject is too narrowly defined, there will be little possibility of a bargain. It is desirable to expand the negotiating agenda until it is wide enough to allow a bargain which benefits each party if not to the same degree then at least to some degree.

Recent contributions to the debate on neo-functionalism have suggested that spillover retains some explanatory power but that it should be understood as depending on the conclusion by political leaders of major political bargains (Keohane and Hoffmann, 1990; Sandholz and Zysman, 1989). Certain types of political bargains by the member states of the Union give the supranational institutions scope for manipulating linkages with a view to further extending the scope or capacity of the integration system: an example is the Commission's White Paper on the creation of the internal market which defined the common goal in broad terms as a 'border-free Europe'. Critical questions have been raised about the capacity of national interest groups to act as vehicles of spillover. After all, there is some evidence that government administrations have often succeeded quite well in co-opting interest groups (Harrison, 1990). But the fundamental point in neo-functionalism, that the satisfaction of material interests is generally a stronger incentive to integration than is the appeal to vague ideas about European unity, appears to remain valid (Webb, 1983, p. 17).

The neo-functionalist literature has yet to establish the nature and level of integration necessary to unleash the forces of (partly) undirected and self-reinforcing integration. What kinds of bargains facilitate and hamper spillover processes have not been studied in depth. But historical evidence suggests that under certain conditions processes of market integration (that is negative integration) tend to become very dynamic and breed strong incentives for positive integration. A priori it therefore seems appropriate to apply the spillover concept to an analysis of the market liberalizing EC–EFTA negotiations – even though there are no common institutions and therefore no genuinely supranational actors which may facilitate task expansion. The EEA negotiations nevertheless constitute a clear example of a sectoral approach to integration. It thus seems pertinent to ask whether the sectoral approach to EC–EFTA integration created imbalances considered intolerable by the EFTA governments.

Of particular relevance in neo-functionalist theory is the proposition that supranational and national political elites may fashion integration plans in ways that create deliberate imbalances, the underlying objective being to influence the political incentives of the actors participating in the integration process. Spillover as a deliberate integration strategy implies the manipulation of imbalances in the sense that short-term decisions are made with a view to longer-term consequences – but without these consequences being made clear to all actors when decisions are made. It also implies an incrementalist approach to integration, a strategy of fractionating the inevitable element of conflict involved in transferring national sovereignty to a new territorial level of decision making. The vices of a short time horizon are described with subtle humour in one of Hans Christian Andersen's tales, 'What Father does is Always Right', which tells the story of a man who takes his cow to the market but on the way to the market-place makes a series of exchanges. The cow is exchanged for a horse, the horse for a pig etc. Each exchange seems logical on its own merits, but the man ends up with a bag full of rotten apples. (It is only in fairy tales that such stupidity is rewarded in gold!)

15

Incrementalist strategies are part of the stock-in-trade of Commission negotiators. Manipulation of linkages and imbalances appears to have been an important factor behind the transition from the internal market to the EMU. It has been shown that the Delors' Report on Economic and Monetary Union contains a considerable number of references to the neo-functionalist logic of task expansion. It seems that the (early) success of the EMU project was due in part to the Commission's skilful cultivation of spillover (Kelstrup, 1990). It thus seems natural to enquire whether one can point to evidence of the use of 'linkage' rhetoric in the arguments used by EFTA elites to rally support for full membership of the European Union.

To sum up, neo-functionalist theory suggests two competing explanations of the transition from the EEA to the membership option which deserve attention as possible supplements to the explanations offered by Wallace. One explanation proposes to interpret the evolution in the EC policy of the EFTA states as a result of undirected and perhaps even unintended developments. Following classical neo-functionalism, one could argue that having embarked upon the ambitious plan of creating a Single West European Market, the two parties were soon forced to recognize the powerful logic of functional spillover characteristic of market liberalizing projects on a regional scale: the negotiating agenda had to be extended to avoid imbalances, and at the same time the integration process was accelerated by pressure from organized interest groups in EFTA which shifted their loyalty from the national level to the European level. This resulted in an expansion of the EEA agenda which placed the EFTA governments on the horns of a serious dilemma: the greater the commitments implied by the EEA agreement, the greater the need for EFTA involvement in the decision-making structures governing an EEA. A second explanation would instead focus on directed change. One may thus interpret the apparent failure of the EEA as a success in disguise, as part of an incrementalist strategy aimed at integrating EFTA in the EC. Modern neo-functionalists emphasizing the role of political leadership would see this as an instance of 'cultivated spillover'.

Explanations focusing on societal and inter-state interaction between the EC and the EFTA countries provide only partial explanations of recent changes in formal patterns of integration between the two sides, although, as is argued here, the importance of such explanations may have been underestimated. It is obvious that changes in the external environment such as the collapse of the cold war system have affected

EC–EFTA relations, notably the EC policies of the neutral EFTA countries. Likewise, domestic politics and specific internal structures have affected the formulation of policies in both the EC and in the EFTA countries. As is well known, there have been considerable differences in the timing of individual membership applications, and one of the major EFTA governments, the Swiss, has in practice had to give up or at least postpone its policy of seeking membership of the European Union.

In order to explain these national differences, we shall have to study foreign-policy changes in the light of specific internal structures and demands and not least the interplay between internal factors and changes in the wider European and international system of which the EC and EFTA are a part. Two of the EFTA countries, Norway and Iceland, are part of NATO and have been less dramatically affected by the transformation of the European security complex than the four EFTA neutrals, Switzerland, Austria, Finland and Sweden. As pointed out by Carlsnæs (1993), comparing the foreign policies of the EFTA neutrals is not an easy task. What they have in common apart from being small West European states is 'a similarly expressed policy in time of war'. While two of them have 'neutral' policies with long historical roots, the 'neutral' status of the other two is a post-World War II phenomenon. Only one of them has been totally unfettered by constitutional or international treaty obligations (Sweden), whereas the other three are signatories to such agreements in some form or other: ranging from an international confirmation of 'perpetual neutrality' at the Congress of Vienna in 1815 (Switzerland); to a highly ambiguous and ambivalent friendship (rather than neutrality) agreement with a neighbouring superpower (Finland); to a full-fledged State Treaty in which neutrality plays a central constitutional role (Austria). While all neutral EFTA countries opted for a special status of non-alignment with the two blocs during the cold war and were therefore to some degree sensitive to changes in the overall structure of the European security complex, the external constraints varied from country to country, and in one of the neutral EFTA countries (Switzerland) neutrality was as much a domestic political as a foreign-policy instrument. The EFTA neutrals can thus be placed in two categories. Some have developed an endogenous form of neutrality. This is the case with Sweden and Switzerland, although Swiss neutrality is more formalized than the Swedish. Swedish neutrality is based on two substantive tenets: that Sweden will make no international commitments with regard to her neutrality; and second that she will at all times pursue a policy that sustains confidence in her political will and military ability to remain neutral in the event of war. The endogenous nature of Swedish neutrality has historically given Swedish decision makers a flexibility which their counterparts in Finland and Austria did not possess. Other EFTA neutrals have thus basically pursued an exogeneous form of neutrality. This is the case with Finland and Austria, although Austrian neutrality is more formalized than Finnish (cf. also Hakovirta, 1988).

2 From the Maudling Plan to the internal market

A whiff of continuity

In a sense, EC–EFTA relations came full circle in the late 1980s. In the 1950s the West European countries had engaged in multilateral negotiations on a Wider Free Trade Area. Though more ambitious than the Maudling Plan, the multilateral EEA arrangement is reminiscent of the trade liberalization plans of the late 1950s. In both cases, the ambition was to create a wider free-trade area in Western Europe. The context is also very similar. As in the late 1950s, in the mid-1980s EC–EFTA relations received a boost from a dynamic EC venture. EFTA's policy has been a reactive policy, one of direct or indirect adaptation to EC developments. Not surprisingly, EC–EFTA cooperation has always been most successful in periods of EC dynamism. Thus, the countries which were later to set up the European Free Trade Association (EFTA)— reacted to the dynamic integration process centring around France and West Germany by launching their own initiative. The United Kingdom first proposed in 1956 the creation of a wider free-trade area in Western Europe. The idea was discussed for two years in the so-called 'Maudling negotiations'. The Nordic countries in 1957–8 seriously considered an ambitious plan for the creation of a Nordic Customs Union. When the United Kingdom realized that the Maudling negotiations had no chance of succeeding, it thus faced the double challenge of a continental and a Nordic common market. The British reaction was to propose EFTA. EFTA constituted a wider and more attractive free-trade scheme than the small Nordic grouping, and consequently EFTA was set up in

1960 and immediately joined by the United Kingdom, Sweden, Norway, Denmark, Austria, Switzerland and, soon thereafter, Portugal. Norway and Denmark both had relatively low tariffs and viewed the Customs Union of the EC with scepticism. Yet, for Denmark with its big agricultural export to West Germany, EFTA was not an ideal solution, an economic iron curtain having been drawn between Denmark's two main markets, but Denmark was at the time still heavily dependent on the United Kingdom market and in philosophical terms sceptical about Franco–German plans (Thune, 1987). Sweden and Switzerland had low tariffs and were strongly opposed to any raising of their own tariffs, which harmonization with the tariffs of the Six in the EC would imply. Austria also joined EFTA, although it had higher tariffs and was not particularly troubled by the economic consequences of harmonization (Camps, 1964, p. 211). Finland became an associate member of EFTA in 1961.

The birth of EFTA effectively killed the plans for a Nordic economic community which had been prepared since 1947, illustrating the fundamental logic in Nordic cooperation that when faced with a choice between smaller Nordic and wider European cooperation, the leading actors in Scandinavia always opt for wider European cooperation. But EFTA also provided the external catalyst and the leadership necessary to set up a binding economic cooperation among the Nordic countries, which were separated by conflicting economic interests in areas like agriculture as well as by historical animosities and the lack of a hegemonic leader. Of course Nordic cooperation survived in its typical informal and low-key fashion. The Nordic Council established in 1952 through parallel national decisions continued its work, and in 1962 the Helsinki Agreement gave Nordic cooperation a kind of formalized basis. The Nordic Council was in principle comprehensive in scope but had very weak institutions. It was organized as a consultative body consisting of both governments and parliamentarians from the member states. Yet, only the parliamentarians were to have voting rights. This was due to a Norwegian fear that a vote by a member of its government would be interpreted as binding for the government as a whole; Norway was wary of any attempt to make Nordic cooperation legally binding (Vibe, 1992, p. 64).

From the very beginning, EFTA was designed as a 'bridge' to the EC. It was foreseen that many of its provisions would have to be altered once the EC and EFTA reached an understanding. Thus, the aims of EFTA were much more limited than those of the EC. While the EC was both a Customs Union and a Common Market, EFTA merely aimed at removing internal trade barriers on industrial goods, and the member states remained free to maintain their own external barriers. EFTA did not envisage a common policy on agriculture. Nor did it envisage joint policies with a view to preventing internal trade distortions, since EFTA would not set up a common market (Griffiths, 1992). EFTA contented itself with establishing a complaints procedure. Unlike the EC, EFTA thus had a very small institutional framework.

The main political function of the EFTA was to strengthen the hand of the free-trading fringe countries in their dealings with the new EC. It soon became apparent that the United Kingdom did not take its EFTA commitments too seriously. In the mid-1960s the United Kingdom thus imposed an import surcharge against all the world, including its part-ners in EFTA, a step which could not but raise eyebrows in the rest of EFTA. Several events prompted a reappraisal of the United Kingdom's policy towards Europe in the early 1960s. First of all, it became appar-ent that the United States was cool, almost hostile, towards EFTA. While the EC was welcomed by the Americans as a bold and politically attrac-tive venture, EFTA was seen as a defensive move with no long-term political purpose to offset its economic disadvantages for the United States. Besides, EFTA was widely portrayed by its members as merely an intermediate step on the way towards a large European trading area. Such an area, were it to become a reality, would obviously increase the area of discrimination against the United States (Camps, 1964, p. 237). What is more, seen from London, the American sympathy for the EC raised the spectre of a special American–EC relationship replacing the Anglo–American relationship. Second, and more importantly, the emergent plans for adding a political dimension to the EC made a strong impression in London as did the new partnership between de Gaulle and Adenauer. Finally, the Macmillan government came to the conclusion that the kind of Europe envisaged by de Gaulle provided a context which would mitigate the impact of supranationality and could provide a platform for British influence on the continent (Griffiths, 1992). The French proposals for a closer political cooperation based on intergovernmental principles reinforced that view.

In the summer of 1960, a cabinet report on the implications of joining the EC was completed, the contents of which can be summa-rized in four points: (i) in the long term the interests of the United Kingdom lay in giving higher priority than heretofore to its European relationship; (ii) joining the EC might be the only way to achieve the close relationship with the Six which was now felt to be desirable; (iii) joining the EC was technically feasible but only provided certain modifications in the Community's arrangements could be negotiated; and (iv) the political case for close association or membership was stronger than the economic case (Camps, 1964, p. 293).

Thus, the United Kingdom applied for membership of the EC only a year after the formation of EFTA, a decision that prompted immediate applications from Denmark, Norway and Ireland. The United Kingdom application was vetoed twice by de Gaulle in 1963 and 1967. In 1963 Denmark was offered an isolated membership but decided to remain loyal to the United Kingdom. The United Kingdom, Denmark and Ireland eventually managed to join the EC in 1973 following de Gaulle's departure. Norway had been expected to join as well, but the government was voted down on the issue in a referendum and Norway remained outside the EC. Once again wider European developments overtook Nordic endeavours. In 1968 Denmark had proposed a Nordic Economic Cooperation (NORDEK) (Miljan, 1977). The plan built upon the earlier plan for a Customs Union, but at Danish insistence included agriculture and also a certain coordination of economic policy. Moreover, the institutional framework was to be stronger than that envisaged in the plan for a Customs Union. The inclusion of agriculture encountered some opposition in Finland and Norway. More importantly, once it became clear in 1969 that Denmark regarded NORDEK as a step towards membership of the EC, Finland stalled. In 1970 the Finnish government indicated that political considerations precluded its participation in the proposed NORDEK (Vibe, 1992, p. 83). However, Nordic cooperation was strengthened in the early 1970s: in 1971 the Nordic Council was given a permanent secretariat and the Nordic governments established the Nordic Council of Ministers. The Council of Ministers, the composition of which varies according to the issues debated, was given the task of implementing specific agreements between the Nordic countries. Ministers for Nordic cooperation in each member state were to coordinate Nordic cooperation. The Council of Ministers was given a small secretariat in Copenhagen.

The accession of the three EFTA countries to the EC was accompanied by the conclusion of bilateral free-trade agreements between the Community and the rest of the EFTA countries. The United Kingdom and Denmark insisted that no new trade barriers should be erected between them and the remaining EFTA countries, thus illustrating the positive secondary effect of enlargements on relations with third countries. Bilateralism was considered necessary because of the considerable differences between the EFTA countries. While Sweden sounded out the EC about the possibility of a Customs Union, Finland wanted to preserve maximum political freedom and Iceland was mainly concerned about fish. Apparently, the EC went to great lengths to keep Finland and Iceland on board, not for economic but for geopolitical reasons (cf. *EFTA from Yesterday to Tomorrow*, 1987, p. 162).

The Free Trade Agreements (FTAs) which took effect on 1 January 1973 provided for the gradual elimination of tariffs for industrial products and a number of processed agricultural goods. The agreements all followed the same general pattern but included special provisions for each country. The FTAs stipulated a general transitional period of four and a half years. For sensitive products, the transitional period was extended to 1980 and for paper products until 1984. The timetable was much the same as that for the EFTA countries about to join the EC. Though limited in scope and not very spectacular, the FTAs created in the 1970s an area of trade stability in an increasingly unpredictable trade environment. During the period 1972–86, trade between the EC and EFTA quintupled (de Lange, 1988, p. 311). Among the results achieved during the 1970s were an acceleration of the timetable for dismantling the tariff barriers, a modest extension of the product coverage for trade in agricultural products and consultations in new areas of common interest.

One may ask why it took the West Europeans 30 years to create a common free-trade area. After all, the high degree of economic interdependence must have exerted a strong pressure for closer formal links. Yet, political considerations prevailed over economic incentives during the whole period. This was the case for the EFTANs as well as the EC core. Several West European states (Sweden, Finland, Austria and Switzerland) saw advantages in keeping a certain distance from the two blocs in the bipolar balance. Additionally, the West European states drew different conclusions from their experiences of World War II, the continentals being much more concerned about the need to foster political integration than the EFTANs. Furthermore, France and the United Kingdom were in competition for the leadership of Western Europe and used all sorts of institutional devices as weapons in that struggle. For many years, EC–EFTA relations were a function of the Franco–British relationship, in a sense the continuation of Franco–British rivalry by other means. Only in the late 1960s, faced with a newly powerful and East-leaning Germany, did France modify its view of the United Kingdom's role in Europe, with immediate consequences for relations with the other EFTA countries.

After World War II there was a general readiness in Western Europe to look for new ways of overcoming the nationalism which had led to Europe's self-destruction both as a model civilization and as a dominant global power. All governments realized the need to go beyond the modest and loose intergovernmental forms of cooperation which had existed before the war. There were also significant differences in view, however, previously reflected at the 'Congress of Europe' held in the Hague in 1948. While a number of countries, led by the United Kingdom, were aiming for a wide European free-trade area, a core of continental European countries had more ambitious plans. They preferred a Customs Union to a Free Trade Area and wanted to set up a system of political integration based on supranational principles (Pedersen, 1991b). From 1956–8 at the insistence of the United Kingdom, attempts were made to bridge these differences, but eventually the two groupings parted ways, the 'outsiders' forming the EFTA in 1960. The Maudling Plan proposed by the United Kingdom excluded agriculture, thus keeping the Commonwealth happy. Besides, it was well known that Belgium and West Germany had been reluctant to embrace a commitment for a common agricultural policy (Griffiths, 1992). The plan also played upon serious divisions within the European Coal and Steel Community (ECSC) between France and the 'free-traders' in the Netherlands and West Germany who were far from keen on the upward revision of their tariffs implied by the West European Customs Union.

What the United Kingdom failed to understand was the strength of the political commitment behind the EC and the determination of the 'federalists' in both France and West Germany. The French centre and centre-right as well as West Germany led by the anti-Prussian Adenauer all saw a politically unified Europe as the way to political rehabilitation on the international stage. Besides, the French were looking for new ways of containing Germany, while the Germans placed major emphasis on the stabilizing effect of a supranational community. For many Germans active in the formative period of European integration, the European construction was an *Ersatz Nationalismus*, an outlet for national feelings that could no longer be expressed at national level and at the same time an essentially idealist project inspired by federalist thinking. Much the same can be said about the Italian political will. At the same time European integration for Italy was also a matter of self-interest, a way of importing modernization. The Benelux countries had of course already set up their own Union which they regarded as a model for the wider Europe. Indeed, the Benelux countries played an important part in bringing the plans for a Common Market to fruition.

The victor in World War II, the United Kingdom, on the other hand, was psychologically prepared to reform but not to revolutionize European politics. Unfortunately, as Jean Monnet put it, the price of victory was the illusion that it was possible to keep what one had without having to change (Charlton, 1983, p. 307). The Brits were the conservatives in the grand debate in the 1940s and early 1950s on European cooperation. Not only did they reject supranationalism, they also underestimated the ability and political will of the continentals to make supranationalism work (Griffiths, 1992). Moreover, in the back of the minds of all the 'fringe countries' also lurked a certain suspicion of the political culture of the continentals. The very national instability and democratic fragility that caused the Six to opt for supranationality and federalism caused the Anglo–Nordic countries to keep a certain distance from the rest of Western Europe. The EFTANs also feared that their high standard of living and social welfare systems would prove difficult to uphold within a European Economic Union. Yet the most important reason for the collapse of the Maudling negotiations was France's fear that in a wider free-trade area the ECSC and the EC would dissolve like a piece of sugar in a cup of tea, as a perceptive observer put it (*EFTA from Yesterday to Tomorrow*, 1987). For France the supranational structures in the new Europe were essential both as a means of exerting control over Germany and as a vehicle for France's global ambitions. Consequently, the EC led by France refused to discuss in parallel the opening of the Common Market and the wider free-trade area as suggested by the United Kingdom. The dominant forces in the EC wanted first to set up the EC and then to make suitable arrangements with the rest of Western Europe, a view which can be recognized in the position adopted by the EC in the European Economic Area (EEA) talks. While national interests were important in all countries in Europe, in some countries national interests were given a radically new interpretation in the light of the recent wartime experience.

The origin of the split between the EC and a group of highly developed economies in Western Europe cannot be interpreted solely by reference to differences in domestic policy preferences. Certainly, as stressed by Milward (1992, p. 445), it is important to understand the 'instrumentality of the Community as an integrationist solution to national problems'. But it would be wrong to dismiss entirely the factor of innovative ideas, and it would be incorrect to portray the 'national problems' guiding European policy as mainly economic and short term. The decision to opt for the 'smaller Europe', even at the cost of postponing wider European cooperation, was in essence motivated by politics – French and German high politics, one ought perhaps to add. The predominance of politics over economics is particularly striking in the case of West Germany given the fact that economically speaking the EC was widely held to be something of a straitjacket for the FRG. It also appears that Milward fails to understand fully the element of strategic thinking in France's foreign policy (and by implication in early EC thinking) so alien to the British tradition of elegant improvisation and haphazard muddling through.

As will be argued in this book, the fundamental logic in European integration has not changed since the 1950s. In 1990 once again the West European core opted for a deepening of integration within a smaller Europe when faced with the possibility of widening and a rapid healing of the divisions of Europe. Politics once again prevailed over economics or, to be more precise, a certain political thinking concerned with the 'politics of scale' in a hostile world prevailed over the logic of economic interdependence and political arguments stressing the wider community of ideas and traditions of which the Union is a part. This is not meant to imply that the Union has turned its back on its neighbours. What it does suggest is that the fundamental changes in the European security complex which took place in 1989–90 did not cause any fundamental reappraisal of the *finalité* and strategy of European integration but on the contrary were interpreted as challenges which could be met most effectively through a renewed emphasis on supranationalism.

The internal market and the 'Luxembourg process'

The new impetus in EC–EFTA cooperation dates back to April 1984, when the 18 EC and EFTA countries held their first meeting at ministerial level. The meeting had a dual purpose. It celebrated the successful implementation of the FTAs, and it provided ministers with an opportunity for looking ahead and identifying new common tasks. With tariffs and quantitative restrictions on trade removed, EFTA had fulfilled its main function and was on the lookout for a new role. The formal initiative for a closer multilateral dialogue came from the EFTA side. The then Swedish Minister of Trade, Mats Hellström, apparently suggested the idea to his French counterpart, Claude Cheysson, during a routine meeting in 1984 and was somewhat surprised to hear Cheysson respond altogether positively. The Swedish idea fitted in well with the new pro-integrationist line of the French socialists, and with the European Parliament (EP) elections approaching, the French government welcomed this opportunity to launch a new European initiative (Pedersen, 1988). Apart from that, the second enlargement of the Community with Greece had already created a need for closer cooperation with the Alpine countries so important for the linkage of Greece with the rest of the Community (de Lange, 1988, p. 312).

In his opening statement at the Luxembourg meeting Claude Cheysson, speaking on behalf of the EC as President of the Council of Ministers, outlined four areas in which the EC and EFTA should expand cooperation: (i) research and development; (ii) industrial cooperation through measures such as a truly free internal market; (iii) common action at the international level with special emphasis on appropriate reactions to 'the international monetary disorder'; and (iv) cooperation with regard to the Third World (*Agence Europe*, 9–10 April 1984).

The new multilateral dialogue came to be known as the 'Luxembourg process', named after the location of the first meeting. In 1984 a joint EC–EFTA High-Level Contact Group (HLCG) was set up, and there were several joint ministerial meetings and meetings of EFTA ministers with the participation of an EC Commissioner. The Luxembourg process had a loose agenda, the main emphasis being placed on the removal of technical barriers to trade in goods and technological cooperation. The approach was sectoral and pragmatic. From 1984 to 1988, the EC and the EFTA countries achieved a number of practical results. After cumbersome negotiations the FTAs were extended to Spain and Portugal. Multilateral conventions on a Single Administrative Document and a common transit regime were signed. Some progress was achieved on rules of origin and a multilateral agreement on rail/road transport was concluded. Bilateral framework agreements for science and technology were also concluded, and EFTA participation in specific Community programmes in the field of research and development was agreed (de Lange, 1988, p. 321). Although the results were far from negligible, the limitations of the pragmatic ad hoc approach soon became evident when the internal market process started in 1987–8.

Economic considerations were crucial in drawing the EC and EFTA closer together. From an economic perspective, it was only logical that the EC's internal market programme should be accompanied by a scheme which ensured that the EFTA economies would not be excluded from the more liberal trade regime created by the EC's internal market. The economic rationale for EC–EFTA integration has always been strong. But it has become more compelling over the years as the two economic groupings have grown more interconnected at the transnational level. The stimulus to preferential trade liberalization is especially strong in countries which are one another's best customers, since reducing trade barriers between such economies provides strong reciprocal benefits. Symmetrical trade dependence is thus a factor favouring the formation of trade blocs. The pattern of trade between the EC and EFTA is symmetrical, although there are significant internal variations and an overall power asymmetry. The share of intra-regional trade in total trade is high in Europe and has been growing during the past decades. Trade flows are evenly spread among countries within the EC–EFTA area, and it is not possible to group countries in two separate blocs purely on the basis of the direction of their trade. In fact, EFTA countries on average take a larger share of their imports from the Community than do EC countries themselves. (Wijkman, 1990). The common interest of the EC and EFTA negotiators was thus to avoid the erection of new barriers to the activity of exporters in the EC and EFTA and to trans-european companies.

Trade with the EC is of crucial importance to EFTA. There has been a steady growth in EFTA's export dependence on the EC as reflected in the figures displayed in Table 2.1.

One notices the marked increase in EFTA's trade dependence on the EC market during the period from 1986 to 1991. But the increasing dependence on the EC is not only a phenomenon related to the internal market project. Apart from the recent rather dramatic increase, there has been a gradual acceleration in dependence dating back to the late 1970s when the Free Trade Agreements were fully implemented and access to alternative markets started becoming more difficult. Having said that, it is beyond doubt that the EC's internal market project created an urgent need for a new cooperation that would ensure EFTA access to its West European market. Economic necessity was compelling. The main interest of the EFTANs was to protect the

Table 2.1 Shares of main areas in EFTA countries' exports (in %)

	EFTA	EC	USA	Japan
1959				
Austria	8.9	52.7	5.9	0.4
Finland	4.5	52.9	5.8	0.2
Iceland	16.5	22.0	16.9	—
Norway	14.0	53.1	10.3	0.1
Sweden	15.7	52.8	8.0	0.3
Switzerland	9.1	47.4	11.2	1.4
Total EFTA	11.1	50.5	8.7	0.6
1979				
Austria	12.2	53.5	2.5	0.7
Finland	24.2	41.0	4.3	1.1
Iceland	13.7	38.6	28.0	3.0
Norway	15.1	63.9	4.0	1.2
Sweden	20.0	49.0	6.0	1.3
Switzerland	9.1	49.8	6.9	3.0
Total EFTA	15.4	51.3	5.4	1.6
1986				
Austria	11.8	60.1	4.0	1.2
Finland	21.9	37.8	5.4	1.5
Iceland	10.1	54.2	21.7	4.8
Norway	13.4	64.9	5.4	1.2
Sweden	20.7	50.0	11.4	1.4
Switzerland	7.6	54.9	9.5	3.2
Total EFTA	14.5	53.7	8.1	1.9
1991				
Austria	9.2	65.8	3.2	1.6
Finland	20.2	49.6	6.1	1.5
Iceland	7.7	66.8	12.6	7.9
Norway	14.6	66.2	4.8	1.9
Sweden	17.9	55.0	8.1	2.1
Switzerland	6.4	58.8	8.2	4.3
Total EFTA	12.7	59.4	6.4	2.6

Source: EFTA Trade, EFTA office Geneva, various years.

economic and commercial interests of the EFTA countries in an integrated Europe without having to pay a political price. For Austria,
Switzerland, Finland and Sweden that meant without having to give up

neutrality. For Norway and Iceland that meant without having to give up national sovereignty in sensitive areas.

The economic costs for EFTA of not participating in the internal market are difficult to quantify as there are both static and dynamic effects. An Austrian economist has pointed out that since as a result of the internal market intra-EC border costs would be reduced by approximately 5 per cent, EFTA's terms of trade might fall by around 5 per cent. Besides, the EC countries would tend to purchase more from each other, which would result in a decline in EFTA exports. Trade diversionary effects would hit EFTA more than other third countries because of geographical proximity. To compensate for this, EFTA countries would have either to try to produce their goods more cheaply, or the EFTA industries would have to transfer the production of specific goods to the EC countries (Woschnagg, 1988, pp. 346ff.). There would be positive effects as well, such as the positive effects on Community growth of the supply-side elements of the internal market programme, but these were difficult to assess and rather uncertain (Wijkman, 1990, p. 66).

Trade with EFTA is also of great importance to the EC. It exceeds trade with the United States and is about the size of trade with the United States and Japan combined. EFTA takes up about a quarter of EC exports in value terms. In 1991, EFTA absorbed 25.1 per cent of the value of (extra) EC's exports and supplied 22.4 per cent of (extra) EC's imports. By comparison, in the same year only 16.6 per cent and 5.2 per cent of the EC's exports went to the United States and Japan, whereas 18.2 and 10.6 per cent of its imports came from these two countries (*EFTA Trade*, 1991, p. 52). What is more, EFTA is the only trading partner with which the EC runs a major surplus (see also appendix).

Changing investment patterns was another factor pushing the EFTA governments towards an agreement with the EC in the late 1980s. In the years after the launching of the internal market plan, big EFTA companies were anticipating the creation of the internal market by investing directly in the EC on a massive scale, thereby gradually erod-ing the productive base of their home countries.

One notices the dramatic growth in EFTA countries' FDIs in the EC area from 1987 and onwards. While there was only a very small increase from 1985 to 1986, in 1987 the FDIs in the EC area rose significantly and in 1988 they more than doubled. A relaxation came in 1989, but in 1990 there was a new dramatic rise. Within EFTA, Switzerland and Sweden were the major investors, accounting for four-fifths of EFTA's

Table 2.2 EFTA's outward FDI flows (net) by region* (in mill. ecus)

	EFTA	EC	North America	Other	Total
1985	527	2,086	3,481	1,739	7,833
1986	1,054	2,400	2,130	2,385	7,970
1987	1,229	4,591	416	2,043	8,279
1988	2,512	10,904	2,179	4,049	19,643
1989	2,896	9,270	5,741	4,765	22,672
1990	1,601	16,732	703	7,609	26,644

* See EFTA Trade, 1990, p. 44

Source: Central Banks in EFTA countries.

total outward FDI stock. Compared to these two countries, the other EFTA countries were operating on a more modest scale, but Finland increased its FDI activity rapidly in the second half of the 1980s (Leskela and Parviainen, 1990). There is a clear correlation between these changes in the patterns of EFTA FDI and internal EC developments: in 1987 the Single European Act was put into effect and the internal market programme took off. In 1989–90, the plans for EMU were placed firmly on the agenda, reinforcing EFTA companies' fears of having to face a worsening of their competitive position.

It would be simplistic to portray the new EC–EFTA *rapprochement* as simply a spin-off from the '1992 project'. Interestingly, the launching of the Luxembourg process predates the formal presentation of the internal market programme. The EFTA side was actively involved in preparations for the internal market project through the presence of powerful EFTA multinationals in the influential European Roundtable of Industrialists set up in 1983. Well before the debate on the internal market took off, there were weighty arguments for a closer cooperation with the EC. The emergence of a new economic partnership between the EC and EFTA can thus be interpreted as reflecting broader trends towards a regionalization of the international economy evident already in the early 1980s (Gilpin, 1987; Hine, 1985; Wijkman, 1993). In the early 1980s, both the United States and the EC introduced more protectionist policies. With the Caribbean Basin Initiative the United States started granting special trade concessions to regional groups of developing countries. And pressure groups in the United States were lobbying hard for the introduction of more sectoral reciprocity in trade relations with major competitors. The EC started making more frequent use of voluntary export restraint mechanisms and in April 1984 introduced a so-called 'new trade policy instrument' speeding up the EC's response to unfair trading practices by competitors (Hine, 1985, pp. 93ff. and 259ff.). The snag was that because of West Germany's close links and substantial trade with the EFTANs, to be acceptable to the FRG, a European protectionist solution had to be defined so as to include these countries – which is probably a central reason why the strategists in the Mitterrand government decided that the '1992' project had to be accompanied by an initiative *vis-à-vis* the EFTA countries (cf. also Hager, 1983). The EFTA countries would of course have been among the first casualties of a more protectionist EC and therefore had a strong incentive to ensure that the EFTA economies would be given special treatment (Wallace and Wessels, 1989).

Although there are also countervailing factors, for example transcontinental links between TNCs, there is considerable evidence pointing to the emergence of a new regionalized world economy centring around three trading blocs – Europe, America and the Pacific each with its economic core and periphery (Wijkman, 1993). New research done by the UN's Centre for Transnational Corporations shows that not only trade but also investment patterns are becoming more 'regionalized'. Overall, the EFTANs were adapting to an intra-European interdependence logic and to a global 'neo-mercantilist' logic, both of which pushed the EFTA-periphery in the direction of closer links with Europe's economic centre.

3 The European Economic Area (EEA) initiative

During 1987–8 doubts began to be voiced about the Luxembourg process, especially on the EC side. There were concerns about the enforceability and coherence of the process. At the same time, dramatic changes in Eastern Europe placed the process in a new perspective. In January 1989 in a speech to the European Parliament, Commission President Delors proposed a more 'structured partnership' between the EC and EFTA (Delors, 1989, p. 10). Prior to this initiative, Jacques Delors had held informal talks with, among others, the Norwegian Prime Minister and Labour Party leader, Mrs Brundtland (Eide, 1990). In his speech Delors sketched out two options for the future relationship between the EC and EFTA: one could either retain the present relationship, essentially bilateral, and gradually create a free-trade area encompassing the EC and EFTA or one could look for a new, more structured partnership which could take different forms, for example a Customs Union. In institutional terms, there seemed to be two possibilities: a 'Two-Pillar structure', which was apparently Delors' preferred solution, or powers could be transferred to joint decision-making and administrative institutions in which all EEA countries participated. The Delors initiative was well received and started what in the EFTA countries became known unofficially as the 'Oslo-process' and in the EC as the 'Delors-process'.

The EEA and the 'Europe of concentric circles'

EC enlargement strategy and tactics in the context of a rapidly changing security environment is the key to understanding the Delors initiative in 1989. That politics, even Community high politics, was the central concern behind the initiative is indicated by the fact that only a year before Willy de Clerq, Commissioner for External Relations, had told a Colloquium at the College of Europe that '*la fuite en avant* into a more ambitious approach would be counter-productive' (de Clerq, 1988, p. 29). Less than a year later, Delors considered it important to 'highlight the political dimension of the cooperation between the two groupings'. The latter statement should be interpreted in the light of the growing concern in the Commission and most member states at the prospect of applications for membership from the EFTA countries. Delors' initiative was an attempt to buy time; to avoid a time-consuming enlargement debate at a time when the Community was in the midst of an ambitious process of deepening integration. But the plea for a new type of structured partnership should also be seen as a first attempt on the part of the EC to respond to the call from Central and Eastern Europe for closer relations with the Community. The new type of partnership described by Delors could both be interpreted as a temporary arrangement for prospective members and as a more permanent form of affiliation with the EC. The Commission, supported by the French and West German governments, was at the time developing a strategy of 'concentric circles', which was a way of combining 'deepening' and 'widening' of the Community, while giving priority to deepening in the short term. The strategy essentially consisted in offering to neighbouring European countries differentiated models of cooperation depending on their economic and political conditions.[1] There would be a 'first circle' around the EC core, bringing together the EC's closest partners in EFTA. This circle would offer the EFTA countries membership of the internal market at a price but without the burdens of foreign policy and security integration – a model well suited to German economic interests (Schmieding, 1989). There would then be a 'second' and 'third' circle for countries with weaker economic and cultural ties to the EC countries. The idea was that as countries – whether by their own efforts or by virtue of changing circumstances – became more fit for integration with the EC, they would shift circle and move closer to the core.

By 'highlighting the political dimension of the EC–EFTA dialogue', the Commission wanted to create an alternative to EC membership, attractive to EFTA countries which wished and needed to take part in the internal market. While diplomats involved in the EC–EFTA negotiations stress the strategic nature of Delors' initiative, which had the backing of the Quai D'Orsay and incidentally bore some resemblance to Mitterrand's notion of a 'European Confederation', the idea of a structured partnership as indicated also contained tactical advantages. For the EC Commission, the Delors initiative was a way of postponing new enlargements, at the same time protecting the new process of deepening in the EC. One should recall that the 'Delors Group' had started work on an EMU in the summer of 1988 and was due to present its report in April 1989. Delors was anxious to prevent outsiders from 'rocking the boat'. In the United Kingdom and Denmark he already had two rather restless passengers. This interpretation is supported by a Commission official, Eric Hayes, who in a rare article by a Commission official confirms that Delors was trying to protect the process of deepening integration by offering a short-term alternative to enlargement. In so doing, Delors was not acting entirely on his own, although there appears to have been some divergence between Delors' position and the position of de Clerq. At a meeting in the Dutch town of Consendonck in April 1988, the Commission had reached the clear conclusion that priority had to be given to the EC's internal development which meant that new accessions were unwelcome in the short term (Hayes, 1990, p. 58).

The general attitude that collaboration with the EFTA countries must not be allowed to delay the EC's own plans can be traced further back to the so-called 'Interlaken principles', enunciated by EC Commissioner de Clerq prior to the meeting with EFTA ministers in Interlaken in May 1987 (*EC-Bulletin*, 5–87, p. 65). On this occasion de Clerq had mentioned three principles which were to guide the EC's negotiating posture:

(1) priority would be given to internal EC integration;
(2) the EC's autonomous powers of decision should be preserved;
(3) there would have to be a fair balance between benefits and obligations.

Giving priority to internal EC reforms meant that enlargement had to await the completion of the internal market. It also implied that although the EC was willing to accommodate EFTA on issues of common interest, there could be no question of creating arrangements that would delay the Community's own programme of integration. Decision-making autonomy was a code word for the view that a sharp demarcation line should be maintained between membership and non-membership and that the *acquis institutionel* should be protected. The European Parliament in particular guarded its modest influence jealously and was wary of any attempt by outsiders to influence the normal decision-making process in the EC.

Balancing burdens and benefits

Yet, as Hayes also points out in his article, there were other important motives behind the initiative: the Commission wanted to extend the agenda of the talks *inter alia* in order to achieve a higher degree of reciprocity. There was also concern about the lack of coherence characteristic of the Luxembourg process. Most importantly, however, the Commission was getting increasingly concerned about the problem of implementation. This latter consideration has subsequently been stressed by Frans Andriessen in an interview with *Neue Zürcher Zeitung* and is also reflected in the Interlaken speech when Willy de Clerq, Commissioner for External Economic Relations at the time, talks about the need for balancing. The problem was that there was a risk of asymmetry in the implementation, enforcement and interpretation of common rules and agreements in the EEA. A Commission official explained the need for a more structured approach as follows (Biroli, 1988, pp. 333ff.): first, interest balancing would be easier if the agenda was widened. Besides, there was an increasing technical convergence between trade, monetary and investment issues; and policies of allocation, stabilization and distribution had to be coordinated to maximize benefits. The piecemeal approach adopted so far had emphasized balance within individual negotiating areas rather than overall balance. Matters related to the internal market which constituted preconditions for achieving the internal market had received only scant attention.

Second, he argued that it was difficult to envisage a EEA without a Customs Union which, in turn, implied a common external trade stance. Some in the Commission thus defined the new 'structured partnership' in quite maximalist terms. A Customs Union was considered necessary because different import regimes applicable to products originating outside the EEA would create unequal competition conditions within the EEA. Furthermore, the coexistence within the EEA of a single internal regime with different external regimes would lead to a lack of coherence between internal and external actions. Third, and this point was stressed, there was a need for 'financial solidarity and ... complementary policies geared to the needs of peripheral regions' without which these poorer regions would stand to lose from the double competition of the rich Community partners and the new EFTA partners. This point was stressed by Spain who clearly felt that its own accession negotiations and the negotiations on Spanish adaptation to the EC–EFTA Free Trade Agreements had been harsh. Accordingly, it was loath to give the EFTANs a too generous treatment (Perez, 1988). Last, and not least, there was the problem of compliance. The absence of regulatory and executive powers at supranational level was seen as a serious weakness of the Luxembourg process.

The emphasis on balancing and reciprocity reflected a general toughening of the EC's external trade stance. The EC thinking was that the EFTA countries would only obtain access to the internal market if they were ready to submit to the same binding rules as the EC countries. Delors therefore proposed the creation of a 'two-pillar' structure, which would imply a major strengthening of EFTA's institutions and working procedures and joint mechanisms of enforcement and jurisdiction. The idea was that there would be a kind of 'osmosis' between the two pillars at the decision-shaping stage (Laursen, 1991). Additionally, EFTA would have to accept the overall package deal, of which the internal market was a part. In trade-policy terms, this could be seen as reflecting a move from 'diffuse reciprocity' to more frequent use of 'specific reciprocity' (Nedergaard, 1991). 'Specific', however, should not be understood as sector-specific. On the contrary, the Community wanted specific concessions but within the context of a global approach allowing broad package deals. A final consideration behind the 'two-pillar approach' was that EFTA should introduce more efficient decision-making procedures. The EC was getting impatient with the often cumbersome internal procedures in EFTA. Clearly, a more efficient EFTA input into the EEA talks would also serve to neutralize those in the EC who argued that the EEA talks were delaying the EC's own plans.

Though the call for a more structured partnership came primarily from the EC side, it met with considerable sympathy in EFTA and among experts. Sven Norberg, head of EFTA's legal service, attacked the approach adopted so far shrouding his criticism in a quotation from Parkinson 'if you don't know where you are going you will end up somewhere else' (Jamar and Wallace, 1988, pp. 327ff.). There was also considerable dissatisfaction on the EFTA side with the limited results of the Luxembourg process. As Wallace and Wessels point out 'the Luxembourg process had had too low a profile to force a quickening of the pace of substantive output' (Wallace and Wessels, 1989, p. 4). The Austrian government had also for some time been calling for a 'global approach' to EC–EFTA cooperation (Woschnagg, 1988, p. 347), partly as a way of proving its *Europafähigkeit*, partly perhaps in the hope that a global approach might imply early EFTA participation in some of the Community's attractive new policies.

EFTA's response

In his speech in January 1989, Delors had raised a number of critical questions regarding the Luxembourg process. He had said:

> Are our partners [in EFTA] prepared to abide by the common commercial policy that any customs union must apply to outsiders? Do they share our basic conceptions? The Single Market also implies harmonization. Are our partners willing to transpose the common rules essential to the free movement of goods into their domestic law and in consequence accept the supervision of the Court of Justice? [*Agence Europe*, doc. 1542/1543, 26 January 1989]

These queries represented a major challenge to EFTA, which was internally divided on a number of issues. EFTA countries shared a commitment to create some kind of successor regime to the FTAs, but there was considerable disagreement especially with regard to the introduction of supranational mechanisms. EFTA responded to Delors' proposal in a declaration from a summit meeting in Oslo on 15 March 1989. Although the Swiss government had serious reservations about the idea of introducing supranational elements in EFTA, the joint response from EFTA was broadly positive and did not close doors. The declaration reads in part:

> [we] give our positive response to Mr. Delors' initiative and declare our readiness to explore together with the EC ways and means to achieve a more structured partnership with common decision-making and administrative institutions in order to make our cooperation more effective … We are ready to explore various options and ways and means to strengthen the institutional links. We would not exclude any such option. [*EFTA Bulletin*, April–June 1989, p. 6].

The EFTA countries also declared their readiness to strengthen their internal decision-making process and their mechanisms for surveillance and enforcement of treaty obligations. An informal joint ministerial meeting in Brussels on 20 March 1989 referred to the 'special relations' between the two groups, and the ministers 'confirmed their determination to continue and step up their cooperation'. In concrete terms, it was decided that the Commission and the EFTA countries would initiate talks in the near future (EC Press Release 5483/89, Brussels, 20 March 1989). Thus, a new level was added to the EC–EFTA relationship making the management of the relationship even more complex and time consuming. There were now three levels of negotiations:

(1) Bilateral talks, which were important for countries with particular problems like Iceland, Switzerland and Austria;
(2) the Luxembourg process, which mainly dealt with technical barriers to trade, research and development, environmental issues and training and education;
(3) the EEA process.

In practice, priority was soon given to the EEA track, and there was to be some overlapping between the Luxembourg process and the EEA talks particularly with regard to 'flanking and horizontal policies' such as research and development, the environment, education, consumer policy, small and medium-sized companies (SMEs) and social policy.

Note

1. Significantly, the strategy of 'concentric circles' appears to have had the support of the German Chancellor. Cf. an influential article in the *Frankfurter Algemeine* by two officials in the chancellor's office, 'Der verhängnisvolle Irrtum eines Entweder-Oder', *Frankfurter Algemeine Zeitung*, 19 July 1989.

4 Negotiating the EEA treaty

The fact-finding phase

EC–EFTA negotiations now became much more structured. Work on the EEA started with a fact-finding phase lasting from April to October 1989. On 17 April 1989 it was decided to set up a joint EC–EFTA high-level steering group (HLSG) as a follow-up to the Oslo and Brussels meetings. Five working groups were established: four groups on the substance of the negotiations (free movement of goods, capital and services, persons and 'flanking' and horizontal policies) and a fifth group which was to deal with legal and institutional questions. The EFTA countries decided to present common views in the talks which were then presented by a representative of the country in the chair.

The agenda of issues in the EEA negotiations concentrated on the following categories (cf. Wallace, 1991):

- the core internal market legislation
- institutional and legal issues
- relevant 'flanking and horizontal policies'
- solidarity measures ('cohesion')
- side issues

The two first categories constituted the core of the EEA process, although in the final stages attention was to shift to EFTA financial aid to the southern EC countries and fisheries ('solidarity') and to the side issue of transit. Generally speaking, given the high degree of trade interdependence referred to earlier, there was strong mutual interest in extending the core internal market legislation to the EFTA area. This included the extension of competition rules, regulation of state aids and public procurement. Both sides recognized the need for equal conditions of competition and equally strong and reliable surveillance throughout the EEA. While EFTA would have preferred a negotiated agreement on a common trade regime, the EC side argued that it would be impossible to unravel the numerous internal compromises on standards and rules which had been reached only with great difficulty.

The EC approach prevailed. The general approach chosen was to let the rules in the Treaty of Rome form the basis for the substantive rules to be included in the EEA treaty with special arrangements in some areas. This meant that basically the EFTA countries had to introduce the EC's extensive body of market regulations in their economies. This constituted a major concession on EFTA's part, and the EFTA negotiators therefore linked acceptance of the Community *acquis* to the adoption of a decision-making arrangement in the EEA, which would give EFTA countries real influence on future internal market legislation.

The EC's negotiating goals were primarily related to legal issues (enforcement and implementation), solidarity measures and side issues such as transit. EFTA's attention was focused on the institutional questions (first of all co-decision). But sensitive aspects of the internal market legislation (for example environmental protection and product safety), and some horizontal policies were also considered important by EFTA countries. Participation in collaborative ventures in areas such as education (for example COMETT, ERASMUS) and research and development (for example CREST) would involve tangible benefits for EFTA citizens (*EFTA Thirtieth Annual Report*, 1991, pp. 21ff.). The main goal of EFTA in this field was thus to obtain a legal basis for full and equal participation in EC activities.

Preparing the EEA agenda

EFTA cohesion was damaged even before the start of the EEA negotiations. The Delors initiative failed to stop Austria's march towards Brussels. On 17 July 1989 the Austrian government submitted its application for full EC membership. The Austrian 'defection' weakened EFTA's negotiating position and threatened to inspire other EFTA governments to apply as well. A chain reaction was a distinct possibility. But this could not stop the EEA process if only because the Austrians insisted that the EEA negotiations were important to them as well. On 20 October, the HLSG was thus able to submit a fact-finding report to the Commission and EC and EFTA ministers concluding that the positions of both sides were now sufficiently close to envisage negotiations on a future EEA agreement (*EFTA Twenty-Ninth Annual Report*, 1990, pp. 9ff.). The report first noted that in order to achieve the objective of the fullest possible realization of free movement of goods, services, capital and persons, the relevant Community *acquis*, which would be identified jointly, should be integrated into an agreement as the common legal basis for the future EEA. Exceptions justified by considerations of fundamental interests and transitional arrangements would be matters for negotiation.

On agriculture, different possibilities were examined for improving market access. It was not considered realistic to aim at an EEA-wide common agricultural policy. On fish and other marine products, EFTA stated that an agreement should ensure the free circulation of fisheries' products. Regarding the free movement of capital, the HLSG noted a general trend towards liberalization of capital movements evident in most OECD countries. It appeared possible to aim at the creation of an EEA-wide market for all services. With regard to free movement of persons, it appeared realistic to work towards the free movement of employees/self-employed persons and members of their families throughout the EEA, based on the equal treatment with nationals of the host country. Given the particular situation in some EFTA countries regarding free movement of persons, the EFTA side underlined that particular arrangements, quantitative or otherwise, would be a prerequisite for any negotiations in this field. The EFTA side also thought that simplifications of border formalities should be included in the negotiations.

An expanded cooperation on flanking and horizontal policies was envisaged. On legal and institutional questions, the HLSG pointed out that a good deal of common ground had been identified. On the central issue of decision making in respect of future legislation, a number of options had been examined, *inter alia* a structure based on separate EFTA and EC 'pillars' with constant interaction, 'reciprocal osmosis' throughout the decision-shaping stage. Both sides recognized that the aim should be to reach at the end of the process a joint decision to be adopted by consensus by the contracting parties. The EFTA side stressed that a genuine joint decision-making mechanism in substance and form would be a basic prerequisite for the political acceptability and the legal effectiveness of an agreement.

EC and EFTA ministers in their joint meeting in Brussels on 19 December 1989 took the political decision to start negotiations as soon as possible in the first half of 1990. The joint declaration from the meeting spelt out the objectives of the negotiations and the principles which were to guide them (*Agence Europe*, 23 December 1989, p. 9). It was pointed out that the ministers felt that this framework (for the EEA) should ensure 'the global and balanced character of their cooperation'. In more concrete terms, the objectives would be:

- to achieve the free movement of goods, services, capital and persons on the basis of the relevant *acquis communautaire* to be identified jointly;
- to strengthen and to broaden cooperation in the context of the Community's action in other areas such as research and development, the environment, education and the social dimension;
- to reduce economic and social disparities between the regions.

It was added that this framework should *inter alia* respect in full the decision-making autonomy of the parties and that negotiations should provide for:

- procedures which effectively ensured that both parties' views were taken into account;
- appropriate formulae to ensure the direct effect of common legislation, surveillance of its implementation as well as judicial monitoring and the proper functioning, in general, of the agreement.

In conjunction with the joint ministerial meeting, two EC–EFTA agreements were signed, both results of the Luxembourg process. The first agreement dealt with the EFTA countries' participation in the Community's COMETT II programme, the second with mutual information on draft technical regulations (*EFTA Twenty-Ninth Annual Report*, 1990, pp. 6ff.).

The exploratory phase

During the first half of 1990, the HLSG conducted exploratory talks in preparation for the start of formal negotiations. The HLSG held three meetings in which it tried to identify the central problems in each negotiating area. The EFTA side was anxious to speed up the EEA talks.

It was feared that the dramatic events in Central and Eastern Europe might distract the EC from its negotiations with EFTA. EFTA also watched with some concern the acceleration of the EC's internal reform process. In January 1990, Swedish Prime Minister Carlsson was quoted as saying that in his view the EEA negotiations ought to be finalized by the end of the year (Reuter, Stockholm, 14 January 1990). The EC Commission did not feel the same time pressure. The Commission spokesman, Nikolas Wegter, stated in early January that there was no deadline for the EEA talks, but that there was an expectation that the EEA treaty would be ready at the same time as the internal market (Reuter, London, 6 January 1990). He also said that Austria must await the right moment for consideration of its application, submitted in July 1989. He added mischievously that no one knew when the right moment was.

On 17 January 1990, Jacques Delors in a speech to the European Parliament once again made reference to the EEA process. The speech was a considerable disappointment to EFTA. Delors said that although an EEA agreement would involve some sort of osmosis between the Community and EFTA, this process must stop short of joint decision making (Delors, 1990). This was an early warning that the institutional and legal issues would cause problems. The reason for the toughening of Delors' position was undoubtedly the changes which had taken place in Europe since early 1989. The two Germanies were moving closer to each other, and Eastern Europe was undergoing a democratic revolution which looked set to redraw the political and economic map of Europe. These developments set the alarm bells ringing in the Commission. Would it be possible to resist calls to relax the timetable for creating a European Union? In his speech, Jacques Delors emphasized the risk of a neo-nationalist trend in Europe accompanied by a 'building-down' of the Community.

> The risk for the Community itself is enormous, for the rapid developments have reactivated the debate on the European construction. I already hear voices demanding that the cooperation between the 12, seen as an off-spring of the Cold War, should cease to exist along with this. [Delors, 1990]

Behind these concerns lurked a more fundamental and longer-term worry: might not the Bonn government be tempted to pursue an ambitious bilateral foreign policy towards the new Eastern Europe and the changing Soviet Union which would imply a *de facto* downgrading of the multilateral EC framework (Petersen, 1991, pp. 112–13)? The conclusion drawn in Brussels – as indeed in Paris and other capitals – was that the EC now had to accelerate the process of European unification and extend it to the political sphere in order to forestall a new German unilateralism.

Despite Delors' warnings about the need to protect the Community structure, the public and academic debate on the EEA kept revolving around the issue of co-decision for the EFTA countries. There was a general and a more specific aspect to this discussion. The general question was how the EFTA countries were to be involved in regular decision making on legislation relevant to the EEA. As pointed out by the Swiss Ambassador Benedict von Tscharner, the EEA regime being negotiated raised a problem of democratic legitimacy. How were EFTA governments to explain to their parliaments that they now had to follow EFTA rules in a number of areas? (*Financial Times*, 27 November 1990). EC officials had in the course of the talks developed the twin concepts of *decision making* and *decision shaping*. The rather vague concept of decision shaping referred to an arrangement whereby the EFTA countries would be involved in the early stages of decision making but without being granted the same influence in the actual decision making as the EC member states themselves. Commission President Delors stated in early May 1990 that in his view EFTA had demanded too much. 'If they [the EFTA countries] want access to decision making, they must apply for membership [of the EC]', he said (Reuter, Copenhagen, 4 May 1990). The more specific aspect of the problem of co-decision was related to the EC demand for a financial contribution from EFTA to cohesion. Originally, it had been intended that EFTA should contribute to the EC's regional development fund. But the EC gradually realized that it was difficult to impose taxation without allowing representation. It therefore changed position, suggesting instead that the EFTA countries pay directly to selected EC countries. There was also a shift in emphasis in the cohesion talks from financial contributions to concessions on fish and agricultural products.

Internal bargaining in the EC and EFTA

In the course of the spring of 1990, EC and EFTA officials started identifying the issues to be put on the negotiating agenda. It was evident that although both sides wanted the negotiations to be structured as group-to-group negotations, individual member states had many special interests which they wanted to protect. This made the multilateral talks very cumbersome and more time-consuming than originally expected.

The problem was most acute for EFTA, in part because of the weakness of the organization's decision-making apparatus and the absence of a strong broker like the EC Commission. From the point of view of EFTA, the most sensitive areas (apart from the institutional issues) were: agriculture, fisheries, the free movement of persons, the right of establishment, EC direct investments in EFTA countries, rules for transit and consumer protection (*Agence Europe*, 13 January 1990). While most of the areas mentioned above were problem areas for only some of the EFTA countries, consumer protection constituted a problem for all of them. In all EFTA countries product standards were above the EC level. EFTA thus wanted to retain a high standard for both domestic and imported goods. From the EC's point of view it was important to maintain the homogeneity of the internal market and the EEA. Besides, it was regarded as impossible to introduce changes in EC rules on environmental protection and product standards in order to facilitate agreement on an EEA treaty since the EC rules were the result of compromises accomplished with great difficulty (*Agence Europe*, 12 April 1990). What made the problem manageable, however, was the fact that the Community was gradually beginning to pay more attention to environmental issues so that in most areas EC standards were expected to converge with EFTA standards over time. In most cases this made transition periods an acceptable solution to EFTA.

Within EFTA economic divergence is limited; in some respects this facilitated agreement on a negotiating strategy *vis-à-vis* the EC. Yet, there are important differences between the EFTA countries in terms of production structure, internal political structures and domestic politics.

Switzerland adopted by far the toughest bargaining position. For Switzerland the fundamental concern was to retain its autonomy and to protect Swiss direct democracy and Swiss federalism. In asking for a right of co-decision on EEA-relevant legislation, the Swiss therefore went further than their EFTA partners by demanding a unilateral right to opt out of future legislation and a right to participate in relevant EC committees. Regarding the four freedoms, for Switzerland the most sensitive issue was the free movement of persons. It was feared that this would lead to an increase in the already high number of immigrants in the country. Besides, there was concern about a possible reduction in health and environmental standards as a consequence of an EEA treaty; the Swiss also wanted to retain the right to place restrictions on the right of foreigners to buy property. They refused to raise their 28-ton limit on lorry transit to 40 tons as demanded by the EC. Finally, the Swiss government raised objections to mutual recognition of professional qualifications (Reuter, Luxembourg, 18 June 1990).

Iceland was a hardliner on a par with Switzerland. For Iceland, fisheries was the main worry given that exports of fish account for some 75 per cent of its hard currency earnings. The intensity of Icelandic fishing interests was of a kind that made compromise difficult. Iceland's commitment to maintaining control over fishing resources was so strong that its partners in EFTA found they had to accommodate Iceland.

Norway was also concerned to preserve its fishing rights and to improve market access for its fishing products. But Norway had other special worries. It wanted to safeguard the special Norwegian laws and regulations which place restrictions on foreign ownership of Norwegian natural resources (the so-called 'concessionary laws').

Finland had special problems in areas like shipbuilding and public procurement. It also saw problems in the field of free movement of capital, fearing that foreigners might buy up Finnish forests (Reuter, Brussels, 16 October 1990). But generally Finland was not among the most demanding EFTA countries. Unlike its foreign-policy cousin, Sweden, Finland did not seem to regard loss of influence as a serious risk. Helsinki expected that irrespective of the formal agreements, it would be possible to obtain a *de facto* co-decision.

Austria was in a special position having submitted an application for membership of the EC in July 1989. Thus, for the government in Vienna, the EEA process was a second-best. Austria was not satisfied with the minimal influence granted EFTA countries in the EC proposals presented so far (*Agence Europe*, 23 February 1990). The Austrian ambassador stated in the spring of 1990 that Austria entered the EEA negotiations with few concrete demands (*Guardian*, 5 March 1990). Yet, there were problems with consumer protection and transit for lorries.

Along with Austria, *Sweden* was the country with the fewest specific demands. Sweden had few problems with the free movement of goods, services, capital and persons but was somewhat concerned about the risk of a loss of sovereignty in a number of policy areas under an EEA regime (*Guardian*, 5 March 1990).

Economic divergence is greater in the EC than in EFTA. This raised the problem of compensation to the weaker economies in the EC for the opening of their markets to EFTA producers. Inter-institutional rivalry and bureaucratic politics on the EC side added to the difficulties. In the course of the spring of 1990, a certain amount of tension developed between the EC Commission and the politicians in the Council of Ministers. While the politicians were eager to start negotiations, fearing that otherwise the Community would be facing more membership applications, the Commission had to grapple with the enormously complicated technicalities and at the same time protect the Community structure (Reuter, Brussels, 7 May 1990). Besides, the European Parliament had signalled that it would not accept an agreement which gave the EFTA countries more influence on EC legislation than the European Parliament. This was no empty threat since the Single European Act had given the Parliament the power to reject association agreements.

In May 1990, after some delay, the Commission was able to submit to the Council of Ministers the draft which would be the basis for the start of negotiations. The draft contained four main items:

- the greatest possible free movement of goods, services, capital and persons on the basis of the Community *acquis*;
- equal competition, including adequate removal of state aid;
- the inclusion of agriculture and fisheries, taking into account the sensitivity of these matters;
- no compromise as regards decision making (*Agence Europe*, 9 May 1990).

Formal negotiations commence

The formal negotiations between the two groups commenced in June 1990. The first meeting of the negotiators took place on 20 June. Negotiations were conducted by the same officials who had conducted the exploratory talks, the name of the high-level group being changed to the High-Level Negotiating Group (HLNG). It was decided that HLNG negotiations would proceed with monthly two-day meetings. The five working groups were maintained, but it was decided to add a sixth group which would deal with the drafting of the proposed treaty (*EFTA News*, no. 5, 2 July 1990). Both sides wanted the agreement to be operative as of 1 January 1993, that is concurrently with the internal market. However, the time pressure was clearly felt more acutely in EFTA than in the EC.

The first phase of the negotiations was dominated by the attempt jointly to define relevant *acquis communautaire*.[1] The relevant parts of this legislation were to be integrated into the treaty as the legal basis of the EEA. The negotiations in September and October centred on two key issues: the request of the EFTA countries for a number of permanent derogations from the *acquis*, a request which had already been voiced in the opening statement from EFTA on 20 June, and the reluctance of the Community to enter into substantive talks on institutional arrangements for the EEA. Negotiations made little progress during the first two months. The meeting in the HLNG on 17–18 October appears to have been a downright disaster. In the course of the following weeks the situation changed. In order to escape from the impasse, at an informal meeting of EFTA ministers on 23 October it was decided to withdraw the request for permanent derogations and to explore the possibility of replacing them with transition periods, safeguard arrangements or non-discriminatory measures. However, this concession was made conditional upon the willingness on the part of the EC to *inter alia* 'accept legal and institutional arrangements allowing for common management and development of the EEA, in particular a genuine common decision-making mechanism' (*EFTA News*, no. 8, 13 November 1990). The background to this initiative should probably be found at the level of domestic politics in individual EFTA countries. On 18 October Norway had linked its currency to the ECU. In Sweden there was growing appreciation of the limitations of the EEA strategy. In fact, Sweden appeared headed for an early membership application. The new Swedish signals suggested to the EFTA partners that unless more rapid progress was made in the EEA negotiations, the whole EEA process risked being overtaken – and reduced to near insignificance – by a series of EC membership applications. Against this background, the new concessions from EFTA made sense. On the other hand, anonymous officials in the EC Commission expressed concern lest the Swedish change in position hamper the EEA negotiations (Reuter, Brussels, 26 October 1990). What they had in mind was the risk that some EC member states might lose interest in bringing the talks forward or perhaps toughen their demands aware of the fact that more and more EFTA countries saw an EEA treaty as a prelude to membership.

At a meeting in late October in Luxembourg, the EC council responding positively to EFTA's initiative regarding derogations recognized for the first time that questions concerning the institutions and legal mechanisms should be dealt with in parallel with other parts of the treaty negotiations.

This was the quid pro quo to which EFTA had been looking forward. During a meeting of chief negotiators from the two sides in early November, the new EFTA position was discussed and a major breakthrough was achieved. EFTA indicated that in the context of an overall balanced solution, it was prepared to recommend to its member governments that they consider withdrawing their requests for permanent derogations. This offer was conditional upon a satisfactory legal and institutional set-up, as well as on transition periods for the implementation of appropriate non-discriminatory legislation and adequate safeguard mechanisms for more specific situations. It was added that this position did not cover matters related to transit, which were dealt with bilaterally by the EC and Switzerland and Austria, or Icelandic fisheries.

EFTA's new offer was conveyed to the EC in writing at an HLNG meeting on 22 November. As a result of the initiative, considerable progress was made on a number of points in December, and the way was paved for a joint ministerial meeting on 19 December 1990 in Brussels. However, the issue of joint decision making remained unresolved. It was still not clear what would happen if no consensus was reached (*Neue Zürcher Zeitung*, 14 December 1990). Would individual EFTA countries have a right to opt out of new legislation, as demanded by Switzerland? The EC was sceptical, fearing that this kind of generalized differentiation, which was not permitted within the EC, might come to serve as a precedent and damage the EC's internal cohesion.

In late November, the EC suddenly presented new demands in the agricultural field. While recognizing that agriculture was not formally included in the EEA negotiations, the Community nevertheless demanded concessions in terms of improved market access for 72 agricultural products (*Neue Zürcher Zeitung*, 17 November 1990). The demand for improved market access in EFTA countries was originally formulated by Spain, which was looking for a belated compensation for what Madrid regarded as an unsatisfactory accession agreement. Thus, the products involved were primarily products of major importance to Spain and Portugal such as tomatoes, nuts, citrus fruits, and flowers (*Neue Zürcher Zeitung*, 18–19 November 1990).

A week before the joint ministerial meeting, on 12 December 1990 a large majority in the Swedish Parliament, consisting of liberals, conservatives, social democrats and centrists gave the government a mandate to apply for EC membership. Only the Green Party and the Left Communists voted against (*Dagens Nyheter*, 12 December 1990; *Neue Zürcher Zeitung*, 16 December 1990).

The joint ministerial meeting on 19 December was able to register progress in a number of key areas particularly regarding the institutional set-up. In this field it was decided that there would be:

(1) A continuous information and consultation process in the decision-shaping phase;
(2) EFTA countries would have the possibility of raising a matter of concern at any moment and at any level without causing additional delays (*droit d'évocation*);
(3) decisions at EEA level would be taken by consensus, the EFTA countries speaking with one voice, and have the character of public international law (Europe Documents no. 1683; *Agence Europe*, 15 January 1991).

Thus, the distinction between decision making and decision shaping was maintained. And the decision that EFTA would be speaking with one voice implied that there would be no individual opting out. EFTA had been asking for the formation of joint decision-making bodies. At the December ministerial meeting, the EC accepted the idea of an EEA council. The joint declaration reads:

An EEA council composed of the members of the EC council, members of the EC Commission and ministers of the EFTA countries, will be set up responsible in particular for
– the general political guidelines
– the global assessment of the functioning and the development of the agreement
– the political decisions leading to modifications in the EEA agreement.

Finally, it was agreed to establish an EEA joint body 'responsible for the implementation and operation of the agreement including the decisions regarding the EEA, to be taken by consensus of the EC on one side and the EFTA countries speaking with one voice on the other'.

On the substantive side, it was noted that the joint identification of the relevant *acquis* had largely been completed. Approximately 1,400 legal acts were to be included in the EEA treaty. However, there were still problems in reconciling a high level of protection of the environment and high standards of product safety with free circulation of goods. It was stated that efforts should be made to sign the EEA agreement before the summer of 1991 in order that the agreement might take effect on 1 January 1993.

Notwithstanding the results mentioned above, the December joint ministerial meeting left some crucial questions open: the financial mechanism, agriculture and fisheries – that is the issues relating to 'cohesion' and balance – and it did not give guidance to the negotiators on some important institutional questions such as the participation of representatives of the EFTA countries in EC committees and the composition and competence of a joint judicial body.

A new series of HLNG meetings in the first months of 1991 first concentrated on agriculture and safeguards. The HLNG started talks between the Commission and individual EFTA countries in the field of agriculture. The talks were made bilateral in view of the differences in agricultural structure and policies in the EFTA countries. An evolutionary clause was envisaged for the agricultural field. Progress was made on the issue of competition. EFTA accepted the EC demand that an independent EFTA structure for the application of competition rules be established and that this structure should be entrusted with equivalent powers and similar functions to those exercised by the EC Commission. At the March meeting in the HLNG, Switzerland and Liechtenstein further signalled a willingness to reduce transition periods required for putting the full *acquis* for free movement of persons into effect (*EFTA News*, no. 1, 31 January 1991; *EFTA News*, no. 3, 2 April 1991). On the negative side, the negotiations on fisheries were in deep crisis. Iceland boycotted meetings in the HLNG because of the EC's insistence that it wanted access to Icelandic fishing waters. An EC diplomat commented that Iceland's absence had not even been noted (*Dagens Nyheter*, 3 May 1991).

Progress on institutional and legal issues

The joint ministerial meeting in Brussels on 13 May 1991 achieved significant results in several areas. First of all, a solution was found to the problem of a judicial mechanism. EFTA wanted an independent judicial body with competence in EEA matters, whereas the EC wanted the EC Court of Justice to play the central role. The solution arrived at in this field was the establishment of a mixed court of justice with five judges from the EC and three from EFTA. The EEA court would be independent but functionally integrated with the EC Court of Justice, a vague and contradictory formulation that would require a lot of subsequent work. Second, as a quid pro quo, the EC obtained an assurance from the EFTA countries that they would introduce provisions in their internal legislation to the effect that rules of the agreement establishing a European Economic Area should prevail in cases of conflict between these rules and provisions of the EFTA countries' internal legal order (the joint declaration from the meeting is printed in *EFTA Information*, 8/1991/F, 14 May 1991). This meant that the EFTA countries had now *de facto* accepted supranationality.

Third, the issue of an EFTA role in decision making was finally resolved. Spurred on by the Swiss government, EFTA had demanded that EFTA countries be given the right unilaterally to opt out of new EEA relevant rules and that EFTA countries be given the right to take part in the EC's committee work. On both issues, the EC was reluctant to make concessions. The EC was adamant in its resistance to a system of individual opting out. As mentioned earlier, in the EC's view there was a risk that such differentiation would be regarded as a precedent by EC member states. What is more, it would jeopardize the legal homogeneity in the European economic area with negative consequences for the balance of advantages and costs as well as for the business climate. Thus, as regards the question of opting out, EFTA's demand was rejected. This was accepted by most EFTA countries, but the Swiss government reserved its position.

On the issue of comitology, on the other hand, a compromise was reached according to which experts from EFTA would be included in the work of some of the committees under the Commission. It was added that as far as the committees relating to the flanking policies were concerned, the status of the EFTA countries would 'take full account of their possible financial participation in the projects concerned'. A footnote was added stating that the Commission would send to the EFTA side a letter explaining the modalities of the paragraph – a good example of the lack of clarity which was to characterize major parts of the agreement. It was not made clear to which committees this arrangement was to apply.[2]

The May ministerial meeting thus to all intents and purposes closed the institutional and legal dossier. The meeting also made progress in other fields: EFTA obtained a general safeguard clause which 'could be triggered into action, whenever serious economic, societal and/or environmental difficulties of a sectoral or regional nature were arising'. However, at the insistence of the EC, eager to preserve the maximum legal homogeneity of the European Economic Area, it was added that before making use of the safeguard clause, EFTA countries would submit the difficulty in question to a joint committee which would try to find a mutually acceptable solution. Finally, the meeting took note of the progress achieved in the agricultural area. The EFTA countries committed themselves to abolishing or reducing import duties from 1 January 1993 on a range of products of particular importance to the less-developed regions of the Community. Further, the parties committed themselves to facilitating trading conditions for processed agricultural products. It was decided that an evolutionary clause would be included in the EEA agreement in this area. Agreement was also reached in a number of horizontal areas such as social policy and environmental policy. In these areas, it was decided that transitional periods would in general apply.

With regard to environmental issues, the meeting in May found a pragmatic solution: different transition periods would apply. Thus, in relation to the EC rules on exhaust emission for motor vehicles, it was agreed that there would be free circulation as of 1 January 1995 on the basis of the Community *acquis*. For certain other products (for example fertilizers containing cadmium, CFCs, Halons) a so-called 'open-ended transitional period' – a major challenge to logic – was agreed subject to review in 1995. Unsolved problems remained regarding dangerous substances, chemical substances and pesticides. A transition period was foreseen for the free movement of persons and for the purchase of property in the EFTA countries.

Most EFTA countries took the view that the meeting had been a success. The Norwegian Prime Minister, Gro Harlem Brundtland, said that 'the most difficult issue has now been solved. The central thing for us was to get an independent EEA court'. The Finnish Minister for Foreign Trade, Pertti Salolainen, similarly regarded the agreement on the EEA court as the biggest breakthrough (*Dagens Nyheter*, 15 May 1991). Sweden and Austria did not have strong views about the meeting, as both countries now had their eyes set on the pending accession talks. The Swiss government, on the other hand, had become marginalized during the meeting, blocking progress in several areas. An observer characterized the result of the meeting as 'a piece of Swiss cheese with holes – holes made by Switzerland itself' (*Financial Times*, 15 May 1991).

Solidarity issues and transit

By the middle of May 1991, there were three major issue areas outstanding: fisheries, an EFTA financial mechanism for the less-developed regions of the Community – both aspects of the cohesion issue, pitting north against south – and transit. The compensations sought from

EFTA could for the most part be seen as side-payments to the EC countries which would be negatively affected by an EEA regime. The southern EC countries argued that they had a right to be compensated for opening up their markets to the efficient EFTA producers.

Thus, it was envisaged that Spain and Portugal would be the main beneficiaries in the field of fisheries and agriculture, whereas Greece (and Italy) would be the main beneficiaries of a relaxation of transit rules in Austria and Switzerland. A linkage was established between the issue of fisheries and the financial mechanism. The message from Brussels was that politicians in Oslo and Reykjavik could buy themselves peace with their fishing community. The EEA negotiations were now considerably behind schedule. The two parties had committed themselves to signing the EEA treaty at a solemn gathering in Salzburg on 25 June. A final breakthrough was sought at a joint ministerial meeting in Luxembourg on 18 June. Whether because Austria's partners in EFTA did not want to see Austria, 'the defector', take the credit for finishing the EEA negotiations or for other and sounder reasons, the negotiations moved forward at a snail's pace. These now focused on fisheries. In the run-up to the joint ministerial meeting, the Spanish Minister for European Affairs, Carlos Westendorp, reasserted his demands, saying that Spain wanted a right to fish 30,000 tons of fish in Norwegian and Icelandic waters. He added that 'unless we get an agreement on fish, we shall use our veto in Luxembourg' (*Dagens Nyheter*, 19 June 1991). Confronting the Spanish was the Icelandic government, whose Foreign Minister, Jon Baldwin, stated that his country was prepared to contribute to a regional development fund but that it was not prepared to let Spanish fishermen into its waters (ibid.).

The joint ministerial meeting on 18 June 1991 resulted in a tentative political agreement on fisheries and the financial mechanism, but the two sides' interpretation of the agreement varied considerably. The Norwegian Trade Minister, Eldrid Nordbø, left the negotiating table convinced that a historic agreement had been reached. Nordbø told the press in Oslo that Norway would get free access to the EC market for raw fish and processed fishing products. In return a small group of EC member states would get the right to fish around Svalbard. Shortly after the meeting it became clear that the EC interpretation was markedly different. As a result the Norwegian Prime Minister Mrs Brundtland was placed in a difficult position on the domestic political scene.

The Salzburg meeting on 25 June was held in a sombre mood. Instead of the expected final agreement, the meeting produced an empty statement of one and a half pages. A hectic HLNG meeting at the end of July did not bring a solution either. It was therefore decided to resume negotiations after the summer recess. At a meeting in late September, the EC General Affairs Council decided that the EEA accord would be a 'mixed agreement', that is on the part of both the EC and its member states. The reason was that a political dialogue was to be attached to the agreement. This implied parliamentary ratification in all member states (*Agence Europe*, 27 September 1991).

On 1 July the Swedish government submitted its application for EC membership. Prime Minister Carlsson held a press conference at the Swedish Embassy in Brussels in which he said that Sweden supported the plans for an EMU, including a common currency. He also underlined that Sweden would not join the EC as a passive member. Sweden would participate and try to influence the EC's and Europe's future. Commenting upon the crisis in Yugoslavia, he said that 'the EC has not done anything which we cannot support. But we think that a military force should be supported by the UN or by the CSCE' (*Dagens Nyheter*, 2 July 1991). Unlike Austria, Sweden submitted an application which contained no neutrality clause. The Swedish application went almost unnoticed in the European media. In one of the few international comments, the Dutch prime minister, now President of the EC Council, called the Swedish neutrality 'antique'.

Just before the summer recess, the Commission adopted its opinion on Austria's request for membership of the EC (Europe Doc. 1730, *Agence Europe*, 3 August 1991). While favourable towards Austrian membership, the document also conveyed the message that membership negotiations would not begin before 1993; that applicant countries should accept the *acquis communautaire*, not as it would be at the time of their application for membership but as it would be at the end of the two intergovernmental conferences on Political Union and Economic and Monetary Union. Norway, Iceland, Finland and Switzerland thus returned to the negotiating tables after the summer recess reminded of the growing fragmentation within EFTA.

Finalizing the formal negotiations

After intense negotiations in the early autumn, the EEA agreement was finally concluded on 21 October – almost a year later than originally envisaged by the EFTA countries (*Le Monde*, 23 October 1991). What appears to have unblocked the negotiations on fish was the EC

Commission's decision to halve its demands for access to fishing resources to 11,000 tons in 1997. Although this concession was balanced by the removal of some 'sensitive' species of fish from the list of fish which would get free access to the EC market, it did represent an opening (*Dagens Nyheter*, 18 October 1991).

But the EC also used the stick, taking advantage of the EC's greater freedom of action. In late September, the Commission told Norway and Iceland to be more flexible in negotiations on fisheries or face being left out altogether from plans to build the world's biggest common market. A Commission official also reminded EFTA that the EC was incurring heavy opportunity costs as a result of the delay in the EEA talks. The EC had other ways of using its scarce administrative and political resources. It had alternatives which EFTA did not have. Plans for EEA had slipped well down on the EC's list of priorities as EFTA countries opted one by one for outright membership and Eastern European countries joined them in knocking at the Community's doors. In the words of the Commission official, 'when the world is crumbling, is it really serious to begin negotiating about 20,000–30,000 tons of fish? It is a secondary issue. I do not think the Community will devote much energy to it' (Reuters, 22 September 1991). Significantly, EC diplomats went on record saying that although the EEA accord might be supplanted by bilateral agreements, the EC would only be prepared to negotiate bilaterally with those EFTA countries which had applied for Community membership or who did so before 1993 (ibid.). The statement was part of the negotiating tactics but also reflected the EC preference for a binding and balanced cooperation, whether through membership or through EEA affiliation.

At the ministerial meeting in late October, Iceland – true to its tradition – stuck to its refusal to admit EC fishing vessels into its waters. Norway, on the other hand, agreed to raise the EC's share of Norwegian catches. Spain obtained an additional catch of 6,000 tons in 1993, rising to 11,000 in the following years until 1997. Seen with Spanish eyes this was a meagre result. Prior to the negotiations in October, Spain had demanded 30,000 tons, and its original demand had been 90,000 tons (*Neue Zürcher Zeitung*, 20–21 October 1991). However, as earlier EC concessions on fishing resources were balanced by EFTA concessions on market access, EFTA had to give up its demand for full free-market access for fish products and other marine products. The United Kingdom, Ireland and to some extent also France did not want to expose their producers to full-scale competition from EFTA

(*Financial Times*, 21 October 1991). But EFTA did obtain duty-free access as from 1 January 1993 for a number of products. For other categories of products there would be transitional periods with a reduction of duties by 70 per cent before 1 January 1997. For sensitive products including herring, salmon and mackerel, however, EFTA did not obtain tariff reductions (*Financial Times*, 23 October 1991). An evolutionary clause was added to the agreement.

The breakthrough on fish should also be seen in the context of the agreement on the financial mechanism. Some EFTA countries, notably Finland, had been reluctant to contribute financially to cohesion partly because of domestic economic difficulties, partly because they regarded aid to Eastern Europe and the former Soviet Union as more important. The EC for its part recognized with reference to the Finnish situation that 'there had been financial changes provoked in the EFTA countries by the upheaval in Central and Eastern Europe and in the USSR and it would take them into account during discussions of the cohesion fund' (*Agence Europe*, 27 September 1991).

At the meeting, EFTA nevertheless agreed to a financial transfer in the form of soft loans and grants. The loans offered to selected south European EC countries would amount to Ecu 1,500 million, the interest rate subsidies amounting to 3 per cent. Additionally, there would be a grace period of two years for the repayment of loans. As for grants, the EFTA countries committed themselves to paying Ecu 500 million over five years. The financial mechanism would give priority to environmental and educational projects. The beneficiaries would be Spain, Portugal, Greece and Ireland (*EFTA News*, no. 8, 24 October 1991).

On the issue of transit, an overwhelming majority on the EC transport council supported agreements concluded by the Commission and the Austrian and Swiss governments. Greece rejected the agreement with Austria but was outvoted in the council by 11 to 1. For a while Greece threatened to veto the whole EEA agreement unless it got more licences for heavy lorry transit, but it eventually accepted the agreement. The agreement with Switzerland would maintain the Swiss weight limit of 28 tons as the general principle. However, 50 trucks of up to 38 tons would be allowed to pass through Switzerland every day, if they were under two years old, carried perishable goods and provided rail transport capacity was full (*Financial Times*, 22 October 1991). The agreement with Austria, which had caused more difficulties, provides for a maximum of 1.3 million transit licences for EC heavy lorries. This would freeze the level of permits for all EC member states except Greece, which would get a 29 per cent increase to 60,500 licences a year (*Neue Zürcher Zeitung*, 21 October 1991). Austria had also wanted a reduction in the pollution from transit traffic of 65 per cent over the next 10 years but eventually accepted a 60 per cent reduction over 12 years (*Financial Times*, 23 October 1991). Some other issues were discussed in the final stage of negotiations. Thus, the EFTA status in the so-called 'category three committees' was discussed. It was agreed that the EFTA countries would have access to nine such committees by the entry into force of the agreement. EFTA countries would also be involved and present on the CREST committee, concerned with research and development cooperation (*EFTA Information* 21/91/FS, 25 October 1991).

There were a number of official reactions to the negotiating result. Predictably, all EFTA governments were satisfied that an agreement ensuring participation in the internal market had been achieved in the eleventh hour. The Swiss Foreign Minister, Rene Felber, said that his country was prepared to sign the agreement but only as a step in the direction of full membership. Finnish Prime Minister Aho said that Finland would take a position on membership early in 1992. Commission President Delors stated that the EEA was a useful experience for EFTA countries wanting to become EC members. Frans Andriessen, EC Commissioner for External Relations, told the press that 'Europe is much too heterogeneous to have only one form of integration' (*Financial Times*, 23 October 1991). Willy de Clerq, liberal Chairman of the Committee for External Economic Relations in the European Parliament (REX-Committee), while welcoming the final agreement, said: 'Do not forget that we [the European Parliament] have the final word' (*Financial Times*, 24 October 1991).

The European Court of Justice intervenes

On 18 November 1991 it became clear that the celebrations had been premature. On the day that the EEA was due to be initialled, the EC Court of Justice sent the Commission a series of questions. This step caused the Commission to delay the initial signing of the treaty (*Financial Times*, 19 November 1991). Later in a 52-page opinion on the EEA agreement, the Court of Justice claimed that the plan to set up a new court would contravene EC law (*Financial Times*, 16 December 1991).

The court's objections were quite serious. Pointing out that according to Article 164 of the Treaty of Rome it had the sole right to interpret Community law, the Court argued that there was a risk that the proposed EEA court would effectively pre-empt its ruling on matters of EC law, on which EEA rules would be closely modelled. The interpretation of the EEA Court might not conform with that of the ECJ, as the objectives of the EC and EFTA differ in crucial respects.

The court also pointed out that the new arrangements would have uneven legal effects. The EEA court would have more impact on EFTA countries than EC states, where the supreme legal authority would still be the European Court. On the other hand, when national courts sought advisory rulings from the European Court, courts in EFTA states would not be obliged to heed such rulings, whereas national EC courts would have to obey. Professor Pierre Pescatore, himself a former member of the court, argued in an article in the *Neue Zürcher* that the court was right in attacking the agreement for its complexity and lack of clarity. But he also criticized the purism and ridigity of the court's written opinion and expressed his surprise at the quick acceptance of the court's verdict by the EFTA countries, implying that if the EFTA governments had the political will, they could find a way out of the impasse (*Neue Zürcher Zeitung*, 7 January 1992).

In principle, there seemed to be two solutions to the problem. One could drop the idea of a special EEA court, in which case the EFTA countries would have to accept undiluted EC jurisdiction. But this solution would directly violate the principle of legal autonomy cherished by the EFTA countries. Besides, and perhaps more importantly, it could create serious domestic political problems for some EFTA governments – particularly the Norwegian and Swiss – which were facing considerable opposition to the EEA agreement. The Norwegian government thus had to muster a three-quarter majority in Parliament to be able to ratify the agreement. Alternatively, EC ministers could decide to overrule the court. But this could well imply the convening of an inter-governmental conference, since according to Article 238 in the Treaty of Rome, if association agreements call for changes in the Treaty of Rome, such changes shall be adopted according to the Article 236 procedure.

In mid-January 1992, the chief negotiators of the two sides met to discuss the matter but without making progress. Apparently, the European Commission had been considering a proposal according to which disputes would be solved by means of political consultations in a mixed committee instead of by legal proceedings (*Neue Zürcher Zeitung*, 17 January 1992). But the proposal had been dropped, as several of the larger EC member states regarded it as a potential threat to the effectiveness and legal homogeneity of the regime.

The court's intervention presented a serious threat to the EEA agreement. There was a risk that in several EFTA countries the EEA would now be seen to be causing more political and administrative trouble than it was worth to them since they were in any event actively preparing for full membership (*Financial Times*, 17 December 1991). However, on 13 February 1992 a compromise was found (*Dagens Nyheter*, 15 February 1992). The original idea of a joint EEA court was dropped. Instead, the EFTA side would set up a counterpart to the EC's surveillance mechanism and court of justice. In case of discrepancy in the application of rules between the EC and EFTA, a solution would first be sought within the framework of an EEA committee consisting of representatives from the EC Commission and high-ranking EFTA officials. The committee would ask the ECJ for a binding prejudicial decision. In case agreement could not be reached on this procedure, the two parties would be allowed to use the safeguard mechanisms or the suspension clause. Only in competition cases dealing with EFTA internal trade would the 'EFTA pillar' have the sole legal competence. In pure EC cases and in 'mixed cases' involving firms having a significant turnover in both the EC and EFTA (above 33 per cent), the ECJ would have the final word. In the majority of cases the EFTA countries would thus *de facto* be forced to accept the ECJ's case law. In domestic political terms, the final compromise was more in keeping with EFTA preferences than the solution reached in the autumn of 1991. The negative features of the agreement had become less visible. An EFTA judicial mechanism would probably be more palatable to EEA sceptics in Norway and Switzerland than an EEA court with 'foreign judges'.

The Commission would have preferred not to have subjected the new compromise to ECJ scrutiny. But on the very day of the breakthrough, the European Parliament endorsed a proposal by the liberal and conservative groups demanding that the agreement be sent to the ECJ once more – a further example of the now common inter-institutional haggles on association and enlargement policy. Legally the Commission was in a position to ignore the demand. But seeing the sword of Damocles hanging over the treaty by virtue of the need to ensure Parliament's assent, the Commission decided to let the ECJ review the treaty a second time. This time, however, the ECJ accepted the agreement.

The EEA Treaty was challenged once more when the Swiss rejected the treaty in a referendum on 6 December 1992. Of the Swiss, 50.3 per cent voted 'no', but more importantly 15 out of 23 cantons and half-cantons opposed the treaty (*Agence Europe*, 7–8 December 1992). Interestingly, all French-speaking cantons supported the EEA, whereas all German cantons, except for the half-cantons of Basel-Land and Basel-City and Italian-speaking Ticino, were opposed. Given the enthusiasm for closer ties with the EC in the French part of Switzerland, one can see how, as in other parts of Europe, the process of European integration will accelerate internal processes of fragmentation in Switzerland. Precisely fear of such a development may impel many Swiss to adopt a more cautious approach to European integration.

To the Swiss government which had recommended a 'yes' and had publicly portrayed an approval of the EEA treaty as the first step towards full membership of the EC, the outcome of the referendum evidently came as a shock. The official reaction, however, was that all options would be kept open. In Brussels, the Swiss 'no' was seen as yet another psychological blow (after the Danish 'no' to Maastricht) to the dynamic process of European unity begun in the mid-1980s. As far as Switzerland's future in Europe was concerned, the Brussels view was that Switzerland now had to withdraw its application, since it evidently had no political basis. Yet, although the Swiss application must now be characterized as dormant, the Swiss have not formally withdrawn it.

The Swiss 'no' also presented the battle-hardened EEA negotiators with new problems. While the bilateral transit agreement was in principle still valid, the EEA treaty had to be revised to take account of the Swiss 'no'. Things were further complicated when a week after the Swiss referendum, Liechtenstein, which is closely integrated with Switzerland, voted 'yes' to the same treaty. The ensuing negotiations were mostly but not entirely technical in nature. The EC demanded that the remaining six EFTA countries make up for Switzerland's contribution to the EEA financial mechanism. Furthermore, the EC demanded that the EFTA countries grant greater market access to agricultural products from the southern regions of the EC than originally agreed (*EFTA News*, 1/93, 3 March 1993).

The compromise solution stipulated that the total amount of loans for which the EFTA countries would grant interest rate subsidies would remain the same – Ecu 1,500 million – but that the interest subsidy for each individual loan would be reduced from 3 to 2 percentage points. Second, the agreements on liberalization of trade in agricultural products would enter into force earlier than the EEA agreement itself (that is by the middle of April 1993). Both sides would do their utmost so that the EEA agreement could enter into force on 1 July 1993. On 25 February 1993 negotiations on an adjustment protocol were finalized and on 17 March the protocol was signed (*EFTA News*, 2/93, 25 March 1993). On 1 January 1994, the EEA treaty finally came into force.

Notes

1. Defined as legal acts published in the official journal of the EC.
2. Ibid. The footnote reads in all brevity, 'The Commission will send to the EFTA side a letter explaining the modalities of this paragraph'. This almost amounted to giving the EC Commission *carte blanche* to interpret the agreement as it pleased.

5   The EEA treaty

A brief overview of the treaty

Assessing the outcome of negotiations is not an easy task. A common approach consists in comparing the outcome of the negotiations with the opening positions of the parties. Yet, this is not an ideal approach. Opening positions may be deliberately inflated for tactical reasons. Besides, they are likely to be vaguely stated (Zartman, 1988, p. 39). An additional method for assessing the outcome of an agreement is the study of reactions to the agreement as reflected in the media.

With these provisos, we shall try to provide an overview of the outcome comparing the outcome for each side with opening positions. In terms of structure, the EEA treaty builds upon the Rome Treaty. There is a preamble, a section on 'objectives and principles' and a main section containing the substantial provisions regarding the four freedoms, competition and state aid; company law; horizontal policies and flanking policies. A final section contains provisions on institutions in a broad sense. There is a small section on the financial mechanism and final provisions. The EFTA countries take over the bulk of the *acquis communautaire* regarding the four freedoms and some related policies. Formally this is done by adding to the main treaty text a number of annexes (around 20), containing lists of the legal EC acts included in the treaty. Additionally, around 45 protocols are attached to the treaty. These supplementary provisions regulate derogations (few in number), transitional arrangements, definitions, etc. (*Agreement on the European Economic Area*, Danish Ministry of Foreign Affairs, 1992).

Originally, EFTA had hoped that the *acquis communautaire* would constitute a basis for negotiation. The EC refused, wanting the swift creation of a homogeneous enlarged internal market, a goal held to be incompatible with a renegotiation of the *acquis communautaire* (*Neue Zürcher Zeitung*, 25 October 1991). Significantly, EFTA accepted that the provisions of the EEA treaty which are identical in substance to corresponding rules of the Rome Treaty and the Paris Treaty shall be interpreted in conformity with the accumulated case law of the European Court of Justice (Agreement on an EEA, Article 6). EFTA had also originally demanded permanent derogations from EC rules in a number of areas such as safety standards. As we have seen, this demand was dropped during the negotiations. Instead, EFTA obtained a general safeguard clause and a number of temporary derogations. Permanent derogations were on the whole not permitted. But two exceptions were made. First, all EFTA countries were allowed to ban alcohol commercials on television. Second, Norway and Iceland obtained permanent derogations in the field of direct foreign investments. These derogations allow the two countries to protect their domestic shipbuilding industry and fishing fleet against foreign purchases. Norway will also retain a restriction on foreign investment in banks and insurance companies with a ceiling of 33.3 per cent. The EC gave these concessions in recognition of the domestic political controversy surrounding these issues in the countries concerned.

Otherwise the derogations granted were temporary. In most cases a two-year transitional period will apply. In exceptional cases, a longer transition period has been granted. Thus, Switzerland was given five years to implement rules on the free movement of persons which will affect laws on immigrants (*Financial Times*, 23 October 1991). As far as the right of establishment for the medical profession is concerned, Switzerland obtained a four-year transition period. In the sensitive field of chemicals, a rather special solution was found: the EFTANs were granted an open-ended derogation, which in practice means that the EFTA countries will not have to alter standards until the EC has caught up with EFTA standards. EFTA standards for exhaust emission for cars, which are stricter than EC rules, would remain in force for a period of two years until 1994. By 1995 the EC was expected to have caught up with EFTA in this field.

In the field of freedom of movement for goods, the EFTA countries would take over the *acquis* relating to technical barriers of trade as well as the *acquis* relating to public procurement. Trade in agricultural products and fisheries are regulated in separate protocols. Essentially what has been agreed here is to include an evolutionary clause in the treaty providing for two-yearly reviews aiming at a gradual liberalization of trade. In addition, the treaty provides for a certain liberalization by means of modifications of the bilateral FTAs which the EC concluded with these countries in the 1970s. The EFTA countries thus make concessions for some 72 agricultural products, the bulk of which are products exported by the southern EC member states. As for fisheries, the EFTA countries are to be granted restricted access to the EC market. Fishing products have been divided into three categories for which the rules of access vary. For the first group there was to be free access as of 1 January 1993. For the second category there was to be a progressive reduction in custom duties from 1 January 1993 to 1 January 1997 with a final level of 30 per cent of existing custom duties. Finally, there is a third category of so-called 'sensitive' products for which access will not be liberalized. This category includes salmon, mackerel, herring and certain shellfish (Agreement on an EEA, Protocol 9).

For its part as of 1 January 1993, the EC was to obtain full market access to the EFTA countries for fishing products, with certain derogations for Finland, Sweden, Switzerland and Liechtenstein. On the resource issue, EFTA also made concessions. The EC's share of the total allowed catches (TACs) would be raised to 2.9 per cent against 2.14 per cent at present. Outside the bilateral agreement, Norway would cede an additional quota of cod, rising from 6,000 tons in 1993 to 11,000 tons in 1997. According to an internal EC decision, this additional quota would be allocated to Spain and Portugal as so-called 'cohesion fish'. Iceland cedes 3,000 tons of haddock. In return, it would receive 3,000 tons of the EC's quota of capelin in the waters of Greenland.

Apart from the improvements in market access, the EC has obtained a considerable levelling of the unequal competitive conditions which have existed so far. The EFTA countries have undertaken to adjust as far as possible their policies of state aid and their competition policy to EC rules in these areas. Among other things, this is an advantage for the Danish fish-processing industry.

As far as free movement of labour, services and capital is concerned, the EFTA countries would take over the basic EC rules, including the right of establishment (Agreement on an EEA, Protocol 9). The free Nordic labour market would remain unaffected, the only change being that in some respects Nordic citizens would have rights in other Nordic countries which citizens from other EEA countries will not have. As far as summer houses and recreational houses are concerned, the EFTA countries have been given the right to introduce legislation similar to the Danish legislation which bans foreign purchases. The EFTA countries would take over the common transport policy as far as road transport is concerned. A separate agreement on the conditions for transit traffic has been concluded between the EC and Austria and Switzerland. Switzerland managed to retain its 28-ton limit, but it had to accept the introduction of a quota system for heavier trucks. Austria managed to avoid an increase in the transit burden except for a small concession to Greece.

The treaty contains a general safeguard clause, which inserts a measure of differentiation and flexibility into the regime. The idea of a safeguard clause was introduced as a way of accommodating the concerns of some EFTA countries regarding free movement of capital. The EC argued that some EC member states had had similar worries which, however, had subsequently proved unfounded. It was therefore largely a question of the EFTA countries having to go through a learning process. The EFTA countries were to be 'brought up not to fear to be bought up', as an insider put it. Yet, the EFTA negotiators insisted on some sort of formal guarantee. Thus emerged the idea of a safeguard clause. EFTA had wanted a safeguard clause specifically mentioning problem areas. After lengthy negotiations this proved very difficult to achieve. When eventually the clause exceeded three-quarters of a page, the issue was referred to Negotiating Group Five which produced an agreed clause of only five lines. Thus Article 112 stipulates that each party can unilaterally take safety measures 'if serious economic, societal or environmental difficulties of a sectorial or regional nature arise. Such safety measures shall be restricted with regard to their scope and duration to what is strictly necessary in order to remedy the situation. Priority shall be given to such measures as will least disturb the functioning of the agreement' (Agreement on an EEA, Article 112). One notes how the EC has managed to remove the teeth of the clause. The existence of this safety clause is nevertheless expected to help ensure that the transformation of new EC legislation into EEA legislation in relevant areas runs smoothly and that the accompanying negotiations do not often end in a deadlock with the consequence that parts of the treaty are suspended. Yet, it is a measure of the EC's impressive negotiating power that EFTA has been forced to retreat from its original demand for permanent derogations to the point of accepting a restricted safeguard clause.

In relation to the FTAs of 1973, the EEA treaty implies a considerable tightening of discipline in state aid and competition. This is due to EFTA's acceptance of a supranational element in the surveillance and enforcement of these rules, a point stressed by the EC. Unless EFTA producers are subjected to some sort of supranational discipline, EC firms risk being exposed to unfair competition because of abuse of a dominant market position, cartel formation, subsidies, etc. on the part of competitors in the EFTA countries where legislation is generally more lax. By way of compensation, the EC (that is formally the contracting parties) has undertaken not to use anti-dumping or countervailing duties.

Horizontal issues are issues which are considered relevant to the internal market but which cut across the four areas of liberalization. In this field, EFTA has taken over rules on the environment, on health and safety, the equal treatment of men and women, some labour market provisions, consumer protection, company law and statistics. As mentioned above, in the environmental area there would in some cases be transitional arrangements. In certain other cases the solving of a problem has been postponed (for example dangerous chemicals).

EFTA also wished to be involved in a number of the EC's collaborative ventures in areas such as education and training, cooperation on high technology and environmental protection. These areas are called 'flanking policies' or 'vertical policies' because they do not involve one party taking over the other party's legislation. The guiding principle is cooperation expressed in the equal participation of EFTA in framework programmes, specific programmes and projects, etc. In this field, EFTA achieved a number of results, particularly in the field of high-technology cooperation where the EEA treaty allows the EFTA countries to participate fully in the EC's framework programmes.

As part of the overall cohesion package (which also includes concessions on agricultural exports and fishery exports), the EC obtained a financial contribution from the EFTA countries (Agreement on an EEA, Articles 115-17). A cohesion fund would be set up. It would dispose of a total sum of Ecu 2 billion over five years, of which 1.5 billion will be in soft loans and 500 million in grants. Spain had to accept that only a minor part of the money would be paid out as grants.

From EFTA's point of view, the institutional and legal part of the treaty was always the crux of the matter. EFTA linked acceptance of the *acquis communautaire* to agreement on a satisfactory institutional and legal order. The results of this linkage must be judged as meagre. EFTA had demanded a form of co-decision over future EEA legislation. The EC had on the other hand insisted that its decision-making autonomy be preserved. EFTA obtained an institutionalized right of information and consultation concerning new internal market legislation and a collective right to opt out. But the treaty does not oblige the EC to refrain from new legislation merely because EFTA cannot accept the inclusion of this legislation in the EEA framework.

The procedure envisaged for the introduction of new rules is the following: ideally, new legal acts would be put into effect simultaneously in the EC and the EEA. This presupposes a consensus among all 19 countries in the EEA committee. In case of disagreement, the EEA partners would have six months in which to find common solutions. If, after this period, an EFTA country is opposed to the new compromise, it could veto the agreement but only if joined by the other EFTA countries. In other words, EFTA would only be granted a 'group veto'. In the event of an EFTA veto, the relevant part of the EEA treaty would be suspended unless a common solution is found within six months (Agreement on an EEA, Articles 97-104). As EC firms are interested in retaining a homogeneous West European market including EFTA, EFTA's collective veto right would give the EC an incentive to pay attention to EFTA's point of view. But the EC is not *de jure* obliged to pay attention to the EFTA view. Furthermore, the EC can take countermeasures in case of an EFTA veto.

As mentioned before, the Swiss government had demanded an individual right of opting out. This was rejected by the EC on the grounds that it would damage the legal homogeneity of the EEA regime. The EC Commission and some of the larger member states were also of the opinion that non-members should not be given the same leeway (in terms of special 'a la carte' arrangements) as members.

Another EFTA demand had been the right to participate in EC committees. In this area, EFTA also made some headway. EFTA countries would have access to a number of committees, but some would remain closed to EFTA in order to safeguard the EC's decision-making autonomy, keeping in mind in particular the sensitivities *vis-à-vis* the European Parliament. Nor would EFTA have a voting right in the committees in which they are represented.

As far as the legal issues are concerned, EFTA had to accept supranational mechanisms. It agreed to set up a counterpart to the Commission with surveillance functions in the field of competition, state aids and public procurement. Significantly, EFTA also accepted that EC law would have primacy over EFTA law. On the issue of a judicial mechanism, EFTA was more successful. The joint judicial mechanism had been one of the really sore points in the negotiations. Several EFTA countries, Norway, Switzerland and Austria, had for a mixture of constitutional and domestic political reasons fought hard to avoid an arrangement which could force their countries to accept the rulings of 'foreign judges'. This was a sensitive issue in domestic politics and one which was certain to take centre stage in pre-referendum debates in these countries. The solution found was not ideal for the EFTA side but did represent a significant concession to Norwegian and Swiss domestic opinion in particular.

The EEA as a case of variable geometry integration

How then should one characterize the EEA? First of all, the EEA has an in-built asymmetry. It does not accord the two parties equal rights as regards the evolution of EEA law (Krenzler, 1993). This is quite exceptional, considering normal practice in international negotiations. To characterize the EEA as 'legalized hegemony' is not far off the mark, since what we are talking about is the extra-territorial impact of EC rules.[1] Second, the EEA constitutes a form of partial or à la carte membership of the European Union. The following parts of EC cooperation are kept outside the EEA regime:

- *The Customs Union.*
- *Fiscal harmonization.*
- *The common agricultural policy (CAP).*
- *Fishery policy.*
- *Monetary policy.*
- *Judicial and internal affairs.*
- *The common foreign and security policy (CFSP).* This is an advantage for those neutral EFTA countries which need time to adapt their foreign policies to the new European security situation or want to preserve a high degree of freedom of action in security and defence policy.

Unlike the internal market, the EEA maintains the autonomy of the contracting parties *vis-à-vis* third countries. The EEA is negative integration (in John Pinder's sense) taken to its extreme. It does not include areas requiring common decision-making and management institu-

70

tions such as a customs union, a common agricultural policy, a common fisheries policy, an EMU or income transfers on a major scale. From the point of view of national autonomy and the wish to preserve essential structures in the EFTA countries, this à la carte element was obviously a significant achievement. At the same time, the failure to create a West European Customs Union and to harmonize taxes means that a costly border control would have to remain in place between the EC and EFTA. Furthermore, national autonomy in the field of foreign and security policy implies a rather weak presence in the European and international political arena. A la carte membership is only available at a price.

Third, in the course of the negotiations the context of the EEA changed, and the objective and function of the EEA changed accordingly (Pedersen, 1992a). For most EFTA countries, the EEA negotiations came to be seen as a prelude to accession negotiations. This placed the EEA treaty in a different light. Some of the drawbacks of the treaty which would have been regarded as unacceptable, had the EEA been a permanent solution for the EFTA countries, became more bearable as the EEA acquired the function of a transitional arrangement. This is true of the lack of real political influence as well as the scarcity of mechanisms for democratic control in the EEA regime.

Even if the two parties had failed to solve the new problems raised by the European Court of Justice, this would not have made the EEA negotiations a complete waste of time. As far as the substance of the talks is concerned – especially the whole trade section including the transitional arrangements – the agreed arrangements will form the basis of accession negotiations. An Austrian business magazine has estimated that for Austria the EEA agreement means that two-thirds of the EC accession negotiations had already been finalized when the accession negotiations started (*TREND*, no. 6, June 1991, p. 159).

However, given the decision of most EFTA countries to apply for EC membership, the element of wasted effort cannot be ignored. Sources close to the negotiations stress that those on the substance (the four freedoms) were not the most time-consuming. What took up time was the search for special institutional and legal formulae for the EC–EFTA relationship. With most EFTA countries now headed for membership, this part of the exercise may prove to have been a waste of time unless the EEA acquires a new role as a permanent element in Europe's institutional architecture. One positive feature is the learning process which all participants went through. The EFTA governments as well as the EC became increasingly aware of the difficulties involved in carving out a 'third way' between membership and free-trade arrangements.

If most EFTA countries regard the EEA as a short-term solution, what will become of the idea of the EEA as an original element in the construction of a new European architecture? The immediate response would seem to be: not much. Apparently, forces in the Commission have had their doubts as to the wisdom of continuing with the EEA regime if most EFTA members opt for EC membership. In an interview with *Dagens Nyheter* in early 1992, the Vice-president of the Commission, Frans Andriessen, said that 'the situation may arise when one must foresee individual negotiations with [the remaining] EFTA countries [instead of the EEA]' (*Dagens Nyheter*, 14 February 1992). Since it is now a common view that the Central and Eastern European economies will not be able to countenance taking part in the internal market for quite some time, there is a risk that the EEA may 'lie fallow' for up to five years with only Iceland and Liechtenstein and perhaps Switzerland as members. If that should happen, there will be voices in the EC asking whether keeping the EEA alive is worth the considerable effort. Moreover, it may prove difficult and time-consuming to 'generalize' the complex EEA regime so as to make it applicable to the Central and Eastern European economies which after all differ markedly from the EFTA economies. Quite apart from the EC's second thoughts about the EEA, it is open to doubt whether the Eastern European states themselves would find the halfway-house of the EEA an attractive home. In terms of political influence, the distance between the Europe agreements and the EEA is small. Some will undoubtedly regard the EEA as the political equivalent of Schubert's *Unfinished Symphony*. Moreover, the EEA lacks a political dimension. What the Central and Eastern Europeans are looking for is a framework which provides strong political anchorage and soft economic integration. The EEA is not such a framework.

One wonders, however, whether at the end of the day the Commission will want to replace the multilateral EEA framework with time-consuming bilateral talks even if only a few EFTA countries remain in EFTA. To this should be added the uncertainty regarding both the likelihood and timing of membership. The European situation is ripe with uncertainties. The EFTA governments may well regard the EEA as merely a short-term solution, but domestic politic pressure may force politicians to reconsider it. Popular support in the applicant EFTA countries for full membership of the Union can no longer be taken for granted. Were the policy of accession to be voted down in, say, two of the four applicant states, there is a good chance that the EEA would get a new lease of life. Even if only one applicant country rejects membership in a referendum this would raise the odds for the EEA's continued existence. What is more, if the Union sticks to its current policy of 'bunching' entrants, this means that the pace of negotiations with the last (in practice Norway) might determine the accession date of the others. It might therefore take longer to finalize the accession negotiations than originally foreseen. It would seem that the EFTA and EEA might in the short term continue to play a role for the EFTA applicants as a 'safety net'.

A crucial question concerns the EEA's attractiveness to the Central and Eastern Europeans (CEECs). It seems clear that there is a need for multi-speed integration in the wider European economy. While politically fit for full membership the CEECs cannot realistically fulfil the requirements of Union membership in the short term, even taking into account the problems facing the EMU and the possibility of a relaxation of the convergence criteria. Jacques Delors thus proposed in a speech to the Institute of Strategic Studies in London in September 1993 that the EEA be kept open to the CEECs. In order to cushion the shock of adaptation to Western capitalism one could envisage a set of concentric circles leading to progressively deeper integration. A CEEC could move from the Europe agreement to an institution providing primarily free trade in industrial goods (EFTA), via embracing the four freedoms (EEA) to membership of the Union. It used to be argued that such an approach would merely serve to deflect attention from membership of the Union. But this worry lacks solid foundation. The preamble of the Europe Agreements notes that 'the final objective of the country is to become a member of the Community and this association, in view of the parties, will help to achieve this objective'. Moreover, the communiqué from the Copenhagen European Council in June 1993 clarifies the objective of full membership for the CEECs. The internal economic difficulties in the Union can be expected to add to the pressure for gradualism in the enlargement policy towards the CEECs. Given the fact that the market challenge to the EC is probably most acute in the agricultural sector, which is not part of the EEA regime, the Union may feel tempted to shift the emphasis in its dealings with the CEECs from the membership option to the EEA, especially if the current economic recession in Western Europe continues. After all, economically enlargement poses a threat not only to employment in Western Europe but also to political stability (see also Chapter 9).

73

If, contrary to conventional wisdom, the EFTA and the EEA do have some value as building stones in a new European economic architecture, which countries in the European periphery can be expected to find the two institutions attractive? It seems reasonable to expect that those CEECs which are at the head of the queue to enter the Union will not find the EFTA and the EEA attractive, whereas those countries which have so far only made slow progress in the transition to a market economy may find EFTA membership attractive. This suggests that the EFTA will mainly be of interest to countries such as the Baltic states, Albania, Bulgaria, Romania and Slovenia. Of these Albania and Slovenia have as yet no free-trade agreements with EFTA and may therefore be particularly keen to join the organization. A further consideration is that the applicant EFTA countries will adopt the Union's external commercial policy once they become members. Since at present, the Union does not have free-trade agreements with the Baltic states, EFTA membership might be a way of maintaining the benefits of existing free trade with the EFTA applicants.[2]

Explaining the nature and outcome of the EEA negotiations

The EEA negotiations tested the patience of all involved. More than once observers wrote (premature) obituaries on the EEA process. Why did the EEA negotiations prove so lengthy and cumbersome? Underdal's observations regarding the importance of the pluralist structure of multinational negotiating parties do appear to provide an important part of the answer.

The EC's negotiating position was on the whole quite uncompromising especially on the institutional and legal issues, but the main explanation does not seem to be the decision-making procedures. Although the EC's external negotiating behaviour reveals some of the features described by Underdal, our analysis of the EEA talks shows that the countervailing factors are important. The Commission acted as an active mediator during the negotiations. A good example is the EC initiative on fisheries in the final stages of the negotiations which helped find a solution acceptable to EFTA in the face of tough Spanish demands. The Commission's mediation was quite effective because unlike the EFTA Presidency it was able to put together comprehensive package deals, linking the EEA result to other internal EC policies.

The EC position was particularly rigid on the crucial issue of institutions and legal matters. This appears to have been mainly due to three factors. First of all, the EEA case shows to what extent the EC has become a highly institutionalized international actor with a rudimentary system of semi-federalist checks and balances. One of the con-sequences of this development is a growing tendency for the EC's external policy to re-flect the mechanisms of interinstitutional rivalry and what in international relations theory is called 'bureaucratic politics'. This is seen most clearly in the interplay and conflictive inter-action between the Commission, the European Parliament (in particular its powerful external economic affairs committee, the REX committee) and the Court of Justice in the final stages of the EEA process.

Second, the connection between rigidity in negotiating posture and internal pluralism hypothesized by Underdal appears to be confirmed by our case. There is a general and a more specific aspect to this. The general point is that the looser and more pluralistic a regional political unit is, the more uncompromising its external negotiating stance is likely to be. The case of the EEA demonstrates the difficulties involved in any attempt to create 'quasi-membership' arrangements. Whatever the circumstances, an outside plea for a 'quasi-membership' status will always pose problems for a pluralistic organization with a weak internal cohesion. The problem is compounded if the organization is relatively open or the 'partner country' is contiguous because this will allow outsiders to join forces with the less committed internal actors in demanding such adjustments in the organization's structure as will be necessary to establish a new type of loose membership. If the majority of the old members want to make the organization more cohesive, the risk of organizational dilution through differentiated membership will gain in importance. This was what happened in 1990 in the case of the EC and EFTA. This brings us to the specific reason for the rigidity of the Union's position. The democratic transformations in Eastern Europe and the prospect of German unification led a number of EC actors – including the German Foreign Ministry – to the conclusion that priority must be given to safeguarding the autonomy of the EC structure and to strengthening its overall cohesion. In other words, had EFTA been negotiating with a fully fledged European Union with a high degree of internal economic and social homogeneity, it would probably have found it easier to obtain a partial membership status. An actor with a weak cohesion like the Union as we know it will be forced to maintain a sharp demarcation line between members and non-members of the unit. Otherwise, new privileged partial membership arrangements risk reopening sensitive debates inside the regional unit.

The point can be backed by historical evidence. There is a striking parallel between the Maudling negotiations in the 1950s and the EEA negotiations: in both cases the fear of some EC member states that a link between the EC and a less binding arrangement would dilute the EC was the main obstacle to an agreement. Miriam Camps puts it succinctly:

> There were only two ways in which the free trade area could be made acceptable to the 'Europeans'. Either it could be transformed into an arrangement as far-reaching as the treaty of Rome ... so that the prospect of the wider group superseding the narrower group became irrelevant, or it could be so different that there would be no temptation to opt for it in preference to the Treaty of Rome and no danger of an automatic undercutting of the tighter, more far-reaching arrangement. [Camps, 1964, p. 168]

The tactic of the French and its allies in the EEA was precisely to ensure that the outcome of the EEA talks was sufficiently unattractive so as to make dilution unlikely. Thus, just as in the 1950s, the hard-line attitude of the EC was in a sense born of the recognition of its weakness. The case of the EEA differs, however, from the Maudling case in one important respect: the balance of forces between the two sides had changed with the United Kingdom now on the side of the EC. Still, to some French the presence of the United Kingdom on the EC side undoubtedly felt like having a Trojan horse in one's inner sanctuary.

The problem of heterogeneity and pluralism was of course compounded by the special features of the decision-making system. With lowest common denominator bargaining a regional political unit which includes a number of vulnerable 'developmental' economies will inevitably be pushed towards a rigid external stance. In a liberalizing regional economy with a growing number of economically weak but politically influential countries, there will be a growing burden of adjustment which will somehow have to be compensated. In this situation, the temptation will soon arise to pass this burden on to third countries, especially once the regional economy reaches the point where a very large part of economic activity takes place inside the region's borders. In other words, thinking further ahead, the geographical expansion of the European Union is likely to create growing pressure for the creation of a 'Fortress Europe' (cf. Chapter 9).

We have described the outcome of the EEA talks as asymmetrical.

This asymmetry can be explained first of all by EFTA's economic dependence reflected in the fact that while the EC could live with a postponement of the agreement, the EFTA countries were in a hurry – keen as they were to reach an agreement before 1 January 1993 when the internal market was to enter into force in the EC. Second, as pointed out earlier inter-institutional rivalry and demands for compensation from the southern European members placed significant constraints on the EC negotiators but also made EFTA 'the negotiating party able to move'. Third, the emergence of new democracies in Central and Eastern Europe, all of them eager to join the EC, had a certain crowding-out effect on the EFTANs. Suddenly, the EC negotiators in DG I (Directorate General I) had quite attractive alternative uses for their precious time, and as we have seen they did not hide this fact from the EFTA side. Fourth, the uniting of Germany and the collapse of the cold war system caused a majority of the EC countries as well as the EC institutions to place renewed emphasis on deepening of integration and by implication to oppose any venture that might weaken the EC's cohesion. In other words, in the course of the negotiations the Union's commitment to the institutional status quo grew considerably. Finally, and not least, the success of the EC side, notably on the issue of co-decision, can be explained by the weak and over time declining political cohesion within EFTA. Cohesion thus seems to be an important factor in multilateral negotiations and one that probably ought to be included in a comprehensive analytical framework for the study of asymmetrical negotiations like the one suggested by Habeeb (1987).

Yet, our analysis of the EEA negotiations does not warrant the conclusion that EFTA or the EFTA countries did not benefit from the treaty at all. The seven EFTA countries were given almost free access to the internal market and to a number of sectoral cooperation projects such as COMETT and ERASMUS. Quite apart from the substance of the treaty, for some EFTA governments the EEA was valuable in domestic political terms because it started a process of integration with the EC while deferring the issue of a formal application for membership. How are we to account for these (modest) successes?

Explanations must be found on several levels. First of all, economic interdependence between most EC states and EFTA was not so asymmetrical as to preclude giving the EC an incentive to reach some kind of agreement. The EC's control in the negotiations, though considerable, had its limits. Moreover, although EFTA's negotiating clout was undermined by its weakening cohesion, EFTA's commitment to the conclusion of an EEA treaty was stronger than that of the EC Commission. For the EFTA countries it was essential to obtain free access to the internal market. Without free access EFTA exports would not be competitive and big EFTA companies would continue to shift their investments to the EC area. Even for the EFTA countries which had already decided to join the EC there was a need for a transitional arrangement. The EC Commission's DG I which conducted the day-to-day talks for the Community on the other hand had a lot of other things on its plate. EFTA was competing for attention with the new Eastern European democracies and with the GATT negotiations. Finally, the transnational linkages mentioned by Odell and Keohane and Nye in their analyses of the United States and Latin America, Canada and Australia, respectively, appear to have had some effect, although the concrete evidence remains scarce. Big business in the EFTA countries was well represented in the European Roundtable of Industrialists, formed in 1983, which lobbied hard for the creation of a large and homogeneous West European home market.

Notes

1. See the article by the Swiss Professor Daniel Thürer, 'EWR-Vertrag – eine Form legalisierter Hegemonie?', *Neue Zürcher Zeitung*, 15 May 1991.
2. I am grateful to Per Wijkman for valuable inputs on this issue.

6 Towards membership of the Union

Since the late 1980s, all EFTA countries except Iceland and Liechtenstein have been preparing for membership of the EC/European Union. The timing and pace of these preparations has differed from country to country, but they have all eventually declared their intention to seek membership at the earliest possible moment. One of the EFTA countries, Norway, has tried to join the EC once before but in vain. Others, like Austria and Sweden, have at some point contemplated very close forms of affiliation with the EC – even full membership. Finally, two of the countries, Finland and Switzerland, have no tradition of close political links with the EC. For these last countries, the option of full membership of a supranational community with the ambition to create an ever closer union constitutes a truly revolutionary change in their foreign-policy orientation and in a sense even in their general political development.

6.1 Austria

Austria was the first EFTA country to opt for full-scale EC membership. On 17 July 1989 the Austrian government submitted an application for membership of the EC following a two-year debate on how to adapt to the new dynamic Community (Luif, 1988, p. 167). A large majority in the Austrian Parliament had given its support at the end of June 1989. Apart from the two governing parties (the Socialist Party, SPÖ, and the Conservative Party, ÖVP), the opposition party, the Austrian Freedom

Party (FPÖ), also supported the move (Schneider, 1990, pp. 91ff.). Only the Green Party with 5 per cent of the seats in Parliament opposed the application.

The fact that Austria was the first among the EFTANs to opt for full membership is not surprising. Austria is the EFTA country which has historically had the closest ties to the EC, a reflection of the intimate cultural and economic links between Austria and Germany. In this connection it is also worth recalling that Austrian thinking is not alien to the idea of multinational communities. Indeed, the Double Monarchy of Austria–Hungary provides an interesting example of international power sharing. It should be added that the founding fathers of the EEC considered Austria a serious candidate for membership of the Community (along with Switzerland and Denmark). Paul Henri Spaak appears to have regarded Austria as a valuable 'land-bridge' between Italy and the rest – a function that probably did not fully reflect Austria's own foreign-policy ambitions (Camps, 1964, p. 59).

When in 1961 some EFTA countries took the first step in the direction of EC membership, the neutral EFTANs sought closer relations with the Community through association. Austria was the only country to retain this wish and in 1963 renewed its plea for an association agreement. In 1965 the EC and Austria started negotiations which lasted until 1967 when Italy put a spoke in the wheel linking the association agreement to a solution of the problem in southern Tirol. The Italian move was provoked by terrorist acts in the area. It is, however, disputed whether even without this veto it would have been possible to bring the negotiations with Austria to a successful conclusion.

In the 1970s, Austria was instrumental in revitalizing EC–EFTA relations. In May 1977 at the initiative of the Austrian Chancellor Kreisky the EFTA countries held a summit meeting which gave an important impetus to enhanced cooperation with the EC. In the 1980s, Austria has once more been EFTA's frontrunner. Already in November 1987, Vice-Chancellor Mock from the Conservative ÖVP stated that the membership option with due consideration of the requirements of neutrality could not be ruled out. In 1987 the Austrian government decided to set up a working group on European integration which was to prepare a comprehensive report on Austria and European integration. The group set up 14 subgroups and 30 smaller project groups (Luif, 1988, p. 170). Among its first initiatives was the introduction of an 'EC-conformity clause', the idea being that all new legislative acts were to contain a clause giving information on the compatibility of the act with EC law. In June 1988 the working group presented its report to the foreign minister. The report not only concluded that Austrian participation in the internal market did not pose insurmountable problems. It also indirectly indicated its preference for the membership option. However, the sensitive issue of neutrality had deliberately been kept in brackets awaiting expert opinions from legal experts in the Foreign Ministry and at the universities.

The pressure for membership came not least from Austrian business. The first important interest group to opt for full membership of the EC was thus the Federation of Austrian Industrialists. In a statement published in May 1987, the Federation made 'an urgent appeal to the federal government to do everything so that full membership in the EC can be accomplished at the earliest possible moment'. Membership was regarded as the only way to ensure full and equal participation in the internal market (Luif, 1991, p. 129). The Austrian trade unions adopted a wait-and-see attitude, but in July 1988 issued a statement expressing a 'cautiously positive' attitude to membership (ibid., p. 130).

In its letter to Brussels of 14 July 1989 the Austrian government referred to its 'internationally recognized status as a neutral country' and made it clear that Austria wanted to retain its neutrality as a member of the EC. There were several reasons why Austria was particularly keen to join the EC (Schneider, 1990, pp. 96ff.). First of all, the Austrian government considered that Austria would suffer more from an exclusion from the internal market than other EFTA countries. Austria's foreign-trade dependence on the EC is higher than that of any other EFTA members except Norway, which is, however, a special case because of the importance of gas and oil deliveries. The EC market accounts for 67.9 per cent of imports and 66.1 per cent of exports (see Appendix). Second, it was a widely held view in Austria, even in the SPÖ, that the Austrian economy was in need of radical structural reform. The expression '*austrosklerose*' was coined to reflect the state of Austria's economy. In the early 1980s, Austria was seen as the 'sick man of EFTA', and some observers regarded the Austrian illness as even more serious than the 'Eurosklerosis' of the EC countries. Under these circumstances – and helped along by the change in economic philosophy – the internal market came to be seen as a strong but necessary medicine. Third, in political terms the Austrian government did not consider itself a weak *demandeur* but on the contrary thought that it had something to offer the Community in the new European climate of *détente*, notably its good relations with Eastern Europe and its considerable expertise regarding this area (Mock, 1990). It should be added that Austria had a specific perception of the Community and its likely future development and did not regard its permanent and treaty-based neutrality as incompatible with EC membership. The EC was regarded as an almost entirely economic organization. The predominant view in Austria – and here the Austrians were wrong – was that only a few 'fundamentalists' in the EC took the political dimension of integration seriously.

The Soviet attitude to Austrian EC membership was originally sceptical and this created problems. However, the Soviet attitude to Austrian EC membership seemed determined by assessments of the EC's internal developments. The Austrian government appears to have had some success in convincing the Soviet leaders that the EC would not develop a military role. It was also significant that the signals emerging from Moscow were mixed (Luif, 1988, p. 183; Arnold, 1989).

Economic factors, notably the internal market programme, were decisive in setting Austria off on the fast track to Brussels. During the period from 1984 to 1987 the growth in BNP in real terms was 1.8 per cent in Austria as against an EC average of 2.6 per cent; 2.5 per cent in Sweden and 2.8 per cent in neighbouring Switzerland (OECD Historical Statistics 1960–84, *OECD Economic Outlook*, 1988, p. 170). If politics have generally been seen in Bismarckian terms as the 'art of the possible', EC policy in Austria instead came to be seen as the art of 'making the necessary possible' to use Paul Valery's apt expression (Schneider, 1990).

On 1 August 1991 the Commission *avis* was submitted to the Council of Ministers (Com (91) 1590 final). The Commission regards Austria as highly suitable for membership from an economic point of view. The opinion highlights the monetary stability which now characterizes the Austrian economy due to the special ties between the Austrian Schilling and the Deutschmark as well as the strong growth of the Austrian economy in the second half of the 1980s. The only economic sectors which are expected to cause problems are agriculture and transit policy. In the agricultural area, considerable changes in the Austrian policy are deemed necessary. On the other hand, the opinion regards Austria's permanent neutrality dating back to 1955 as potentially a more serious problem. The opinion thus refers to the possibility of seeking assurances from Austria that the country is legally capable as well as politically willing to fulfil its obligations in this area. However, despite these concerns the Commission does not expect that neutrality will pose insurmountable problems in the accession negotiations (Com (91)1590 final, p. 30).

Austria has since started a reappraisal of its neutrality policy so as to make it compatible with the provisions on the CFSP in the Maastricht Treaty. Neutrality has been redefined in order to enable Austria to conduct a policy of international solidarity. Equally important, since Austria applied for membership, the context of Austrian neutrality has changed quite dramatically. The conflict in former Yugoslavia is a source of growing concern to the Austrians especially since there is a host of other unsolved minority problems around the former Yugoslavia. Much as in the case of Finland, membership of the European Union has thus come to be seen as a solution to new security problems (Sucharipa, 1993). Consequently, the Austrian political elite now fully supports a CFSP including a common defence policy. A large majority in the Austrian Parliament adopted a motion in December 1992 which reads *inter alia*, 'The National Council identifies fully with the goals of the CFSP and intends to take an active part in the dynamic evolution of that policy' (quoted in Sucharipa, 1993, p. 159). However, within the Austrian government there is known to be some tension between the foreign minister, who is prepared to abandon neutrality, and the prime minister, whose party and voters remain attached to the neutrality policy. At the same time, Austria is also very conscious of the importance of its location at the gateway to the East and South-east of Europe and evidently considers that it has something to offer the Union, notably in the field of Eastern policy but also for example in the field of Third World policy (Mock, 1993a).

In his statement at the meeting on 1 February 1993 in Brussels opening the conference on accession of Austria to the European Union, Foreign Minister Mock in general terms listed the areas in which Austria had specific interests and demands. These were: first of all agriculture; second, the preservation of high social and environmental standards; and third, a satisfactory solution of the transit problem in the Alps (Mock, 1993b). Finally, Austria wants guarantees against foreign purchases of real estate and is trying to obtain a special arrangement modelled on the Danish arrangement for summer cottages.

Although it has not formally renounced its neutrality, Austria makes a point of stressing the benefits that will accrue from a European political union. Thus, Austria welcomes the creation of a European security order which will provide effective instruments for the deterrence and sanctioning of aggression and infringements of international law. It is held to be a vital interest of Austria's to support such a development. Austria has therefore declared that it fully supports the goals of the CFSP and that it will be an active and solidary participant in the further development of the CFSP. So far the institutional aspects of Austria's adhesion to the Union have barely been discussed. But the issue is in the back of the minds of the Austrian negotiators, and in the reports to the Parliament on the Austrian negotiating position it has been clearly stated that Austria intends to defend the position of the small states in the decision-making structure of the union.

The Austrian government has repeatedly signalled its support for the Maastricht Treaty, hoping to mollify the opponents of rapid enlargement within the Union. Thus, in June 1992 Austria sent an *aide-memoir* to the member states of the Community in which it declared its unequivocal endorsement of the Maastricht Treaty. A few days before the Edinburgh Summit another *aide-memoir* with essentially the same message was circulated to the EC governments. All in all, the Austrian government has been pursuing an active, coherent and ambitious policy of adhesion to the EC since 1988.

While the political elite enjoys the support of all the major interest groups in the country, public opinion on the issue of Union membership is volatile and increasingly sceptical. The opponents of membership have been gaining ground in recent years. In May 1991, 43 per cent of the Austrians said they would vote 'yes' to membership of the EC; 33 per cent would vote against and 24 per cent said they had not yet taken a stand. In May 1992, only 29 per cent would vote 'yes' in a referendum, 26 per cent 'no', whereas as many as 45 per cent were undecided. Another poll from May 1992 showed that 37 per cent would vote 'yes', 39 per cent 'no' and 24 per cent were undecided. A poll taken in March 1993 showed that 44 per cent would vote 'yes', 52 per cent 'no' and that only 4 per cent would not care to vote. Two recent polls taken in May 1993 suggested that the 'yes' and 'no' sides had almost the same support but with the 'no' side in the lead. The first poll showed that 37 per cent would vote 'yes' and 38 per cent 'no', while 25 per cent would abstain in a referendum.[1] The second showed that 32 per cent would vote in favour of union membership, 38 per cent against, while 30 per cent would abstain (*Trend*, no. 5, May 1993). Thus compared to the situation in 1991, the supporters of union membership have been steadily losing ground. However, the rise in the number of 'no' votes may be levelling off.

It is difficult on this basis to make reliable predictions regarding the outcome of a referendum on Austrian membership of the European Union. The polls shown above indicate first that public opinion is volatile and second that the 'no' side is in a strong position, though not so strong as to make the outcome of a referendum a foregone conclusion. It should be stressed that the two big parties, the Socialists and the Conservatives, and sections of the FPÖ, are in favour of membership. Although this should put the 'yes' side in a strong position in the electoral campaign prior to the referendum, the Danish and Swiss referendums should serve as a warning not to overestimate the ability of political elites significantly to influence the attitudes of their electorates. Furthermore, the Austrian government has already initiated a campaign aimed at convincing the Austrian population of the benefits of Austrian membership of the European Union without this having had any major effect on the strength of the 'yes' side. Particularly worrying for the political elite is the fact that a majority of Austrians (52 per cent) think that Austria's influence as a member of the European Union will be negligible (*Market Archiv M 28*, August 1993). After all, the centre-piece of the government's campaign for membership has been the argument that full membership is the only way to gain influence over domestic and international matters.

6.2 Sweden

Despite a historical preference for confederal forms of integration, the issue of Swedish membership of the EC has time and again appeared on the political agenda (Bergquist, 1969; 1970). The decision of the British government in July 1961 to apply for membership of the EC provoked a long and intense debate in Sweden concerning the appropriate Swedish response. But de Gaulle's veto in 1963 effectively buried the issue. In the spring of 1967 the issue resurfaced and this time Sweden was willing to go farther. The general view in Sweden's political elite was that the presence of de Gaulle, and not least the Luxembourg compromise on the right of veto, had dealt the federalists a decisive blow thus making Swedish EC membership much more realistic. Besides, the French-inspired *détente* initiatives *vis-à-vis* the Soviet Union facilitated neutral Sweden's *rapprochement* with the EC. In the autumn of 1967, the Swedish government submitted a new application to the EC seeking some kind of formalized relationship with the EC. Significantly, the option of full membership (with appropriate escape clauses) was kept open. In November 1967, de Gaulle once again blocked EFTA accession to the EC, and the Soviet invasion of Czechoslovakia in 1968 in any case made Swedish EC membership look less realistic. In 1971 Sweden made it clear that in its view neutrality and EC membership were after all incompatible. The reason was twofold. First, foreign-policy cooperation in EPC though not formally binding aimed at the formulation of a common foreign policy. Second, the Werner Plan on Economic and Monetary Union was regarded as incompatible with Swedish neutrality since it would deprive member states of an essential part of their sovereignty. During the 1970s and early 1980s, EC membership thus became effectively a non-issue in Swedish politics. Instead, Swedish foreign policy concentrated on the further elaboration of committed and active neutrality with its emphasis on global welfare (Sundelius, 1989).

A mixture of economic and security-related factors reinforced by domestic political dynamics explains Sweden's rapid move towards membership of the European Union in the late 1980s. Although the formal change in the position of the leading political parties occurred quickly in the course of the year 1990, commentators and academics had been debating the issue of EC membership for several years (for an early contribution see Hamilton, 1987). The new security context appears to have been an important factor behind the Swedish decision to apply for EC membership. The changing security situation which emerged in Europe in 1989–90 altered the parameters of Swedish foreign and security policy. The bipolar structure and the tensions between the two blocs had created room for neutral go-betweens. With East–West confrontation a thing of the past, the neutrals were suddenly of no intrinsic value to the international community, and what had so far been regarded as a beneficial non-involvement now increasingly looked like self-imposed isolation. With its pragmatic form of neutrality Sweden was able to act with greater flexibility than the other neutrals in EFTA in trying to adapt to new realities (Nordlöf-Lagerkranz, 1990). The stated intention of several Eastern European countries to apply for EC membership also made an impression. It was feared that the Central and Eastern Europeans would so to speak 'crowd out' the EFTA countries unless the latter speeded up preparations for EC membership.

Factors relating to international markets and domestic politics added to the pressure for a reversal of policy. The Swedish economy was taking a dive and the incumbent Social Democratic government was rapidly losing support in the electorate. On top of that, the ideological climate in Sweden was becoming more right wing and everything 'European' was becoming fashionable in intellectual circles. The government could not but note that the opposition's unequivocal commitment to EC membership appeared to be a vote winner. During the spring of 1990, the two main opposition parties, the Conservative Moderate Party and the Liberal Peoples' Party, had made EC membership an election issue. They had found a receptive audience in a changing public opinion when suggesting that Sweden should apply for membership of the EC immediately after the parliamentary elections scheduled to be held in September 1991 (Reuter, 29 May 1990).

The Social Democrats reacted by adjusting their EC policy to economic and domestic political realities. In June, Swedish Prime Minister Carlsson had stated that 'first we want EEA. Then watching what happens in Europe and the EC, we will decide whether we want to seek membership' (Reuter, 12 September 1990). In September there was a clear shift of emphasis in the government's argument regarding EC membership. The timing of a membership application was now linked to the fast changing East–West relationship, about to be codified at the Paris summit. In September Foreign Minister Andersson said that 'if the alliances disappear and there is a different security cooperation [in Europe], the situation will be such that we can become members of the EC' (Reuter, 12 September 1990).

On 26 October 1990 the Swedish government sent a message to Parliament which signalled a U-turn in Swedish policy towards Europe. Without giving details as to the time of application, the government stated that the changing security situation and the developments in Europe had improved the chances of Sweden becoming a full member of the EC without having to give up the principles of Swedish neutrality (*Dagens Nyheter*, 26 October 1990). Swedish Finance Minister Allan Larsson, on presenting a package of proposals meant to counter the economic crisis in Sweden, said that the government wanted Parliament to express itself more positively with regard to Sweden's intention to apply for EC membership (*Dagens Nyheter*, 28 October 1990).

Lennart Pettersson, Social Democratic member of Parliament and chairman of the Industrial Committee said to the Foreign Affairs Committee of the European Parliament that there were good reasons for applying before the election in September 1991 in order that the government might reinforce its position. He added that what had caused the quick Swedish move towards an EC membership application was first of all the signals from the EC that the community would not set up a common defence policy (*Dagens Nyheter*, 28 November 1990). Swedish Prime Minister Carlsson stressed economic motives. He told the *Economist* that the reasons for the change of policy in Sweden were serious economic difficulties, reflected in high inflation, big budget deficits and low growth as well as the change in the position of neutral countries (*Economist*, 8 November 1990).

The influential Swedish Cabinet Secretary, Pierre Schori, expressed himself somewhat differently. He stated in an interview with *Dagens Nyheter* that the changing Swedish EC policy had nothing to do with the Swedish economy. Nor was it a question of the Social Democratic Party having changed its position. The crucial factor was the changing security situation which had made neutrality less significant. He added that the fact that the EC had no common defence policy meant that there was not a big barrier to be crossed. He also pointed out that Sweden was not neutral in the Iraq–Kuwait conflict (*Dagens Nyheter*, 8 November 1990).

The changing signals from Stockholm did not go unheeded in the other EFTA countries. The Nordic neighbours reacted most strongly, but the reactions differed in content and intensity. In Norway the trade unions and the business community were agreed that if Sweden applied for membership, Norway had to follow suit. Prime Minister Syse stated that following the Swedish government statement on EC policy there was a greater likelihood that Norway and Sweden would apply for EC membership simultaneously. The opposition leader Gro Harlem Brundtland was less direct but basically expressed the same view as the prime minister. Her first reaction was that she did not believe that Sweden would apply before Norway. She maintained the current position that first the EEA negotiations had to be finalized (*Dagens Nyheter*, 28 October 1990). The debate on the new Swedish EC policy and its consequences served further to polarize the conflicting positions within the Norwegian Centre-Right government in which two centre parties were opposed to membership of the Union. Already there was disagreement on how to react to the EC's demand that Norway give up its restrictions on the right of foreigners to buy Norwegian property, industry and banks. On 29 October 1990, Prime Minister Syse had to resign, and after abortive attempts to form a Conservative one-party government, Mrs Brundtland took over as prime minister (*Frankfurter Algemeine Zeitung*, 2 November 1990; *Neue Zürcher Zeitung*, 31 October 1990).

The Finnish and Icelandic reactions to Sweden's move were much more negative. The Icelandic foreign minister stated to the press that 'the unity in EFTA has not yet been broken, but Sweden and Norway make negotiations on an EEA more difficult' (*Independent*, 30 October 1990). The Finnish government similarly reacted coolly to the new developments in Sweden. The Finnish Prime Minister, Harri Holkeri, stated that the Swedish signals had no significance for Finland, which still placed priority on the EEA negotiations (*Neue Zürcher Zeitung*, 1 November 1991). In Finland the general view was that Sweden's unilateral gesture had severely damaged EFTA's credibility and bargaining position *vis-à-vis* the EC.

However, the Finnish reaction to the new Swedish EC policy was measured compared to the uproar caused by remarks by the Swedish Foreign Minister Steen Andersson in late October to the effect that the Nordic EFTA countries might consider submitting a joint application for EC membership. The statement came after a meeting of the Steering Committee of the Social Democratic Party. Andersson, whose statements were probably somewhat misinterpreted in the media and in Finland, said that the Nordic countries had moved closer to each other and that gradually this could lead – depending on the internal developments in the EC – to a common Nordic posture regarding membership of the EC and that this would, in his view, be a major asset for all parties (*Dagens Nyheter*, 2 November 1990).

The Finnish reaction was very reserved. In connection with the yearly meeting of the chairmen of the Nordic Social Democratic Parties (SA-MAK), the Vice-Chairman of the Finnish Social Democratic Party, Tuulikki Hämäläinen, said that 'this is not the right time in spite of all the changes. One ought to place priority on the EEA negotiations' (*Danish Daily Information*, 1 November 1990). More importantly, Finnish President Koivisto made a sharp off-the-record remark on a flight back from Portugal, saying that in his view Andersson had humiliated Norway and Finland and that the Swedish foreign minister had made his statements with an eye on the domestic political scene in Sweden (*Frankfurter Algemeine Zeitung*, 3 November 1990; *Dagens Nyheter*, 2 November 1990).

On 12 December 1991, the Swedish Parliament decided on the basis of the government's proposal to prepare an application for membership of the EC. In this connection the government stated *inter alia* that:

A Swedish membership of the EC with maintainance of Swedish neutrality is in our country's national interest. Sweden's economy and society are already very closely connected to the rest of Europe. It seems clear that the EC and its member states are going to play a central role in the continuing development of European cooperation. Our possibilities for influencing this process, politically, socially and economically, will selfevidently be improved through full membership of the EC. In the international field such a participation would improve the possibilities for finding an audience for our national points of view, amongst these our traditional endeavours to improve the conditions of the countries in the Third World (*Konsekvenser av ett svensk EG-medlemskap.* May 1991, p. 3).

The Swedish government submitted its application to the EC on 1 July 1991. There were several early European reactions to the Swedish application. Commission President Delors expressed his happiness with the Swedish move. French President Mitterrand similarly said that Sweden was welcome in the Community. The United Kingdom was much more reserved. 'Sweden will have to join the queue', was Margaret Thatcher's comment (*Dagens Nyheter,* 29 October 1990). Sweden received its response from the Commission well over a year later. The Commission *avis* was broadly favourable towards Swedish membership but did mention what it called 'a few problem areas' (Com (92) 1582 final). It stated that there were no insurmountable problems of an economic nature – the wording used in the Lisbon communiqué – and that as a member of the EC Sweden would contribute to strengthening the Community notably in the areas of economic and monetary policy, social and environmental policy and research and development. Among the EFTA countries Sweden was characterized as special with regard to its ability to contribute positively to the European construction. The document stressed in particular the positive role which Sweden would play in bringing to fruition the plans for the EMU. The problem areas were seen to be agricultural policy – though cognizance was taken of the reforms underway in Sweden which would harmonize Swedish agricultural policy with that of the EC – regional policy, state monopolies notably the alcohol monopoly and most importantly neutrality policy. Clearly, Sweden's adaptation to the planned Common Foreign and Security Policy (CFSP) was regarded as the most serious problem. The *avis* emphasized the obligation to accept *l'acquis politique* and took note of the Swedish reservations regarding the future shaping of a common defence policy and a common defence. In this connection the Commission: 'Recommended that during the accession negotiations one seeks specific and binding commitments from Sweden as regards the country's commitment and legal ability to fulfil its obligations in this field.'

Since submitting its application, the majority of Swedish political forces, headed by the current, very pro-European Prime Minister, Carl Bildt, a conservative, has been preparing for its new role as an active participant in the shaping of Union politics. The Swedish thinking on the European Union is well reflected in a speech by the Minister of Foreign Affairs, Margaretha af Ugglas, at Chatham House, London, in November 1992 (Ugglas, 1992). In her speech the Swedish foreign minister not only supports the federalist-inspired notion of subsidiarity, she also applies the concept in a rather centralizing way listing as tasks which belong to the supranational level a number of economic issues as well as '*defence* [author's emphasis], migration and communications'. The speech leaves one with the impression that Sweden will be a fully committed member of the European Union. The foreign minister also highlights the central geopolitical position of Sweden in Europe. Within the larger framework of Western policy towards the East, Sweden intends to assume specific tasks in relation to the Baltic countries, Poland and the adjoining parts of Russia. The Baltic Council and the Barents Sea Cooperation process, the latter initiated by Norway, are thus institutions in which Sweden intends to adopt a high profile.

Sweden's support for CFSP has similarly been stressed by the Minister for European Affairs and Foreign Trade Ulf Dinkelspiel. In an Information to Parliament on Sweden and Europe in late 1992, Dinkelspiel thus reiterated that 'Sweden would not put a brake on future progress towards the goals which were formulated in the Maastricht Treaty in the area of security policy' (Dinkelspiel, 1992). He added that his country assumed that 'no additional commitments will be required of Sweden beyond those which were agreed by the member countries at Maastricht' (ibid.).

In a speech to the Fondation Paul-Henri Spaak in Brussels on 16 September 1993, the Swedish prime minister gave a broad exposé of Sweden's European policy which contained a few interesting novelties (Bildt, 1993). His main point was that enlargement would strengthen the CFSP. Bildt argued *inter alia* that along with Norway and Finland, Sweden would, as a member of the European Union, be able to make a decisive contribution to the security of the northern part of the Union. Recalling that Moscow regarded the three Baltic states as its 'near abroad', Bildt stated that 'it is our task to make it clear that they are just as much the "near abroad" of the European Union and all its member states'. He also drew attention to the fact that Sweden though not a member of any military alliance makes a far bigger contribution to military peace-keeping operations than the leading members of NATO in Europe. This in Bildt's view demonstrated the limited relevance of dividing countries into those which are part of a military alliance and those which are not. Commenting on the WEU, the Swedish prime minister said that Sweden's relationship with the WEU could only be defined when Sweden had become a member of the Union. In the meantime, he welcomed the growing role for the WEU in the peace-keeping area.

Sweden has presented a number of specific demands in the accession talks. On the occasion of the opening of the accession negotiations on 1 February 1993, Ulf Dinkelspiel outlined the main concerns of Sweden. He first confirmed that Sweden would not hamper the development of a defence union. Then Dinkelspiel stated that 'a final Swedish position relating to the transition from the second to the third stage [of EMU] would be taken in the light of future events and in accordance with the provisions of the treaty'. He went on to state his country's wish to see Nordic cooperation recognized in an appropriate form in the accession treaty. Regarding the more specific negotiation issues, Dinkelspiel mentioned regional policy; the environment; agricultural policy; fisheries; commercial monopolies and Sweden's free-trade agreements with the Baltic states as areas where Sweden had specific interests requiring joint solutions. He also stated that the size of Sweden's budgetary contribution might constitute a problem (Dinkelspiel, 1993). A report prepared by the commerce department in the Ministry of Foreign Affairs in 1991 mentions other specific problems. Thus some of the Swedish excise duties like the package duty and the tax on commercials would have to be abolished. And Sweden must foresee certain adjustments in its on the whole very generous trade policy towards the Third World (*Konsekvenser av ett svensk EG-medlemskap*, May 1991, Ministry of Foreign Affairs). Membership of the Union will inevitably involve Sweden in trade disputes with Japan and the United States which from a Swedish point of view will often appear like 'foreign-trade wars'. This should be weighed against the fact that as a member of the Union Sweden will be able to count on the protection of its partners in disputes with third countries.

In his Paul-Henri Spaak speech the Swedish prime minister also commented upon the accession negotiations, lamenting the limited progress on some technical issues of great importance to Sweden. He stressed the fact that some specific issues like the need to retain a policy regarding the sale of alcoholic beverages designed to limit the abuse of alcohol while of marginal economic interest to the EC were politically very sensitive in Sweden (Bildt, 1993).

Indeed, opposition to Union membership is very considerable in Sweden. Public opinion in Sweden on the issue of membership of the European Union appears less volatile than public opinion in Austria with the Swedes even more opposed to membership than the Austrians. A number of polls taken by the polling institute SIFO show a relatively clear and stable picture. In October 1992, probably under the influence of the Danish 'no' to the Maastricht Treaty in June 1992, as many as 53 per cent of the Swedes said they would vote against accession to the EC, only 30 per cent would vote 'yes', while 17 per cent were undecided. In December 1992 the 'no' vote had dropped to 50 per cent and the 'yes' side had recovered slightly, registering 33 per cent support; 17 per cent were still undecided. By February 1993, following the successful Edinburgh Summit, the 'no' vote had dropped further to 43 per cent with 32 per cent in favour and 26 per cent undecided. It seems that some opponents had now become undecided, perhaps influenced by the concessions which Denmark had obtained in Edinburgh. By March 1993, the picture was roughly the same: 44 per cent were against membership, 34 per cent in favour and 22 per cent undecided. Then in May 1993, the 'no' side seemed once again in the ascendant: 46 per cent said they would vote 'no'; 33 per cent said they would support membership and 21 per cent were undecided (all polls quoted in *Göteborg-Posten*, 29 May 1993). The victory of the 'yes' side in the second Danish referendum on 18 May 1993 appears to have had a certain effect on Swedish public opinion. New SIFO polls showed that at the end of May 1993 a majority of 55 per cent (against 31 per cent) thought the outcome of the referendum would be 'yes', whereas a month earlier only 43 per cent had foreseen a victory for the 'yes' side compared to 42 per cent who had foreseen a victory for the 'no' side (*Svenska Dagbladet*, 1 June 1993). It remains unclear, however, to what extent expectations of a victory for the adherents of membership will translate into a positive vote at the referendum itself.

All in all, public opinion in Sweden is currently more hostile towards Union membership than Austrian public opinion. The 'no' side has a clear majority in the population and this support is at the time of writing at a high level above 40 per cent. However, the adherents of membership have some reason for optimism, pinning their hopes on the big Social Democratic Party which has not yet taken an official stand on the membership issue but whose leadership is known to support the 'yes' side. At the time of writing the Social Democratic voters are, however, overwhelmingly against membership. At a party congress in September 1993 the Social Democrats thus decided to postpone the decision on whether to support membership until after the result of the accession negotiations is known. In the meantime the party will be discussing the issue. Two social democratic organizations, one favouring a 'yes', another a 'no', have already been formed (*Svenska Dagbladet,* 18 September 1993).

6.3 Finland

Finland has travelled a long way from its position as an outsider in EFTA in the 1960s to its current position as a firm supporter of the Maastricht Treaty. This reflects the extreme degree of structural determination in Finnish foreign policy, Finland being highly sensitive to negative and positive developments in its eastern environment. During the first decades of the post-war period, Finland thus remained aloof from the many integration schemes launched. The European federalist movement attracted very little attention in Finland, and in fact until the late 1950s Finland had no specific policy towards European integration (Törnudd, 1969). Aware of the necessity of good relations with the Soviet Union, Finland refused to participate in the European Recovery Programme and consequently did not become a member of the OEEC. It did, however, decide to join the Nordic Council (established in 1952) in 1955 and took part in the Nordic discussion about a Nordic Customs Union. However, when in 1959 the Finns finally declared themselves ready to take part in a Nordic Customs Union, the plan had already been overtaken by the wider European scheme. When EFTA was set up in 1960, Finland had to negotiate a special association arrangement, the so-called FINEFTA agreement of 1961, granting it the rights of an EFTA member, while also guaranteeing its special interests *vis-à-vis* the Soviet Union (Jacobsen, 1982, pp. 158ff.). The Soviet Union, referring to the most-favoured-nation clause, wanted the same treatment as Finland's European trading partners. Finland could have refused this demand by pointing to the GATT rules which allow the establishment of customs unions and free-trade areas under certain conditions. Yet, Finland felt that for political reasons it could not simply brush aside the Soviet demand as did the other EFTA countries. In the late 1960s, the plans for Nordic economic cooperation once again placed Finland on the horns of a dilemma. Eventually it proved impossible to bridge the gap between Denmark, which saw the NORDEK plan as a prelude to EC membership, and Finland, which regarded it as a more permanent arrangement.

As mentioned earlier, in the aftermath of the adhesion to the EC of Denmark, Ireland and the United Kingdom, the EC concluded free-trade agreements with the rest of EFTA. Finland also concluded an agreement with the EC although a year later than the other EFTANs, but for political reasons the Finnish agreement did not include an evolutionary clause (Antola, 1991, p. 149).

In the mid-1980s, the plans for the creation of an internal market in the EC caused the Finns to take several steps. Finland joined the EU-REKA project in 1985 and in the same year became a full member of EFTA. Given the external constraints on Finnish foreign policy, it was useful for Finland to pursue its *rapprochement* with the EC within a grouping with several neutral member states. Finland became one of the firmest supporters of 'EFTA orthodoxy' in the negotiations with the EC on an EEA while being much more reticent on the issue of a possible strengthening of the EFTA pillar.

Over the last five years, Finnish policy towards European integration has undergone a more dramatic change. Beginning as a laggard in EFTA, Finland has become a full and loyal member of EFTA and subsequently a committed supporter of the Maastricht Treaty. It now even supports security policy integration within the Union. Economic interests made it imperative for Finland to follow in the tracks of Norway and Sweden once these countries had decided to move closer to the EC. Since pulp and paper exports are still of great importance to Finland, and Finland competes with Norway and Sweden in this field, Finland would find it difficult to remain outside a preferential trade arrangement which included these two countries and the important customer, the EC. But security policy factors also played an important role in the policy transition which lead to the Finnish application.

Finnish EC policy changed track in the months following the (official) finalization of negotiations on the EEA in late 1991. The EEA was now described as an intermediate solution, and in early 1992 the Finnish government declared its intention to apply for EC membership. During the EEA talks, Finland had been among the most stalwart supporters of the multilateral approach (Carlsson, 1991; Antola, 1990). The EEA had appeared the ideal solution to a country like Finland, economically dependent on the internal market but politically immobilized by a long-standing and largely imposed policy of adaptive acquiescence in relation to the Soviet Union (Mouritzen, 1988, pp. 365ff.). But by late 1991 the parameters of Finnish EC policy had changed dramatically. The EEA talks had been concluded. Sweden was headed for EC membership and to the east Finland no longer faced political intimidation but economic chaos. With the collapse of the Soviet Union and the new CIS economies in deep crisis, the Finnish economy was more than ever dependent on the EC market. There was a risk that Finland would be placed in an economic no-man's land between a collapsing CIS and a dynamic European Union. In security terms, the collapse of the cold war system provided Finland with a 'window of opportunity': adherents of the EC now had an opportunity to make dreams come true. At the same time, the adherents of Finnish membership realized that they might be running out of time. The abortive coup in Moscow in August 1991 had a sobering effect on the Finns, reminding them that a conservative backlash or a civil war in Russia was a realistic possibility. Finland hastened to negotiate a new treaty with the Soviet Union devoid of any special security clauses which, following the abolition of the Soviet Union in December 1991, was transformed into a treaty with Russia signed in January 1992 (Hubel, 1993).

The general view in the political elite was that unless they acted quickly, the Finns might miss an historical opportunity. Besides, if it waited too long Finland might not be able to negotiate an accession treaty with the EC along with Sweden and Austria and thus ran the risk of having to wait until the second round of enlargements, expected to take place at the end of the decade.

Yet, much still depended on the outcome of the on-going debate in the EC regarding defence integration. In late October, Prime Minister Aho pointed out that Finland would have to await the result of the EC summit in Maastricht before making a final decision. He also said that Finland wanted to remain neutral and that with regard to agriculture and regional policy EC membership would not be an advantage for Finland (*Frankfurter Algemeine*, 30 October 1991). The final decision on the membership issue of course lay in the hands of Koivisto, the Finnish president, who much like the French president has extensive powers in the foreign-policy field. In November Koivisto appeared at one of his few press conferences, telling the press that he was doubtful about the idea of Finnish EC membership. He referred to a recent devaluation of the Markka saying that Finland's economy had a narrow export base and was therefore very sensitive to short-term changes in international markets. Under these circumstances Koivisto had his doubts about the wisdom of relinquishing control over exchange-rate policy (*Dagens Nyheter*, 20 November 1991).

In early January 1992, the Finnish government submitted a report to Parliament on the advantages and disadvantages of membership. The report gave a balanced analysis of the membership issue and great efforts had evidently been made to reach balanced policy recommendations (cf. the government report *Finland and Membership of the European Community*, 9 January 1992). Regarding the economic consequences of membership, the tone of the report was upbeat. EC membership would bring 100,000 new jobs and an increase in real incomes of 8 per cent. Additionally, consumer prices would fall and the interest rate would stabilize with positive effects on investment. It was stressed that only full membership could guarantee Finnish companies full equality with European companies. EC membership would also have a positive effect on the prospects for companies to form close relationships with companies in the EC countries, for example in research and development. Finally, the report mentioned that only membership could give Finland influence on EC policies of crucial importance to Finland such as environmental regulations concerning the forest industry (op. cit., p. 26).

Negative economic consequences of membership were on the other hand foreseen in the agricultural field (op. cit., p. 19 and appendix). The report estimated that as a member of the EC, Finland could suffer a 30 per cent drop in its agricultural production. It recommended that in accession negotiations, the Finnish government should try to obtain special arrangements in both the agricultural and regional areas. In the regional area the report recommended that attempts be made to change the EC criteria for granting regional development aid so as to ensure that they took Finland's special conditions into account (op. cit., p. 51).

In the field of foreign policy the report was rather circumspect, arguing that 'membership would represent a stronger foreign-policy channel for Finland's national ambitions'. Membership would give Finland a better platform from which to propagate its foreign-policy views. On the other hand, the report also argued that membership would imply 'restrictions on Finland's freedom of action'. Thus, it stressed that EC membership would involve not only economic commitments but also political commitments such as participation in sanctions and joint interventions. However, it added that if such joint European sanctions and interventions were coordinated with the UN, they would present no problem for Finland. As for defence, the report argued that Finland would retain responsibility for the defence of its territory. At least, there was little likelihood that a Finnish EC membership would increase the risk of Finland being drawn into European conflicts. The report thus argued that EC membership was not incompatible with military neutrality.

As suggested above, this warming to the political dimension of the EC should be seen in the context of the new security situation to the east of the country. Max Jacobson, former Finnish Ambassador to the UN, argued that 'if there is a lot of trouble in the former Soviet empire, Finland is surely more secure as a member of a large powerful alliance than standing alone'. Elisabeth Rehn, Finnish Minister of Defence, similarly argued that Finland would be safer in the EC than outside (Reuters, 8 February 1992). It should be remembered that Finland shares a 1,200-kilometre border with Russia and that the Finno–Soviet border is the steepest with regard to living standards. A new nuclear disaster in Russia could prompt a massive migration to neighbouring Finland. To this should be added the possibility of spillover of any armed conflict between Russia and the Baltic republics (Kivinen, 1993).

As indicated, the other crucial factor behind the change in Finland's EC policy was the deep economic recession caused by the collapse in the traditional Soviet market which used to take up between 15 and 25 per cent of Finnish exports. Unemployment in Finland has been growing steadily and is currently 19 per cent. During 1991 alone Finland's exports decreased by about 14 per cent mainly due to the collapse of the Soviet market, and imports to Finland dropped by as much as 20 per cent. By way of comparison, Sweden and Switzerland also faced a drop in the value of exports during 1991, but only by roughly 4 per cent in each country. The severity of the Finnish recession is further illustrated by the fact that Swedish exports to Finland contracted by 20 per cent in 1991 (*EFTA Trade*, 1991).

The presentation of the government report was followed by a long parliamentary debate on EC membership, a debate called 'the foreign policy debate of the century'. It clarified the position of most of the political parties (*Dagens Nyheter*, 15 January 1992): The four-party government was divided on the issue. The most enthusiastic EC supporters were found in the conservative party Samlingspartiet. This party was supported by the small Swedish Peoples' Party, which feared that a 'no' to EC membership would separate Finland from Sweden and Western

Europe. By contrast, the agrarian Centre Party, now the biggest party in Finland, was deeply divided on the issue.

The prime minister, himself a member of the Centre Party, said during the debate in January that he could only support membership on certain conditions: neutrality must be compatible with EC membership, and one would have to find solutions to the problems of autonomy, agriculture and regional policy. He also spoke about the special needs of 'arctic agriculture', the new buzz word in the Finnish EC debate. A final worry also mentioned in the government report concerned the existing free-trade arrangement with Finland's eastern neighbours. Although Finnish trade with the East has fallen from 25 per cent in the heyday of Finnish–Soviet trade to almost nil, the free-trade arrangement was considered important especially with a view to the future. Prime minister Aho thus wanted a special deal with Brussels that would exempt Finland from ordinary EC Customs Union policy (*Dagens Nyheter*, 12 January 1992). The government report did not mention this option, which in any case seems unrealistic. Instead it pinned its hope on the evolving network of EC cooperation and association agreements with the states in the former COMECON area (*Finland and Membership of the European Community*, p. 17).

The small Christian Union, the fourth party in the government with only one seat in the government, was vehemently opposed to EC membership and went so far as to quote the Bible on the negative features of power concentration (*Hufvudstadsbladet*, 15 January 1992). Outside the government, the biggest opposition party, the Social Democratic Party, was in favour of membership. It argued that it was neither possible nor necessary for Finland to stick to its neutrality. The party wanted a swift application without preconditions. The left-wing opposition party, Venstreforbundet, was opposed to EC membership, arguing that the EC was becoming a 'United States of Europe'. The Green Party, on the other hand, was split on the issue.

In February 1992 the Finnish government went further in the direction of an application. After talks with the EC presidency, Foreign Minister Vayrynen said that it was his government's intention to submit a very simple application with no conditions attached. But he also added that Finland would retain its neutrality in the sense that it would stay outside military alliances and retain an independent defence. The final decision would be taken on February 27 (Reuters, 10 February 1992).

In February, the Social Democratic president also broke his silence and came out in favour of Finnish EC membership. He now clearly supported a membership application. Koivisto contradicted his own prime minister, arguing that in his view agriculture and the peripheral districts would stand to benefit from EC membership. In a speech on the occasion of the opening of Parliament on 7 February 1992, Koivisto repeated this message saying that 'it is important for Finland that the whole country remains inhabited and agriculture remains vital. In the long run it may be easier to fulfil these goals within a European framework than on our own' (Koivisto, 1992). In this connection he also drew attention to the very high prices of food in Finland. In the 1980s, food prices have been roughly double the prices in the rest of northern Europe, the implications being that more competition might be needed in the Finnish economy.

The argument that agriculture and the periphery would benefit from Union membership made a strong impact among anti-EC forces in Norway which have for a long time used precisely the protection of small peasants and regional 'district' policy as one of their main arguments against EC membership. Significantly, Koivisto also argued that 'we rely on decisions taken elsewhere ... and it is better to have a voice where the decisions are taken than not to have one' (*Agence Europe*, 7 February 1992).

On February 27, the government made public its intention to seek membership of the EC (*Regeringens principbeslut om meddelande til Riksdagen angående medlemsskap i den europæiske gemenskapen*, UM Press meddelande no. 84, 28 February 1992). The decision, which represents a dramatic new departure in Finnish foreign policy, was justified by a combination of political and economic arguments. Prominent among these were the new security order in Europe, the decision of two countries within Finland's key reference group to apply for EC membership and the growing economic and political weight of the EC in Europe. However, in the statement's presentation of the background to the application, economic factors are emphasized. The report places the EC's goal of a common defence policy within the context of the CSCE process, which in Finland's view ought to be strengthened. The report characterizes the 'core of Finnish neutrality as military non-alignment and an independent defence'. The central objective of Finnish neutrality policy is to 'maintain and reinforce stability and security in Northern Europe'. While thus trying to carve out a special role for Finland in the EC, the report also signals Finland's willingness to compromise on the issue of a common defence policy. The report reads 'Finland's point of departure in the EC is an independent defence' (op. cit., p. 3). The report reiterates the view that Finland is entitled to special treatment in the area of agricultural and regional policy. One of the central goals in the Finnish accession negotiations with the EC will thus be to 'develop the EC's system for regional support in order that the Northern conditions may be taken into account' (op. cit., p. 4). The report also contains an undertaking to hold a consultative referendum on the issue of EC membership.

On 18 March 1992 the government submitted its proposition for a membership application to the Finnish Parliament. After a marathon debate, 108 members voted for and 55 members against the government proposition. In an earlier vote, 133 members of parliament had voted for an alternative proposition by the Social Democratic Party and 60 members against. Thus, the die-hard opponents could muster less than a third of the Parliament's members (*Politiken*, 20 March 1992).

The Commission delivered its opinion on Finnish EC membership on 4 November 1992 (Com (92) 2048 final). As in the case of Sweden, the opinion on the whole adopts a positive attitude towards Finnish membership. Yet, there are slight but telling differences between the two opinions. Whereas the opinion on Sweden explicitly praises the contribution which Sweden will be able to make as a member of the EC, the opinion on Finland simply repeats the standard phrase (from the Lisbon European Council) that Finnish membership will not pose insurmountable problems of an economic nature. Moreover, the opinion on Sweden talks about 'a few' problem areas, whereas in the opinion on Finland the word used is 'some'. On the other hand, when it comes to CFSP, the European Commission credits Finland for its constructive and open-minded attitude. The document points out that 'Finland has accepted the Treaty's provisions [on CFSP] and has indicated its preparedness to participate constructively in their implementation'. However, the opinion repeats the recommendation found in the opinions on Austrian and Swedish membership that the Community should seek 'specific and binding commitments from Finland' regarding its commitment and legal ability to fulfil its obligations in the areas of defence policy and defence.

On the occasion of the opening of accession negotiations in Brussels on 1 February 1993, Pertti Salolainen, the Finnish Minister of Foreign Trade, explained in which areas Finland would seek special conditions. In particular he drew attention to agriculture and regional development. In the field of agriculture 'special measures were needed to alleviate the disadvantages of a northern climate and long distances'. In the field of regional policy, Finland wanted the specific conditions of the arctic and sub-arctic regions to be taken into account when assessing permitted national support and in identifying regions eligible for support from the Union's funds. The Finnish representative also mentioned Finland's wish to preserve its free-trade arrangements with the Baltic states (Salolainen, 1993). But all in all, the Finnish negotiating position was not very hard and looked less demanding than the Swedish.

Public opinion in Finland on the issue of Union membership must be characterized as remarkably stable. According to regular surveys carried out by the Centre for Finnish Business and Policy Studies (EVA) in November 1992, the number of those in favour of membership was 43 per cent, with 41 per cent against (EVA, 1 July 1993). In July 1993, the figures for and against were exactly balanced at 40 per cent for each side. The number of undecided has thus gone up slightly. Within the government, 78 per cent of the conservatives are in favour, but only 31 per cent of the Centre Party supporters. Within the opposition, 52 per cent of the Social Democrats are in favour of membership, 43 per cent of the Greens are in favour but only 14 per cent of the Left-Wing Alliance. The trade unions are divided on the issue with only 30 per cent of the Central Organization of Finnish Trade Unions backing membership of the European Union. The one big group which is decidedly against membership is the farmers: 81 per cent of the farmers expressed opinions against membership in a survey carried out by the Centre for Finnish Business and Policy Studies (EVA). As many as 77 per cent of the Finns believe that Finland will in fact join the Union in the near future (EVA, op. cit.).

All in all, it seems that the Finnish adherents of membership are in a better position than both their Austrian and Swedish counterparts when it comes to securing a popular endorsement of the policy of accession to the Union. However, it is obvious that the high level of support for membership is to a significant degree determined by contingent factors, notably the current economic crisis. To the extent that the Finnish economy shows signs of recovery, this must be expected to have a negative effect on support for membership of the Union.

6.4 Norway

To an outside observer not familiar with Norwegian domestic politics, it may seem odd that Norway is not already a member of the EC (Sæter and Knudsen, 1991). If Denmark is 'the odd man in', Norway (along with Austria) is the 'odd man out'. After all, like most EC countries, Norway is a member of NATO and a very loyal and active one at that. Moreover, Norway's trade dependence on the EC market is extremely high (around 70 per cent of exports go to the Union). However, a significant part of this trade is in the field of raw materials, where technical barriers to trade are not a big problem. What is more, because of oil and energy deliveries, interdependence with the EC is far from being a one-way-street.

The main barrier to Norwegian membership of the EC is, however, of a different nature. Domestic politics in a broad sense has simply prevailed over economic considerations in Norway's European politics. In the 1972 referendum on EC membership, a majority of 53 per cent voted against. A number of factors explain the outcome (Allen, 1979, pp. 159ff.). History and geography combined to make it a natural reaction for many Norwegians. Centuries of foreign rule first by the Danes, then by the Swedes and the fact of being a young nation made many Norwegians fierce patriots. The word 'Union' used by the EC to describe the Community's goal touched raw nerves in Norway, reviving bad memories of the union with Sweden abolished in 1905. Moreover, the foreign-policy links with continental Europe were rather tenuous, whereas many Norwegians had personal links with America. Most importantly, there was a clear centre–periphery clash in Norwegian EC politics. The EC question pitted the traditionalist north with strong currents of Protestant fundamentalism against the modernist south (cf. Allen, 1979; Martens, 1979; Schou, 1980). To this should be added the problem of remote government in a country of great distances, compounded by the specific interests of the fishing and farming communities in the north. As stressed by Allen, it would however be wrong simply to describe the EC resistance as a periphery phenomenon. The EC opponents in the north had powerful allies both in the conservative cultural groups of the south-west and in metropolitan circles, where many academics regarded the struggle of the farmers and fishermen as symbolizing the defence of certain values and a certain way of life characteristic of Norway. Finally, the 'pro' side was over-optimistic and conducted a rather weak campaign made difficult, it should be added, by unhelpful acts on the EC side. For instance, the Commission made controversial statements on oil policy only a few days before the referendum on 25 September 1972. And the EC's refusal to grant Norway the revision clause in the fisheries agreement which it had asked for obviously did not help the pro-EC side in Norway.

In the 1980s, the leaders of the Social Democratic Party in Norway seemed to have learned the lesson: when the EC question resurfaced, they took great care to move slowly and carefully prepare the ground for the electorate. Against the background of the traumatic EC referendum in 1972, Jacques Delors' proposal in January 1989 to create a kind of partial membership for European countries with close ties to the EC found a receptive audience in the Norwegian political elite. There are even indications that Mrs Brundtland, leader of the Social Democratic Party, was closely involved in preparing the Delors initiative. It is a measure of the politicization and sensitivity of the EC membership issue that Mrs Brundtland was immediately criticized in the Norwegian public debate for conducting a 'Back-door EC policy' (*Management Today*, 30 May 1989).

Thus, the Norwegian government had a special stake in the EEA venture. First of all, there was personal prestige involved. Mrs Brundtland had helped Jacques Delors get the EEA talks off the ground in 1989. Second, and more importantly, incrementalism was more in demand in Norway than in any other EFTA country with the possible exception of Switzerland. Domestic political opinion had to be prepared for EC membership, and both the EC and the Norwegian pro-EC elite knew that this preparation was likely to take time. The Norwegian debate displays some similarities with the Swiss debate in the sense that not only EC membership but also the EEA regime is controversial. By contrast, in Sweden and Finland, the EEA has generally not been politicized.

The Luxembourg declaration in 1984 did not provoke immediate initiatives in Norway. But following the adoption of the Single European Act and the internal market programme, the Norwegian government decided to have the Foreign Ministry prepare a report on the issue. The report called 'Norway, the EC and European Cooperation' was deliberately pragmatic: it did not touch on the question of EC membership directly but merely went through the various technical adaptations required to make Norway fit for '1992'. It also expressed considerable sympathy with the strengthening of the EPC (*Stortingsmelding*, nos. 61 and 63). The Norwegian government was evidently of the opinion that if a structured European pillar was being created within NATO, Norway risked being left isolated within NATO or else becoming more dependent on the United States – unless it joined the EC.

As indicated, when in 1989 Jacques Delors launched the EEA plan, the Norwegian government was enthusiastic. Austria was on the verge of applying for membership. The Norwegian pro-EC camp was well aware of the consequences: there was now a risk that the debate on EC membership might spread to other EFTA countries. From the point of view of Norway's EC supporters, this was premature. Norway needed more time to prepare the population for EC membership. The EEA was needed in order to gain time. Besides, EFTA provided a tactical cover. Like Nordic cooperation, EFTA has always been non-controversial in Norwegian domestic politics. Therefore from the elite point of view it was politically wise to portray the new positive Norwegian EC policy as an EFTA policy and a Nordic policy (Sæter and Knudsen, 1991; Sæter in Laursen, 1990, pp. 115ff.).

The Norwegian debate on the EC issue was subdued during the first and second phases of the EEA negotiations. But the Confederation of Norwegian Business and Industry (CNBI) did come out in favour of membership in February 1990. Arve Thorvik, Vice-Chairman of CNBI, told the *Financial Times* that Norwegian industry wanted to remain competitive when the EC's internal market was introduced. He also pointed to the need for real influence on EC decisions (*Financial Times*, 21 February 1990). Only after the start of detailed negotiations in June 1990 – when the EC began to show its hand – did the Norwegian EC issue receive serious attention. On 18 October 1990 Norway announced that it would shadow the exchange-rate mechanism of the EMS. Norway had wanted a formal association with the EMS. It had signalled its intention to draw closer to the EMS in early 1990 (Reuters, 25 January 1990). However, Norway was rebuffed by the EC, which told Oslo that formal association was not possible. Significantly, the argument used by the EC was that this would complicate the EC's internal monetary reform process. 'Maybe three years ago associate membership was possible, but not now', an EC official said (Reuters, 21 October 1990). At the same time, the EC Commission was delighted that Norway linked its currency to the ECU basket rather than the anchor currency of the EMS, the Deutschmark. This added credibility to the Commission's efforts to make the ECU the future single EC currency.

As the EEA negotiations moved into the sensitive areas, the strain began to show in the Norwegian right-of-centre government. In October 1990 the Conservative Prime Minister Jan P. Syse had to resign because of internal disagreement over the right of foreigners to invest in Norwegian property, industrial firms and banks and because of disagreement over how to react to Sweden's sudden move towards full membership of the EC (*Guardian*, 30 October 1990). At issue was the Norwegian negotiating strategy in the EEA talks. The new Social Democratic government led by Mrs Brundtland declared its intention to push for closer ties with the EC without laying down strict preconditions for a deal (Reuters, 6 November 1990). The new prime minister also said that Norway should speed up a decision on whether to join the European Community. But her minority government also said that it would not decide on EC membership until EFTA had agreed on setting up an EC–EFTA free market. The prime minister told a news conference that 'this debate is due to last until the next party meeting in 1992. But if dramatic things happen in the world around us, which demand a higher tempo, we cannot exclude that we must ask our party colleagues to make faster conclusions' (Reuters, 7 November 1990).

In fact, dramatic events had already taken place. The Swedish decision in late October 1990 to prepare for EC membership could not but make an impact in Norway, if only because Sweden is Norway's biggest trading partner. However, reactions to the Swedish move were not as simple as might have been assumed. Although as expected organizations with a direct economic stake in trade with Sweden concluded that Norway would have to follow suit, reactions in the population were less clear. Norway's democratic history is one of liberation from Sweden (and Denmark), and there is still a certain sensitivity in the Norwegian public to signs of 'Swedish dominance'. The prime minister – who given her positive attitude to EC membership must have had a strong incentive to use the Swedish card as an argument in favour of membership – nevertheless felt it was necessary to stress Norway's independence. 'I think it is wrong to draw simple conclusions that if Sweden does something, Norway will do the same – we are a special country,' she said in December 1990 (Reuter, Oslo, 21 December 1990).

The developments in Finnish EC politics appear to have had a slightly different impact in Norway. When after the Finnish elections in March 1991 it became clear that Finland might be headed for membership, Prime Minister Brundtland used this as an argument in favour of accelerating Norway's own decision-making process on EC membership. In late April 1991, she told a Danish newspaper that in her view the Finnish decision changed the picture for Norway (the Danish daily *Information*, 30 April 1991). In her traditional 1 May speech, Mrs Brundtland reiterated this view saying that if both Sweden and Finland sought EC membership, it was not easy to envisage a situation where Norway would decide to remain outside. Apart from the fact that membership for both Sweden and Finland raised a new problem of marginalization, it should be recalled that Finland's economic structure is much more similar to that of Norway than is Sweden's. It may also be of importance that in the Norwegian public, Finland is perceived as a 'genuine' small state, unlike Sweden. Besides, Norway has no historical 'hang-up' regarding Finland. Yet, at the same time, the Norwegian Prime Minister reacted reservedly to a new Finnish debate about a 'Nordic bloc' joining the EC together. Mrs Brundtland stuck to her view that 1992 was the year when the three Nordic countries would decide on EC membership (*Dagens Nyheter*, 4 May 1991).

The anti-EC parties were led by the agrarian Centre Party. In her 1 May speech in 1991, the new leader of the party, Anne Enger Lahnstein, said in a statement typical of the anti-EC position that the EC had severe environmental problems and was anti-social. She also stated that she wanted Norway to retain control over its own resources. Finally, Mrs Lahnstein said that for her party the EC meant centralization, a centralization that would 'split up families, erode cultural life and impoverish local life when we give up democracy and sovereignty' (*Neue Zürcher Zeitung*, 9–10 May 1991). Another argument used by the anti-EC parties was the risk that EC membership would lead to cuts in welfare benefits and slash subsidies to rural communities.

The Centre Party was also critical towards the EEA, though less so. In an interview with the daily *Aftenposten* in July 1991, Mrs Lahnstein said that 'with EC membership we give up Norwegian sovereignty and independence ... We do this to a lesser degree if we join the EEA, but the subjection to EC's rules will imply an increase in unemployment because market forces will be let loose' (*Aftenposten*, 13 July 1991). This rhetoric apparently struck a responsive chord in the Norwegian electorate. In the local elections in September 1991, the Centre Party and the other major party opposed to EC membership, the Socialist Left Party, made big gains. The Centre Party advanced from 6.5 per cent in the national elections in 1989 to 12.1 per cent. The share of the Socialist Left Party rose from 10.1. per cent to 12.1 per cent.

In press interviews, the prime minister admitted that the election result made it less likely that Norway would apply to join the EC (Reuters, 10 September 1991). Asked at a news conference if she would now back EC membership, Mr. Brundtland declined to answer (Reuters, 16 September 1991). Her own party's share had slumped from 34.3 per cent to 30.4 per cent at the 1989 elections, which had been its worst showing since World War II. The conservative opposition party, another supporter of EC membership, also lost support. It slipped to 21.8 per cent from 22.2 per cent. However, most of these votes were picked up by the pro-EC Progress Party.

The result of the EC Summit in Maastricht in December 1991 endorsing the treaty on the European Union was broadly welcomed by the Norwegian prime minister. She stated that the summit was a milestone in European history which made it vital for Norway to ratify the EEA agreement before 1993. Yet, her specific statements were more balanced. Pointing out that the advantages of membership were mainly to be found in the foreign-policy and security fields she added that 'there are other areas – agricultural policy, taxation – where the benefits of EC membership are not so obvious'. Mrs Brundtland said the Summit would not speed up the party's long-running debate on EC membership. The decision would be taken in November 1992. She also said she had not made a final decision on whether to recommend EC membership to the country, adding that her decision would in part be guided by the development in a debate on membership to be held within the Labour Party in the following months (Reuters, 11 December 1991).

The problem for Mrs Brundtland was that the Labour Party's EC schedule did not match that of the EC. The EC had signalled at the Maastricht Summit that it intended to initiate talks with the first group of applicant countries in early 1993. The incoming British Presidency had even suggested that it might try to accelerate enlargement. The EC was therefore getting increasingly impatient with Norway, wanting a clear indication of Norway's intention. Did Norway want to opt for an early EC accession? Or did it prefer to wait? The Labour Party in Norway and indeed the prime minister were well aware of the problem. In early 1992 she therefore made a statement to the effect that she would make a decision on EC membership in April at the first regional party meeting (*fylkemøde*) at the latest. In this way the Norwegian government would be able to send a signal to Brussels well before the formal decision was taken at the Labour congress in November.

At the same time, Gro Harlem Brundtland began showing her hand. There was no doubt that she wanted Norway to apply for membership. The problem was that opposition to EC membership was very considerable in her own party, indeed the issue could become a serious threat to the electoral fortunes of the party. A speech to the Norwegian Labour Party in Akershus on 14 January is characteristic of the arguments used by Brundtland in trying to convince the EC-sceptical party members (cf. *Norge i et nytt Europa*, Akershus Arbeiterparti, 14 January 1992). Mrs

Brundtland started out referring to the Labour Party's traditional inter-nationalism: 'The Labour Party has always seen the connection between national identity and international cooperation.' She then attacked those in Norway who argued that the EEA and EC membership amounted to the same thing. She stressed the differences in decision-making procedures as well as in terms of the scope of cooperation. In this connection, she indicated that in her view it was not in Norway's interest to stay outside the foreign and security component of EC integration which was becoming a more important part of the EC.

Having stressed the economic costs of political uncertainty, Mrs Brundtland went on to make a crucial point: in an open world, au-tonomy was best safeguarded by securing access to those bodies where the real decisions were taken. Economic internationalization created a demand for political internationalization in more and more areas. In this connection the Norwegian labour leader stressed the social dimen-sion, which the Norwegian government had fought hard to include in the EEA agreement. Yet at the same time she was careful to dispel any fear that the EC was developing into a centralized superstate. In sup-port of this view she referred to the principle of subsidiarity. In the final part of her speech, Mrs Brundtland reiterated that only through mem-bership of the EC could Norway obtain co-decision and political influ-ence and stressed the influence on European foreign- and security-policy formulation as being of particular importance to Norway.

The emphasis on political influence and participation in foreign policy and security cooperation was echoed in Foreign Minister Thorvald Stoltenberg's foreign-policy statement before the Norwegian Storting on 10 February 1992. Stressing the willingness of other EFTA countries and Eastern European countries to take an active part in political integration, Stoltenberg said *inter alia* that 'Maastricht has made it clear for Norway that there are only two ways of adapting to the new Europe: either one can take part in the decisions in the EC and thus take part in the construction of the future Europe or one can adapt to the results of these decisions without having taken part in the process. The latter solution would in reality mean a weakening of Norwegian autonomy' (Stoltenberg, 1992). The rest of the year 1992 saw an intense debate about Norway's European policy, culminating in the decision in November at the Labour Party's congress to apply for membership of the EC. On 25 November 1992, Norway submitted its application for membership of the EC.

In the Autumn of 1991, the government had commissioned a report on the implications of Norwegian participation in different forms of European cooperation. The final report was published in November 1992, timed to have maximum impact on the crucial Labour Party and its constituency (*Norge ved et Veivalg*, 1992). The report highlights a number of differences between an EEA affiliation and full membership of the Union. First of all, full membership would remove the remaining insecurity regarding the possibilities of EEA members achieving the same economic conditions as Union members. Second, full membership would, the report argues, enable Norway to benefit from the Union's regional policy. It is argued, not altogether convincingly, that 'membership entails no new restrictions on the formulation of "district policy" compared to the obligations following from the EEA regime'. The effects of membership on the Norwegian system of taxation and excise duties are not, the report argues, more severe than the adaptations in any case made necessary by lowering of levels of taxation in adjacent countries. In fact, membership would give Norway an influence on the shaping of European policies in this field which it would not have as a member of the EEA. The report describes some general advantages of participation in the EMU but recognizes that the Norwegian dependence on oil might cause problems for Norway were it to join the EMU. The reason is that as an oil economy with a narrow export base the Norwegian economy is particularly prone to cyclical changes caused by sudden changes in prices. As a member of the EMU, Norway would not be able to counter the effect of such shocks on its competitive position by devaluing its currency. Strangely, the report does not mention agriculture at all and only deals in passing with the sensitive area of fisheries. Regarding the budgetary effects of Union membership, the report estimates that Norway would have to contribute a net sum of around Norwegian Kroner 3.5 billion (almost Ecu 500 million) per annum. However, from this figure should be deducted the current Norwegian contribution to the EEA which is around Norwegian kroner .5 billion (around Ecu 65 million).

The Commission submitted its *avis* on Norwegian membership of the EC in late March 1993 (Com (93) 485 final). In its opinion, Norway is clearly eligible for membership of the EC. As a founder member of NATO and an associate member of the WEU, Norway is not expected to cause problems for the Union's CFSP. On the contrary, Norway is expected to be able to make a significant contribution in this area. In Norway's case, the problems are to be found in the economic area. Agriculture would pose problems, although the Norwegian government is undertaking reforms which would bring agricultural policy in line with the CAP. Regional policy would in the Commission's view have to be made compatible with the Community *acquis*. Adaptations are also deemed necessary in the fisheries sector as well as in the field of state aid and state monopolies. There is a specific problem in the field of trade relations with third countries, that is the fact that Norway has signed free-trade agreements with the Baltic states, whereas Union relations are (at the time of writing) still based on most-favoured-nation treatment (Com (93) 485, p. 35). Finally, it is stated rather vaguely that 'competition in general will increase in a number of fields'. On the positive side, the opinion mentions that Norway will bring to the Union important experience in the environmental field.

The Norwegian negotiating position in the accession negotiations has been described in a statement by Bjørn Tore Godal, the Minister of Trade and Shipping, on the occasion of the opening of accession negotiations with Norway on 5 April 1993 (Godal, 1993). While supporting the provisions and goals of the Maastricht Treaty, the Norwegian minister mentions a number of areas where Norway has particular interests which need to be taken into account in the accession negotiations. First of all, the energy policy of the Union poses problems. Norway is very critical of the Hydrocarbon Licensing Directive for which it sees no need, and given the fact that Norway is a stable supplier of oil and gas to the Union, which imports 15 per cent of its oil and gas from Norway, the latter expects its views to be taken into account in the debate on this initiative. Second, the minister refers to Norway's wish to make certain improvements in the Union's Common Fisheries Policy. Third, agriculture poses problems. 'New arrangements within the framework of the CAP are required' to ensure that the specific conditions for agricultural production in Norway are taken into account. Fourth, Norway wants to 'contribute prior to accession to the elaboration of criteria reflecting the country's regional conditions such as low population density, long distances, heavy dependence on fisheries and a cold climate'. Finally, Norway wants to find solutions enabling it to maintain free-trade agreements with the Baltic states (ibid.).

Public opinion in Norway remains highly sceptical of the idea of Norwegian membership of the European Union, and the number of opponents to membership has in recent years been growing.[2] In March 1992 both the 'yes' side and the 'no' side had the support of 41 per cent of the voters, with 18 per cent undecided. Then in July 1992 following the Danish 'no' to the Maastricht Treaty, 34 per cent of the Norwegians said they would vote 'yes', whereas 49 per cent would vote 'no'; 16 per cent remained undecided. Thus, the Danish 'no' may have had a significant effect on Norwegian public opinion by reinforcing the position of the already powerful 'no' side. In January 1993 following the Edinburgh Summit, 35 per cent said they would vote 'yes', 48 per cent would vote 'no' and 17 per cent remained undecided. A poll taken in March 1993 by Gallup showed that 45.6 per cent would vote 'no' and 28.7 per cent 'yes' with 25.7 per cent undecided. Another poll from the same month taken by Scanfact (*Verdens Gang*) showed that 39 per cent would vote 'no' and 25 per cent 'yes' with 35 per cent undecided. A poll taken in May 1993 prior to the second Danish referendum showed that as many as 51 per cent of the voters would oppose membership, whereas 30 per cent would support it. 19 per cent remained undecided. The outcome of the second Danish referendum does not appear to have had a significant effect on Norwegian public opinion, although a certain effect is detectable. A poll taken in early June 1993 showed that 49 per cent of Norwegians were still opposed to membership, whereas 38 per cent were supportive and 13 per cent undecided (*Dagbladet*, 7 June 1993). In September the opponents had grown even stronger with 58 per cent against membership and only 31 per cent in favour (*Politiken*, 15 September 1993). What is more, the parliamentary elections in September strengthened the 'no' side, almost tripling the mandates of the Centre Party. Significantly, this means that with the present composition of Parliament, the opponents of Norwegian membership of the European Union are able to block an accession.

Seen in a long-term perspective, the Norwegian opposition to the EC has been remarkably stable. At the referendum in 1972, the 'no' side obtained 53.5 per cent, in March 1993 it registered 51 per cent and in June 1993 49 per cent. Thus, the inroads made by EC supporters during the last 20 years have been quite modest. This suggests that although a Swedish and Finnish accession to the Union might lead some Norwegians to change their minds, the pro-union forces are facing a herculean task in Norway.

6.5 Switzerland

As stressed by Church (1993), Switzerland is different from the other EFTA countries – not because of its neutrality but because of the longevity and strict interpretation of its neutrality and the crucial domestic functions of that neutrality (cf. Bonjour, 1970). Additionally and related to this, Swiss national feeling is particularly strong. It has been argued, probably correctly, that Union membership can only be sold to the Swiss as a reinforcement of Swiss identity (Kriesi *et al.*, 1993). As we have seen, during the EEA negotiations the Swiss negotiators often adopted hard negotiating positions which alienated their partners in EFTA.

Swiss neutrality dates back at least to 1815. In 1815 five European big powers, Austria, France, Great Britain, Prussia and Russia signed a declaration 'recognizing and guaranteeing Switzerland's perpetual neutrality and the inviolability of its borders'. It added that 'the neutrality and inviolability of Switzerland and its independence from all foreign influences are in the interest of European politics in general' (Frei, 1967, p. 9). Swiss neutrality is thus firmly rooted in international law. Swiss neutrality has always had crucial domestic functions, the most important probably being the preservation of internal unity and the avoidance of over-centralization. Given Switzerland's geo-political location and internal divisions, neutrality was necessary to prevent the Swiss 'states' from entering into alliances with competing foreign powers. Though some internal conflicts have subsided, new ones have emerged in this century notably the linguistic divide which also reflects more fundamental clashes between cultural identities. It would therefore be wrong to neglect the domestic function of neutrality in the current debate about Switzerland and Europe. In fact, the new clashes between German-speaking and French-speaking parts of Switzerland may have led some Swiss to conclude that retaining neutrality is the only way to avoid fragmentation, keeping in mind the signs of fragmentation in neighbouring Italy. Yet, the Swiss elite has been more concerned about the obstacles which Swiss neutrality may create for Swiss accession to the European Union. In recent years, it has therefore started downgrading and re-defining neutrality.

The Swiss debate about closer links with the EC has centred around three options: (a) EC membership, (b) a structured partnership and (c) a special arrangement – '*Sonderweg*' (Meier, 1991). The first government report on Switzerland's relationship with the EC, published in September 1988, put the emphasis on the third option. To quote the report 'it is a matter of adopting a "Europe reflex", building bridges and not erecting new obstacles, and constantly working for an improved environment to enhance the competitiveness of our economy'. The Swiss government talked about a 'third way' between marginalization and membership which would be guided by the three principles of compatibility, reciprocity and bridges. The idea was to introduce rules similar to the internal market rules in parallel with the EC, counting on the EC's willingness to negotiate bridging arrangements. It would be a pragmatic approach combining bilateralism and multilateralism. The same report claimed that 'EC membership cannot be a goal of Swiss integration policy'.

However, the viability of this strategy depended on the EC's willingness to grant Switzerland a special status and to negotiate numerous bilateral agreements with Switzerland (Schwok, 1989, p. 20). In 1989 the EC made it clear that it preferred to deal with the EFTA countries within the framework of a more structured multilateral negotiating framework which would reduce the Commission's administrative burden and at the same time ensure a more uniform implementation of rules in the West European market. This caused a certain shift in the Swiss attitude in the direction of the option of a structured partnership. But the Swiss support for the EEA remained more half-hearted than that of its partners in EFTA. The main reason appears to have been that because of the peculiarities of the Swiss political structure, the political costs of the EEA fell heavier on the Swiss than on its partners.

It was recognized that Swiss direct democracy would be affected by the proposed EEA. In the fields covered by the EEA, the popular right of initiative would have to be abolished. Some decisions regarding changes in EEA rules would have to be delegated to a higher level. The rights of the cantons would be affected in such areas as the right of establishment of foreigners, public procurement, state aids, standards for pharmaceuticals and medical appliances. The EEA was therefore widely regarded as a kind of 'mini-accession' in terms of the duties Switzerland had to accept (Meier, 1991, p. 41). It was therefore logical that the Swiss in the EEA negotiations should try to obtain what they considered the corresponding rights, especially with regard to co-decision.

Another reason for Switzerland's aloofness towards a joint EFTA strategy was its reluctance to set up new supranational structures within EFTA as proposed by Jacques Delors. Switzerland's hardline position was evident even in the early days of the 'Delors/Oslo' process, but the Swiss government soon found itself isolated within EFTA and on a number of points had to bow to peer group pressure.

A new report from the Federal Council published in November 1990 thus stated three goals that would have to be fulfilled in the EEA negotiations (*Informationsbericht des Bundesrates über die Stellung der Schweiz im Europäischen Integrationsprozess vom 26 November 1990*):

- a high degree of Swiss integration in the internal market;
- a right of co-decision that would allow Switzerland to defend its interests effectively;
- permission for Switzerland to retain a significant portion of its special features.

If EEA membership would be burdensome, Union membership is generally considered to pose serious problems for Switzerland. The main barriers are federalism, neutrality and direct democracy. Federalism not only – it should be added – constitutes a barrier to EC entry, it could also be seen as a Swiss asset, since Swiss federalism is in some respects based upon some of the same principles as the European Union (for example subsidiarity). Switzerland might even in some respects serve as a model for the future evolution of the EC. Indeed, the *Wall Street Journal* asked, in an editorial in May 1991, why the Swiss wanted to join the EC. It ought to be the other way around: Switzerland ought to admit the EC countries as members of its confederation! (*Wall Street Journal*, 31 May–1 June 1991).

During 1990 and 1991, several developments changed the parameters of Swiss EC policy weakening several of the arguments against Swiss membership. First of all, during the EEA negotiations it gradually became clear that the EC was not in a position or willing to grant the EFTA countries a genuine equality as regards decision making on new EEA legislation. This made the EEA treaty appear asymmetrical and provoked a public debate on the risk of satellization. In an influential article in *Neue Zürcher Zeitung*, the Swiss Professor Daniel Thürer described the EEA as 'a form of legalized hegemony' (*Neue Zürcher Zeitung*, 15 May 1991). An Action Group for an Independent and Neutral Switzerland called the EEA 'a double satellization' (*Neue Zürcher Zeitung*, 8 October 1991). The then German Foreign Minister, Hans-Dietrich Genscher stated that 'a member of the EC would never become a satellite' (*Neue Zürcher Zeitung*, 1–2 May 1991).

Second, the collapse of the bi-polar bloc system in Europe and the liberalization of the Eastern European states made the protection of Swiss neutrality appear less important as an argument against EC membership. The Gulf War showed what kind of security problems might top the agenda of the new world order. During the Gulf War, Switzerland thus practised a 'differentiated neutrality', taking part in economic sanctions against Iraq but refusing to participate in the military action (*Neue Zürcher Zeitung*, 28–9 January 1991). Third, a number of EFTA and East European states began moving closer to the EC.

These developments placed the membership option in a somewhat different light. The report from the Federal Council on the European Integration Process from November 1990 accordingly signals a change of perception in the Swiss elite. The report compares the situation in 1990 with the situation in 1988 when the previous report was published and cautiously concludes that the membership option has gained in attraction. The report lists six factors that taken together might prompt the Swiss government to review its integration strategy:

- the collapse of the bi-polar security structure in Europe;
- the dominant role of the EC in the new European architecture;
- the new enlargements of the EC which are foreseen;
- the growing tendency for the EC to insist that cooperation with its neighbours be based on the EC's own legal regime;
- the strengthening of the federalist features of the EC, including the more systematic use of the principle of subsidiarity;
- the strengthening of the EC's global role.

The report emphasizes that a possible change in the Swiss EC strategy would not mean that the strategy followed hitherto had been a failure, since the strategy of national adaptation and structured partnership had been the right answer under the circumstances. The point is, the report argues, that circumstances have changed and that these may call into question the wisdom of the old strategy. The report does not conceal what in its view constitutes the most important change in the external parameters of Swiss EC policy: were Swiss EC policy to change in the direction of an EC application, this would be due first of all to the events in Central and Eastern Europe – or in the words of the report [die option EG-Beitritt] 'bezieht sich vielmehr auf eine EG, die mehrere neue Mitglieder, auch Neutrale, umfassen könnte und die angesichts ihrer grösseren Vielfalt in bestimmten Bereichen dezentraler sein könnte als heute [alge-meinere Anwendung des Subsidiaritätsprinzip]', which translates as 'the option of accession furthermore relates to an EU which might have several new members including neutrals and which in view of its greater diversity might be more decentralized in certain areas than today's EU'.

As the EC and EFTA approached the end of the EEA negotiations,

116

the Swiss elite debate shifted from a wait-and-see attitude to an open plea for an EC membership application. Yet, there continued to be considerable uneasiness about the idea of EC membership even at elite level. There was particular concern about the costs to the Swiss direct democracy and to Swiss agriculture, which was expected to lose 50 per cent of its income in the case of membership (Meier, 1991, p. 38). Participation in the EMU, the Customs Union, fiscal harmonization and a possible future common defence policy were other problem areas. However, as Sweden applied for EC membership in July 1991 and Finland and Norway began edging towards EC membership, the Swiss government elite came round to the view that Switzerland could not afford to 'wait and see'.

Switzerland was now prepared to sign an EEA agreement. It could in theory have opted for a *Sonderweg* in the short term, hoping to join the EEA later. But the problem was that the EEA option might not exist in the medium and longer term. If it chose not to sign the EEA agreement in 1991, Switzerland might have to negotiate a framework agreement with the EC later in the 1990s together with some Eastern European countries with which Switzerland had little in common. That would place Switzerland in a weaker negotiating position. If Switzerland did sign the EEA treaty in 1991, it might soon find itself sidetracked anyway because the EC might decide to abolish the EEA and convert it into bilateral agreements if most of the EFTA countries joined the EC. The alternatives to EC membership were thus rapidly losing credibility. Most importantly, however, the Swiss became increasingly aware of the political cost of non-membership. From the Swiss point of view the difference between the EEA and EC membership in terms of costs was simply too small and the difference in terms of benefits too big to make the EEA an attractive deal.

Already in early October 1991, that is before the end of the EEA negotiations, Derek Jacobi, State Secretary and leader of the Political Department in the Swiss Foreign Ministry, for the first time openly talked about a Swiss application (*Frankfurter Algemeine*, 2 October 1991). *Neue Zürcher Zeitung* commented upon the final treaty, arguing that the EEA was only acceptable if it did not close the 'European dossier'. The editorial particularly lamented the *de facto* lack of symmetry between the contracting parties when it came to rights and duties (*Frankfurter Algemeine*, 24 October 1991).

The pattern of Swiss diplomatic activity around the time of the finalization of the EEA negotiations suggests an intensified Swiss effort to win supporters within the EC. In late September Flavio Cotti, President of the Swiss Confederation, said in a speech delivered at the opening of the academic year of the College of Europe in Bruges that 'Switzerland is wholly convinced: Europe will be confederal, or it will not be'. Cotti found the French president's idea of a broad European confederation fascinating. He went on to ask whether the Council of Europe might not become the body on which to transplant the confederal idea. Cotti said he had a 'vision of a Europe giving decentralized structures the greatest possible number of competences' (*Agence Europe*, 27 September 1991). An Italian state visit to Switzerland shortly after the finalization of the EEA negotiations signalled the importance both parties attached to this relationship in the new Europe (*Neue Zürcher Zeitung*, 25 October 1991). But the United Kingdom was evidently also regarded as an important ally despite disagreements regarding the interpretation of subsidiarity. In late October Ulrich Bremi, President of the National Council, visited London giving a speech in the City Swiss Club in which he stressed the need for economic globalism, respect for the principle of subsidiarity and protection – and indeed promotion – of minorities (*Neue Zürcher Zeitung*, 30 October 1991). The EC Commission also paid Switzerland its respects. Martin Bangemann, EC Commissioner for the Internal Market, gave a speech in the Schweizerische Volksbank Luzern in early November on the subject of the EC and Switzerland. In his speech he argued in favour of Swiss membership. Commenting upon the sensitive issue of neutrality, Bangemann said that in case of a military attack on the EC, all member states obviously had to contribute. But in case of a military involvement outside the EC, a neutral state did not have to take part (*Neue Zürcher Zeitung*, 3–4 November 1991).

In early 1992, the EC debate in Switzerland became noticeably more pro-membership. 'Eurovision', a high-level working group in the Swiss Ministry of Foreign Affairs consisting of young diplomats, argued strongly in favour of EC membership in an article in *Neue Zürcher Zeitung* published in January 1992. The article stressed the institutional deficit of the EEA, characterizing the EEA as a transitional solution unsuitable as an independent and permanent element in Swiss European policy (*Neue Zürcher Zeitung*, 9 January 1992). An editorial in this influential newspaper spoke in neo-functionalist terms about an '*aus der Sache kommende Zwang*' to apply for membership. It criticized the government for failing to explain why it wanted to take Switzerland into the EC – except for the 'logical deduction' that whoever wanted to be

118

treated as an equal in integration matters had to become a full member of the EC (*Neue Zürcher Zeitung*, 16 February 1992).

A study group on neutrality set up after a request from Parliament but chaired by a highly placed government official published a report in March 1992. The report argued that neutrality had lost much of its relevance being now merely an instrument in foreign policy. Neutrality was, as in neighbouring Austria, reduced to its military core – that is avoiding participation in wars between other states. The report also recommended abandoning the duties of neutrality in peacetime in the economic and political fields. Were the EC to move towards a common defence policy, Switzerland would have to decide whether neutrality was still relevant (*La Neutralité de la Suisse sous la Loupe*, 1992; Landau, 1993). Furthermore, the report argued that neutrality was no longer crucial to Swiss interests. With the bloc confrontation gone, it was no longer essential. Neutrality did not offer an answer to conflicts in Eastern Europe, blackmail with ABC (atomic, bacteriological and chemical) weapons, terrorism in general, migration or the destruction of the environment. Neutrality was thus not considered incompatible with the setting up of a European system of collective security. The solution recommended for Switzerland was to adopt a so-called 'differential neutrality' in the European Union, taking part in economic measures with a security content and preserving complete neutrality in the military area. The Federal Council did not comment upon the report, awaiting the outcome of the EEA vote.

The Swiss government had now adopted a long-term strategy of seeking EC membership. The open question was when to apply. Should the application be submitted before or after the referendum on the EEA scheduled for late 1992? Significantly, the Swiss constitution requires a majority of both voters and cantons before Switzerland can join the EC, but in May 1992 the Swiss government eventually decided to submit its application.

Public opinion in Switzerland apparently remains strongly attached to the traditional neutrality line. In 1986, the Swiss government recommended membership of the UN but was voted down by 75.7 per cent of the electorate. A referendum in November 1989 on the abolition of the Swiss army, a step that could be seen as a departure from the Swiss commitment to a strong armed neutrality, once again revealed a cleavage between elite and population. It also suggested that the Swiss were not prepared to adjust the policy of neutrality in response to the dramatic changes in Eastern Europe. The proposal was rejected by 64.4 per cent of the voters. The governing elite received some encouragement from the outcome of a referendum in May 1992 on Swiss membership of the IMF, but this was clearly interpreted by the population as a question of functionalist problem solving rather than of transfer of sovereignty (Landau, 1993). The proposal was favoured by 55.8 per cent of the voters. Then in December 1992 the Swiss people with a narrow majority rejected the EEA agreement. An analysis of the outcome has shown that the opponents' motivation was overwhelmingly idealistic, a question of the defence of identity (Kriesi, 1993).

This blockage of the road towards the EEA produced a considerable disarray in the Swiss government. The options before Switzerland were now:

(i) To try to negotiate bilateral arrangements with the Union mirroring the EEA agreement. Unfortunately the Union has indicated that it will not grant Switzerland a 'bilateral EEA' or an 'a la carte EEA'. However, the Union is prepared to consider bilateral arrangements in certain areas where a mutual interest can be identified. After all, Switzerland is the Union's second largest export market (see appendix). A national adaptation to EEA legislation does not appear to be a realistic option since the Union will only grant reciprocity to a third country if there are common structures between the parties permitting the implementation and supervision of the relevant rules.

(ii) To adhere to the EEA agreement later. Already a popular initiative is being prepared which, if successful, will allow a new referendum to be held. However, this option is dependent upon several factors. It is an open question whether the EEA will continue to exist in its present form if Sweden, Finland, Austria and possibly even Norway become members of the Union in 1995–6. Besides, the EEA which the Swiss would join would be a different EEA, revised to account for new Union legislation.

(iii) To seek membership of the Union. The Swiss government has decided to keep the option of membership open but recognizes that given the domestic political situation in Switzerland and the enlargement schedule of the Union, there will be no accession negotiations with Switzerland in 1993. The Swiss government estimates that although a popular initiative on the opening of accession negotiations with the Union is being prepared, the realistic prognosis must be that Switzerland will not be a part of the current round of enlargement and will thus not take part in the next intergovernmental conference among the members of the Union (*Botschaft über das Folgeprogramm nach der Ablehnung des EWR-Abkommens, vom 24 Februar 1993*).

This assessment is borne out by available evidence on the state of public opinion in Switzerland. Swiss public opinion is more hostile towards membership of the European Union than public opinion in any of the other EFTA countries dealt with in this study. Kriesi *et al.* (1993, pp. 57ff.) found that only 29 per cent of the people voting on 6 December were in favour of Swiss Union membership. As many as 59 per cent were against, of which 42 per cent constituted hard-core opponents stating that they were 'certainly against' membership. This finding fits in well with a trend showing decreasing support for Swiss Union membership all through 1992. The hard-core opponents mainly consist of German-Swiss living in rural cantons ideologically belonging to the centre or right. This group mainly justified its rejection of the EEA with the fear of loss of sovereignty, economic motives, fear of unemployment and fear of an influx of foreigners (ibid, p. 68). Underlying the fear of loss of sovereignty is the fear of an erosion of Swiss identity, which essentially has three dimensions: direct democracy, federalism and neutrality (Schwok, 1992, pp. 5ff.).

Briefly, Swiss direct democracy refers to two arrangements. The 'referendum' and the 'initiative'. Any bill approved by the Federal Assembly must be submitted to referendum. The bill comes into force only if no petition is made against it within 90 days. If a petition is submitted supported by the signatures of 50,000 citizens, a referendum is held, thus giving the people the final say. The 'initiative' refers to an arrangement whereby the people, provided it has the support of 100,000 signatures, can demand that the Federal Constitution be amended or partially revised. A change in the Constitution requires a majority of both voters and cantons. The Swiss system of federalism ensures the regions a very high degree of autonomy. Thus, policy sectors like education, health, police, justice, finance, economy and agriculture are to varying degrees under regional control. Opponents of the EEA and of Union membership fear that closer integration will erode this unique system of self-rule, notably in sensitive areas like education and health (Schwok, op. cit.). Finally, as already mentioned neutrality still commands very considerable support in the Swiss population. It may seem strange that EEA membership should have been regarded as a threat to Swiss neutrality, but the anti-EEA forces managed to convince many voters that since EEA participation would automatically lead to membership of the Union,

Swiss neutrality would indirectly be threatened by the EEA.

All in all, like Norway, Switzerland is facing severe domestic political constraints in trying to adapt to the new integrated Europe. Arguments stressing economic benefits and political necessity have difficulty competing with arguments emphasizing the need to defend Swiss identity. Adherents of membership evidently have to integrate the cultural dimension in their rhetoric if they are to succeed in taking Switzerland into the EEA and eventually into the European Union. The government may wait until a number of other EFTA countries have successfully concluded accession agreements with the Union and then reopen the EEA debate and try to convince the Swiss that they cannot manage on their own in the new Europe. In the meantime, it will try to negotiate as many bilateral 'bridging' agreements with the Union as possible. Of particular interest from a Swiss point of view are the areas of transport, research and development and public procurement (Koller, 1993). It remains doubtful whether this strategy of adaptation to outside pressure will succeed. Unlike in most other countries on the Union's periphery, in Switzerland isolation is not generally regarded as something to be feared and, what is more, Switzerland's strong global presence will serve to counterbalance any regional isolation. Besides, this strategy if it is to succeed presupposes that all EFTA countries seeking Union membership do in fact become members, an outcome which can no longer be taken for granted. In the short and medium term Switzerland will probably remain outside both the European Union and the EEA. This will enable the Swiss to preserve their specific identity but they will have to pay a price aptly summarized by Schwok (1992) as political marginalization, political satellization and economic marginalization. The loss of political influence is likely to be felt particularly strongly.

Notes

1. The polls quoted in the foregoing have been compiled by the Danish Foreign Ministry from various Austrian sources.
2. Polling data has been made available by the Danish Ministry of Foreign Affairs.

7 Why membership?

How do we explain the sudden rush for EC membership in five EFTA countries? The pressure from informal economic integration is clearly an important part of the explanation. While trade patterns explain the decision to extend the essence of the internal market to EFTA, direct foreign investments seem particularly important in explaining the decision of internationalized EFTA economies like the Swedish to opt for full membership: the EEA solution apparently did not have the full confidence of the Swedish TNCs (Trans National Corporations), since FDIs in the EC remained exceedingly high even in 1990. Only full membership would stop the erosion of the production structure in the EFTA economies caused by the exodus of capital. There was also a remaining concern in all EFTA governments that the EEA would not after all give EFTA producers the same economic conditions as EC producers.

While affecting all EFTA economies, market conditions are likely to have been of particular importance to Austria because of the extremely high degree of informal economic integration between this country and the EC. But economic factors are also important in understanding the EC policies of Sweden, Finland and Switzerland. Both Sweden and Switzerland have externally orientated export economies with a high degree of outward direct investment. This also made these economies sensitive to the internal market process and the EMU. Yet, there appears to have been one important difference between the two countries: whereas business never completely lost faith in the fundamental soundness of the Swiss economy, the Swedish business community was in the late 1980s convinced that the Swedish economy suffered from severe structural deficiencies. This explains why the EEA regime was unable to stop the outward direct investment flow from Sweden to the EC area, whereas in Switzerland there was a dramatic decrease in outward investments in the EC area in 1989 which can probably be related to the launch of the EEA process (*EFTA Trade 1990*, Tables 13 and 15). The most crisis-ridden of the EFTA economies simply had to pay a risk premium in the form of full membership in order to reassure business. Like Sweden, Finland also had to pay this premium. Although the Finnish economy is less extroverted than the Swiss and Swedish, in Finland there were circumstantial external economic and political factors pushing the country towards the EC in 1991–2. The traditional Soviet market was collapsing, making Finland much more dependent on EC membership as a shortcut to economic recovery. And Sweden's application for EC membership in July 1991 inevitably sent shock waves through the Finnish economy, prompting an exodus of capital from Finland – in most cases with Sweden as first country of destination.

Our analysis of the evolution in the EC policies of the EFTA governments showed that apart from international market conditions, international security and power structures were important explanatory factors. Not only did the collapse of the cold war system increase the freedom of action of neutral EFTANs in general and Finland in particular, it also seriously reduced the value of neutrality as a foreign-policy option. In the post-cold war era there was simply no need for neutral go-betweens, at least not in the European region, and the strategy of non-commitment appeared irrelevant in the context of a new European security order. Suddenly, neutrality was more a hindrance for international influence than an asset.

But our survey of changes in the EC policy of most EFTA governments also pinpoints the importance of political-institutional dynamics including the spillover dynamic. Both politicians and representatives of interest groups in the EFTA countries used neo-functionalist arguments when arguing the case for accession to the EC. There was a keen awareness of the imbalances of the EEA Treaty, and it was argued that more integration was needed in order to correct these imbalances. It is therefore tempting to conclude that the EEA is a clear-cut case of 'cultivated' spillover. Yet, this would be too simple an explanation. In all five EFTA countries, the EEA was widely seen as suffering from a political deficit which could only be eliminated through EC membership. Yet, not all EFTA countries waited until the EEA process had come to

124

an end before applying for membership. Austria even applied before the EEA negotiations had started. This suggests that spillover mechanisms cannot alone explain the transition from the EEA option to the membership option and that incrementalism was not of the same importance to all EFTA countries. Only in the two countries where the EC membership issue created deep divisions in domestic political opinion – Norway and Switzerland – was incrementalism essential. A comparison between the foreign policies of the EFTA countries therefore seems appropriate.[1] For Austria, Sweden and Finland the constraints on EC policy were evidently mainly external and security-related, whereas in Norway and Switzerland they were to a larger extent domestic and political-cultural.

The spillover factor did apparently play a role in EC–EFTA developments, but what was the precise nature of the spillover logic? Should we interpret the use of spillover rhetoric as part of a (long-term) incrementalist strategy dating back to 1989? There is some evidence supporting this conclusion. When the EEA process started off in 1989, none of the neutral EFTA countries except Austria regarded EC membership as a realistic option for the short term. There was a widespread view in the EFTA countries that the EEA regime would be the central framework for regulation of the EFTA's relationship to the EC for a substantial period of time. Yet, the point is that from EFTA's point of view there was no contradiction between the EEA and eventual full membership. Hence the notion of the EEA as a 'waiting room' for prospective members of the EC. In other words, the EEA was a perfect compromise between the advocates of an extended free-trade agreement and the advocates of full membership. And the advocates of EC membership did indeed regard the EEA as part of an incrementalist strategy.

As far as the policy development in the EC is concerned, the spillover factor and the strategy of incrementalism explains very little. From the Commission's point of view, the EEA model was a way of postponing enlargement – perhaps even making it look superfluous. This strategy essentially failed. Far from making the EFTA countries give up the idea of membership, the EC policy appears to have had precisely the opposite effect in several EFTA countries. How do we account for this? In order to understand the 'political deficit' in the EEA agreement, which was the major source of concern for the EFTANs, we must focus on the internal and external factors affecting the policy evolution in the EC. The internal factors which can be placed under Odell's heading 'organization and internal bargaining' (Odell, 1982) mainly but not only have to do with the role of the EP. Supported by several governments, the European Parliament insisted that the EFTA countries not be given a greater political influence on new EC legislation than itself. The crucial external factor was the new politicization of the German problem (although in a new version) as a result of German unification and the accompanying acceleration in the process of deepening integration.

It seems that internal constraints had a greater impact on EC policy towards EFTA than external constraints. After all, if we are right in arguing that during 1990–1 the Commission and a number of EC governments came to feel that for 'high politics' reasons they had to deepen integration and protect the integration system from dilution, we would expect the EC to have gone out of its way to facilitate progress in the EEA talks especially on the tricky issue of institutional and legal structure. It did not do so, although modest concessions were indeed made, notably on the court issue. This element of 'irrationality' in the behaviour of the EC was largely due to the power of some EC institutions and their willingness to use that power. The more recalcitrant member states probably also simply overplayed their hand, underestimating the ability of some EFTA countries to contemplate membership. It should be added that from 1990, EC governments and the Commission increasingly shifted their attention from the talks with EFTA to the Eastern European and Soviet problem and as a consequence tended to neglect the EEA talks. Paradoxically, the factor of commitment (or lack of commitment) by the two sides can explain both the successes of EFTA and the failure of those forces in the EC wanting to avoid early enlargement.

While in all the EFTA countries dealt with in this study the business and political elites are in favour of full membership, as we have seen public opinion is generally very sceptical. This is important since popular participation in constitutional issues in Union politics is much bigger in the EFTA countries than in the Union itself. Our survey showed that overall the opponents of membership have been gaining ground during the last few years, notably in Norway, Sweden and (less markedly) Austria. Switzerland must be regarded as a special case since its application is now dormant. It should be noted however that the Swiss are more opposed to Union membership than any other applicant country in EFTA.

In Table 7.1 we summarize our findings comparing the attitudes of

126

Table 7.1 Public opinion in EFTA-4 on Union membership, 1993 (in %)

	For	Against	Undecided
Austria (May 1993)	32	38	30
Sweden (May 1993)	33	46	21
Finland (July 1993)	40	40	20
Norway (June 1993)	38	49	13
EFTA-4 (average)	35.7	43.25	21

public opinion in the four applicant states which are currently negotiating membership terms with the Union. Unfortunately it has not been possible to find polls taken in the same month in all countries. Although they present a static picture, the figures nevertheless allow some preliminary observations. First of all, the number of undecided is still relatively high and therefore the outcome of the referendums in the EFTA countries is still uncertain. Second, the opponents of membership are generally in a strong position. It is worth noticing that even in Austria, which has been preparing for membership since 1988 and is in the midst of an official campaign to rally support for membership of the European Union, public opinion is quite sceptical and surprisingly many Austrians remain undecided. Third, in three of the applicant countries, the opponents have been gaining ground during the last few years. This can be expected to make the EFTA negotiators adopt tougher positions in the accession talks which implies a risk of delay perhaps even deadlock in the process of enlargement. Indeed, the leader of the Swedish Social Democrats, Ingvar Carlsson, has stated that in his view it will be impossible for Sweden to conclude a satisfactory deal in time for Swedish accession in 1995. Carlsson's recommendation is thus to take the necessary time to ensure that the negotiating outcome can be sold to the Swedish voters (*Göteborg Posten*, 21 July 1993). A delay in the accession process would tend to prolong the life of the EEA.

The evolution in attitudes and the outcome of the referendums will depend on many factors. Two factors, however, deserve mentioning. First and most importantly, the perception of the European integration process will be of importance. Here two conflicting trends can be identified: on the one hand, the recent monetary turmoil and the setbacks suffered by the EMU process may very well, combined with the perception that the EC has failed dismally in the former Yugoslavia, further erode support for membership of the Union in the EFTA countries. To this should be added the new pressure for institutional reforms prior to enlargement aimed at strengthening the position of the big states *vis-à-vis* the small – a debate that, even if in the end it does not lead to major reforms, is likely to have a particularly damaging effect in Scandinavia where the prospect of an influential Nordic 'bloc' within the European Union has so far been a powerful argument for the 'yes' side.

On the other hand, the clarifications added to the Maastricht Treaty at Edinburgh and the opt-outs obtained by Denmark may have served to improve the Union's image. Yet, the effect is probably not going to be big. Although the polls quoted in this study indicate that the eventual Danish 'yes' did have a certain positive effect on attitudes to membership in for example Norway and Sweden, we are talking about a very limited effect. What is more, this positive effect is probably weaker than the earlier effect of the first Danish referendum 'no' which, judging from the figures, seems to have been quite dramatic in Norway and significant in Sweden. Moreover, the fact that the Danish opt-outs cannot be generalized to the new members will – once this becomes clear to public opinion in the applicant states – probably have a negative effect on attitudes to membership. Overall then, we would expect the 'output/image effect' on public-opinion attitudes in the applicant states to be mainly negative, but of course this may change before the referendums take place in 1994–5.

The second important factor will be the timing and sequencing of the referendums and by implication a factor which could be called 'the fear of marginalization'. The timing and sequencing will be planned with a view to maximizing the positive vote. There are known to have been behind the scenes' talks between the applicant EFTA governments on this issue. The countries with the best chances of a positive vote will be the first to hold referendums. We know little about the 'electoral spillover' between EFTA electorates. The case of Norway–Denmark in 1972 where first Norway voted 'no' and then a few weeks later Denmark voted 'yes' – with a comfortable majority in both countries – suggests that even in European societies with close ideological-cultural affinities, the cross-border effect of voting on constitutional EC issues is limited. However, the picture may have changed since 1972 as a result of cumulative informal integration. A European 'general public' is gradually coming into existence. Thus there was some Danish participation in the French pre-referendum debate and some British participation in the Danish Maastricht campaigns.

Certainly, the 'Nordic card' is still regarded by the Nordic governments as being of some importance in Union politics. Opinion polls in Denmark show that if asked to choose between a Nordic and a continental European Union, a majority of 39.2 per cent prefer the hypothetical Nordic Union with 35.2 per cent preferring the European Union (*Information*, 1 March 1993). Similar attitudes are found in the other Nordic countries with the exception of Finland, where Nordic cooperation has always had a lower profile, in part because of the language barrier. The adherents of membership in the Nordic EFTA countries will thus be obliged to pay attention to the Nordic issue. They will have to reassure voters that the *acquis nordique* in areas like free movement of persons (the Nordic Passport Union, the free labour market, the social convention), the informal harmonization of laws and cultural cooperation can be maintained in a European Union.

So far, one of the key arguments of the adherents of membership has been that with Swedish, Norwegian and Finnish adhesion a Nordic voice in European politics would be strengthened: it would be possible to form a powerful Nordic bloc within the Union. If one or more of the Nordic applicants do not become members of the Union, 'the Nordic card' will play into the hands of the opponents. Similarly, any major changes in the institutional set-up of the Union which change the balance between big and small states will remove one of the central pillars in the adherents' strategy and rhetoric.

The fear of marginalization will probably play a certain role for hesitant countries facing a 'yes' trend in other applicant countries. If Sweden and Finland join the Union, this could tip the balance in Norway and ensure victory for the 'yes' side. However, one should not overlook the fact that 'isolation' from neighbouring states may not always be regarded as a big problem. Thus we have seen how Finnish (and to some extent also Norwegian) reaction to Sweden's decision to apply for membership of the EC was rather cool. The concern about marginalization or lack of influence is also in most cases of greater relevance to the political elite than to the citizen. What is portrayed as a 'national interest' is sometimes in actual fact the interest of a rather limited circle of internationalized groups in a national polity.

Notes

1. See Odell (1982) for a useful framework of analysis of foreign-policy change emphasizing the factors international market conditions; international security and power structure; domestic politics; organization and internal bargaining; and ideas.

8 The enlargement policy of the Union

Procedures and conditions

The technical procedure of accession to the European Union is beguilingly simple. A state directs its application to the Council, which, having received an opinion from the European Commission, decides by unanimity whether to admit the country in question. Whereas the EEA negotiations and other negotiations with third countries are conducted by the Union represented by the Commission, the negotiations on enlargement are conducted by the member states themselves, only assisted by the Commission. The Union is normally represented by the Presidency in enlargement negotiations. Given the rotating Presidency and the often considerable divergence between member-state interests, this procedure makes for rather lengthy negotiations. As is well known, there is a considerable distance between the very positive view towards enlargement of countries like Germany, Denmark, the United Kingdom and, with certain reservations, the Netherlands and the more reserved attitude and conditional support found in Spain, Portugal, Italy, Greece and to some extent also France and Belgium (cf. Pedersen, 1991a). Whereas the scepticism of Spain and its supporters in the south is mainly economic, the hesitation of France, Belgium and to a certain extent also Italy is mainly rooted in political considerations. In these countries, the prospect of large-scale enlargement, while welcomed because of the added political and economic resources it will bring to the Union, often provokes the knee-jerk reaction that enlargement will 'dilute' the Union (see also Chapter 9).

The adherents of 'deepening' have of late received some institutional reinforcement. With the adoption of the Single European Act (SEA), it was decided that accession treaties would only take effect after having obtained the assent of the European Parliament. Although it remains to be seen to what extent the Parliament is willing to use this powerful weapon in practice, the Parliament's new role in enlargement politics undoubtedly raises the threshold which applicants have to cross to become members.

There are a number of conditions for admission to the European Union. Some of these are formal and sometimes but not always spelt out in the Union's treaties. Others are informal, often implied in decisions made at European Council meetings. There are surprisingly few formal and explicit conditions for membership. The main reason is that the issue of enlargement is highly contentious among member states and in relation to the European periphery. But apart from that, it is probably fair to say that the Union has been caught by surprise by the events in Central and Eastern Europe and still has not quite adapted its enlargement policy to take account of these changes.

The Treaty on European Union requires that a state seeking membership of the Union must satisfy two basic conditions: European identity, and democratic status and respect for human rights (Articles F and O). Democracy and human rights are concepts which have, not least in recent years, been given a relatively precise meaning through international agreements. It is a much more open question how one should define 'European'. Should one apply geographical criteria? This definition would make Central and Eastern Europe natural candidates for membership, whereas Russia and Turkey would be border-line cases. Or should one apply cultural criteria emphasizing ethnic similarities and religious beliefs? In that case it could easily be argued that European values and the European way of life stretch as far as North America and Australia and New Zealand, whereas Muslim Turkey and a large part of the former Soviet Union would not be eligible for membership. European culture could also be defined as a specific way of organizing society. Jacques Delors has thus spoken of the social market economy as something typically European, setting Europe apart from both the United States and Japan. This definition would make it possible to justify excluding the United States from European cooperation but still leaves the question of whether to erect barriers against societies like Canada, Australia and New Zealand, whose political culture is quite similar to that of Europe. It also raises the question whether countries outside the European continent are eligible for membership if at some later stage they manage to fulfil a cultural criteria of 'Europeanness'.

Just as culture may be defined as ethnic and religious homogeneity and as a specific societal model, it may also be defined as a certain type of civic and political culture. Edgar Morin in his book *Penser l'Europe* cautions against a geographical definition of Europe, since in his view Europe has no stable frontiers (Morin, 1987). From the point of view of geography, the unique feature of Europe is its lack of unity. From a cultural point of view, it is striking that a lot of the philosophical ideas which are today regarded as belonging to the core of Europeanness were in fact imported from the periphery of Europe or from its south-eastern neighbours. The mythical description of Europe as a Phoenician princess kidnapped and transported to Crete by Zeus actually symbolizes the identity of Europe very well. After all, as Morin writes, Europe borrowed much of what is now regarded as 'European' from Western Asia; and classical Greece lived with its back turned against Europe as we know it today. The heartland of Europe did not enter the history of civilization until some time after the fall of the Roman Empire. And only during the Renaissance did Europe transform the classical legacy into something uniquely 'European'. Europe in Morin's view is thus a certain intellectual tradition dating back to the Renaissance and elaborated in the Enlightenment. Humanitarian individualism is Europe's most original contribution to global civilization. It can be defined as a tradition of critical dialogue and perpetual doubt regarding the values of one's society. Europeanness is 'l'esprit qui nie toujours' or 'la problematisation generalisée' and by implication European culture is the laicized and secularized culture *par excellence*. While this may well be a fitting description of Europe's unique intellectual tradition, to ask of new member states that they share the 'European spirit' of self-critical reflection is to ask quite a lot. On the other hand, Morin's concepts are sufficiently vague to allow politicians to bend them to suit their purposes.

So far no attempt has been made to establish an official definition of European identity which is probably just as well, since such a debate could easily become a serious source of conflict that would only serve to prove to the outside world the Union's lack of cultural-ideological cohesion! Apart from this cohesive function, an 'open frontier policy' also has the important external function of defusing latent conflicts with neighbouring big powers like Ukraine, Russia and Turkey. Perhaps we are advised to recall Edgar Morin's proposition that eternal doubt is the essence of European mentality and conclude that to leave the question of its borders open is in keeping with the best European traditions.

It must be added, however, that 'nation-building' rarely proceeds through deliberate decisions made by enlightened politicians. European nation-building – assuming that it will take place – will in large part be the product of undirected events. Developments at the level of public opinion in Europe may well force the hand of politicians. Riker (1964) has shown how external threats have always played a central part in the formation of federations. In the formative period of European integration, the Soviet threat served as a crucial cohesive factor in Western Europe. In the post-cold war period, new types of security 'threats' haunt Europe. Societal security is becoming a central concern for West Europeans (Wæver et al., 1993). The most important of these perceived 'threats' is probably large-scale immigration. It is certainly possible that hostility towards immigration and foreigners in general will, channelled through public opinion, lead to new demands on politicians to exclude certain cultures, states as well as citizens, from admission to 'Europe'.

Apart from the formal requirement of 'Europeanness', there are a number of informal conditions for membership of the Union. First of all, new adherents must demonstrate a willingness to accept the *acquis communautaire* and the *acquis politique*, that is the legal acts and political positions adopted by the Union at the time of accession. Moreover, they must demonstrate a willingness to support the goals of the Union. Until recently, the notion of *acquis communautaire* was not mentioned in the treaties themselves. The Maastricht Treaty changes that. In Articles B and C of the common provisions, the Union refers to the objective of 'maintaining *in full* the acquis communautaire and *build on it* with a view to considering ... to what extent the policies and forms of cooperation introduced by the Treaty may need to be revised with the aim of ensuring the *effectiveness* (author's emphasis in all cases) of the mechanisms and institutions of the Community' (see Michalski and Wallace, 1992, p. 21). This clarification, introduced by the adherents of deepening, without doubt raises the barriers to entry for the membership candidates and makes for tough accession negotiations.

In practice, new adherents are also expected to have a developed market economy and a well-functioning private and public administration. Thus, the Commission report on the challenge of enlargement draws attention to the importance of a well-functioning implementation system (Europe and the Challenge of Enlargement, *EC Bulletin*, Supplement 3/92). It follows logically from the decisions on EMU that new adherents must be prepared to introduce full capital liberalization. They must also in principle be able to fulfil the convergence criteria spelt out in the treaty, though the setbacks which the EMU process has suffered undermine the Union's credibility in this particular area. Economic eligibility also implies a certain level of economic development. But economic structures may be more important than levels of affluence at the time of accession. There is no agreement on this point. Some in the Union consider that applicants have to cross some critical threshold before being admitted as members; others argue that with transitional arrangements, even less-developed economies can be admitted rather quickly provided the right economic structures are in place. The latter position often cites the example of Spain and Portugal, which adjusted very fast to Community standards (Michalski and Wallace, 1992, p. 4). A preliminary report on the consequences of enlargement prepared by the Commission also mentioned the importance of making sure that new members 'demonstrate a broad political and public consensus in favour of membership' (*A Strategy for Enlargement*, Brussels, 14 November 1991, p. 14). However, this is clearly a more controversial position and not one shared by all member states.

Membership of the Union also presupposes membership of a number of other international organizations like the UN, the CSCE, GATT and the Council of Europe. In part this requirement follows logically from the principles on which the Union is built. But apart from that, it goes without saying that exerting influence in international politics will be very difficult if the member states are not members of roughly the same set of international organizations.

The Maastricht Summit in December 1991 took several decisions of relevance to the enlargement issue. First of all, the decisions on the EMU and political union mean that the commitments which new adherents have to accept have become more extensive. At the same time, the finalization of the Intergovernmental Conferences gave the applicants a clearer picture of the kind of cooperation they were about to join. Second, the summit specified that only European states whose system of government was based on democratic principles could apply. This represented a certain toughening of the Community's stance, since the Treaty of Rome had merely stated that applicant states must be 'European'. Third, the summit asked the Commission to produce a report on the implications of enlargement.

During the spring of 1992, the Commission did some preliminary work on this issue. However, following the uproar caused by the Commission president's statement that the report would come as a shock to many in the Community, the preliminary report referred to above was shelved; instead the Commission presented a much shorter and more innocuous report to the European Council in Lisbon in June 1992 ('Europe and the Challenge of Enlargement', Brussels, June 24, *EC Bulletin*, Supplement 3/92). The European Council in Lisbon agreed that negotiations on enlargement could start on the basis of the Maastricht Treaty as soon as the Community had finalized its negotiations on own resources and related issues in 1992. The Council also said that in its view the EEA agreement had paved the way for negotiations on enlargements which could be finalized quickly with those EFTA countries seeking membership of the Union. It called upon the EC institutions to speed up the preparatory work including the preparation of the Union's general negotiating position before the European Council in Edinburgh. Finally, the Presidency conclusions stated that official negotiations would start as soon as the Maastricht Treaty had been ratified and agreement had been reached on the Delors II package. The Council was of the opinion that accession negotiations should as far as possible be conducted in parallel, while allowing each application to be dealt with according to its own circumstances. In a significant concession to the EFTA countries and to Denmark whose population had just voted down the Maastricht Treaty, the Council agreed that an enlargement with the EFTA countries was possible without there being a need for institutional reforms (European Council in Lisbon, 26–7 June 1992, Presidency conclusions).

With regard to the other applicants and potential applicants, the Council agreed to establish a political dialogue with the Central and Eastern European countries. Similarly a political dialogue would be set up with Turkey. In its report to the Council, the Commission proposed to go further and set up a European Political Area (EPA) which would provide an immediate institutional anchoring, while postponing full economic integration ('Europe and the Challenge of Enlargement', op. cit.; Wijkman, 1993, p. 143).

Like the Lisbon Summit the Edinburgh Summit was held in the shadow of the unsolved Danish problem (which was, incidentally, as much a Community problem). While the majority of member states were very reluctant to renegotiate the Maastricht Treaty, speeding up the process of enlargement was a step which it was felt would make an impression on hesitant 'no' voters in Denmark and a step on which most member states could agree. Thus, the Edinburgh European Council agreed that 'given the agreement reached on future financing and the prospects for early ratification of the Treaty ... by all member states, enlargement negotiations will start with Austria, Sweden and Finland at the beginning of 1993'. These negotiations would be based on the general negotiation framework of which the General Affairs Council took note on 7 December. The Council also invited the Council of Ministers to start negotiations with Norway on the same basis as soon as the Commission's opinion on Norway was available (European Council, Edinburgh, 11–12 December 1992, Presidency conclusions).

The agreement reached in Edinburgh on the terms of Denmark's participation in the Union could be argued to contain some 'variable geometry' elements, which might theoretically be used by applicant states in their negotiations with the Union. There was a clear risk that the Danish model might create a precedent. The Commission therefore went to great lengths to stress the principle that new member states could only obtain temporary derogations from Union rules or transitional arrangements. Thus, in the Commission opinion on Norway there is a reference to the statement by the President in Office of the Council of Ministers at the ministerial meeting opening the conferences on the accession of Austria, Sweden and Finland to the Union on 1 February 1993. It said that 'the acceptance of the rights and obligations by a new member state may give rise to technical adjustments, and exceptionally to temporary (not permanent) derogations and transitional arrangements to be defined during the accession negotiations, but can in no way involve amendments of Community rules' (Com (93) 485 final p. 2). In other words, the message was that the Danish opt-outs had changed nothing in the Union's enlargement policy. When asked to explain why new member states should not expect the same favourable treatment as Denmark, EC negotiators referred to the goodwill and credit which 'old' member states automatically accumulate over the years. Much to their regret the Danish opponents of the Maastricht Treaty may well have made enlargement more difficult. To the extent that the first Danish 'no' (and the sizeable 'no' vote in the second referendum) had any effect on the enlargement process, the effect was probably mainly to harden the position of those in the Union who all along have been sceptical about speedy enlargement. To them Denmark's behaviour was but a symptom of the inherent problems involved in admitting small states with neutralist traditions as members of the Union.

The Copenhagen Summit in June 1993 was able to congratulate the hosts on a positive outcome of the second referendum on the Maastricht Treaty with the clarifications and opt-outs agreed in Edinburgh. As regards enlargement policy, the European Council, while taking note of the fact that the initial difficulties in the negotiations had now been overcome, called upon the Commission, the Council and the applicant states to ensure that the negotiations were carried out constructively and quickly. The Presidency conclusions added in strikingly clear language that 'the European Council is determined that the first enlargement of the European Union shall take place on January 1, 1995 at the latest according to the guidelines laid down at the European Council in Lisbon and Edinburgh' (European Council, 21–2 June 1993, Copenhagen, Presidency conclusions). In another significant move, the European Council stated that those associated countries in Central and Eastern Europe which wanted to could become members of the European Union. It was added that accession would take place as soon as the associated countries were able to assume the obligations of membership and fulfil the economic and political conditions. Finally, the European Council decided – inspired by proposals from the Commission and the EP – to establish 'an extended and expanded multilateral dialogue' with the Central and Eastern European countries on a number of political issues. This decision represented a partial implementation of ideas on 'affiliated membership' presented by Commissioner Frans Andriessen in April 1991 (see below).

However, other forces in the Union were mobilizing against a rapid enlargement without guarantees against dilution. The concern over a possible fall-out from the Danish opt-outs agreed in Edinburgh was echoed by the majority in the European Parliament which in its decision on enlargement of 15 July 1993 'stress once more that all applicant states must accept l'acquis communautaire including the Treaty on European Union and the goal of further integration and insists that the applicants not be granted further concessions like the ones granted to the UK and Denmark' (EP decision B3-1017, 1018 and 1043/1993). This position of the EP is of some relevance since the EP has a right of veto over new accessions.

In Lisbon it had been decided that the adhesion of the EFTA countries did not in itself require new institutional reforms in the European Union. This position has since been challenged by the European Parliament and a number of member states. Thus, in a decision on the shaping of the European Union, the strategy of enlargement and the formulation of a global perspective on European cooperation adopted on 20 January 1993, the European Parliament states that it does not share the view of the European Council but on the contrary is of the opinion that at least the most necessary institutional and structural reforms should be agreed on in the context of the enlargement with the EFTA countries (EP decision A3-189/92, *EC Bulletin*, 15 February 1993). In the early autumn 1993 there were calls for the convening of a special summit to discuss institutional reforms to accompany enlargement with the EFTA countries (see also Chapter 9). However, the timetable of the EFTA enlargement is so tight that far-reaching institutional reforms may have to be postponed until the next full-scale inter-governmental conference in 1996. Whereas France and to some extent also the United Kingdom want institutional changes soon, Germany appears to be more divided on the issue with influential sections arguing that the changes are not so important that they cannot be postponed (*Financial Times*, 5 October 1993).

The debate about 'deepening' and 'widening'

It must be stressed that the Union's enlargement policy is not very formalized and is in a state of evolution. The issue has become politicized which makes it very difficult to say anything precise about the enlargement policy except for a few key points. Enlargement has become a 'high-politics' issue in Union politics. With the prospect of comprehensive enlargement, the EC has clearly to define its identity and political goals. The dilemma between deepening and widening is becoming acute. Are the traditional EC goals still valid in the new Europe? If so, can those goals be realized in a wider Union? So far, the Union has preferred to sidestep these issues and apply the well-known incrementalist method to enlargement. But this may be changing.

Widespread concern about the institutional implications of enlargement should not be confused with resistance to enlargement. The debate is mainly about when to enlarge and on what conditions. Some of the member states most anxious about a dilution of integration are also among the countries most eager to admit new states as members of the Union (for example the Netherlands and Germany). More importantly, there is widespread agreement that the Union as a whole will benefit from enlargement – in particular EFTA enlargement. As far as the EFTA countries are concerned, economic factors weigh heavily in favour of membership. The five EFTA countries which have applied for membership would alone add around 14 per cent to the Community's tax base (Baldwin *et al.*, 1992). The EFTA countries are all advanced economies that fit in easily with the internal market and EMU. Other contingent economic factors make EFTA membership attractive to the EC. The EFTA countries will be net contributors to the EC budget. This will help the EC finance its new tasks at a time when Germany is not in a position to act as the Community's 'paymaster' as it used to do. The total yearly net contribution from EFTA members has not been estimated in precise terms. But by way of illustration, Sweden's net contribution to the budget has been estimated at around Ecu 1 billion annually (Dinkelspiel, 1992). The inclusion of the EFTA countries in the European Union might also serve to speed up the process of monetary unification which is currently confronted with serious problems.

To the extent that the admission of EFTA countries creates problems for the Community, these are mainly to be found in the political area. There are at least two dimensions of the debate about the political effects of admission of EFTA countries, both relating to the future development of the community. Firstly, there is what we may call the 'constitutional' aspect. Do the EFTA countries share the view of the majority of EC member states that Community integration should be further developed beyond the Maastricht Treaty? Second, there is the more specific problem of the security dimension. Do the EFTA countries share the EC's commitment to create a common security policy and over time a common defence policy that may eventually lead to the creation of a common defence? With the exception of Norway, the applicants' ability to meet the obligations of the CFSP is a source of some concern, although as we have seen the EFTA neutrals have all begun a reappraisal of their neutrality policy and general foreign policy.

During the second half of the 1980s, there was considerable concern in EC quarters that the admission of neutrals like Austria and Sweden might block progress towards the creation of some kind of EC security and defence entity. However, in recent years EC scepticism about neutralism has been mellowing, as the EFTA neutrals have signalled their intention to redefine neutralism. To a considerable extent it was concern about neutrality – and the indirect effects of having neutral members in the EC on Germany's policy – that caused France and other member states to insist that the goal of a common defence be written into the treaty on the European Union. John Roper, a British security expert employed in the WEU 'think-tank' in Brussels, argued in 1991 that once the objective of defence integration was on paper (in the Union Treaty), the neutrals would be prevented from vetoing future decisions on the development of the defence dimension (quoted in *Dagens Nyheter*, 2 April 1991). It is a matter for discussion to what extent the Maastricht Treaty with its careful wording ('a common security policy including in time a common defence policy that *may* eventually lead to the creation of a joint defence') has succeeded in laying down solid tracks to a future defence union. It would seem that Article B in Section I of the new treaty represents an important change in that the long-term goals of the Community are specified. Moreover, while the creation of an operational defence is clearly an issue that requires a new political decision, Article B is unequivocal about the goal of a common defence policy and there are likely to be powerful functional linkages between a common defence policy and an operational defence.

National political leaders in the EC have so far made only few and vague statements on the issue of enlargement. However, some basic dividing lines among member states can be established. The northern member states are obviously the most enthusiastic about the prospect of admitting as members a group of countries mainly located in the northern part of Europe. But even the southern member states have for budgetary reasons in recent years tended to adopt a slightly more constructive attitude in the accession negotiations. Perhaps one can say that the issue of 'conditionality' is now mainly a question about the institutional prerequisites for enlargement with the enlargement sceptics concentrating on putting together a package of constitutional changes to be adopted concurrently with the admission of the EFTA countries. One detects a significant movement in the French attitude to enlargement. In an interview with the *Financial Times* in December 1992, President Mitterrand declared that enlargement was a high priority goal and he defined 'Europe' in very broad terms, being wary of excluding specific countries (*Financial Times*, 9 December 1992). The Edinburgh Summit thus agreed to accelerate the enlargement process, allowing accession negotiations to commence even before all formal preconditions had been fulfilled. No doubt the main motive behind this French change of policy was a wish to accommodate Germany. But the move was also meant to help the Danish government in its campaign for a 'yes' to the Union in a second referendum.

A substantial debate on deepening and widening has developed in the supranational institutions and among academic analysts in Europe. One of the first in the EC to broach the wider problem of enlargement and integration was Frans Andriessen, Dutch Vice-President of the EC and Commissioner for External Economic Relations. In a speech in April 1991 to the Eurochambers, an organization of firms from all over Europe, Frans Andriessen pointed out that the Community had to start reflecting on its long-term future. Noting the rush for membership of the EC and in particular the Eastern European plea for admission as a way of consolidating democracy, he called for creative thinking to define arrangements whereby the Community could offer the benefits of membership and the accompanying gains for stability without weakening its drive towards further integration (Andriessen, 1991).

Frans Andriessen went on to say that in his view a new kind of affiliate membership might be the solution. Affiliate membership would 'provide membership rights and obligations in some areas, while excluding others, at least for a transitional period. It would give the affiliate member a seat at the Council table on a par with full members in specified areas, together with appropriate representation in other institutions such as parliament.' The particular areas which Andriessen had in mind were political cooperation and monetary affairs. He was well aware that neutrality might pose problems for security cooperation but suggested the use of occasional opting-out, a procedure already used in the case of Ireland.

Commissioner Andriessen's suggestions were not directed at the EFTA countries but rather at the Central and Eastern European countries (cf. interview in *Neue Zürcher Zeitung*, 29–30 November 1992). In Eastern Europe there was a call for political links with the EC or the WEU. The idea of affiliate membership might also appeal to a country like Turkey, which is of considerable geostrategic importance to the Community and NATO. One of the implications of Andriessen's suggestions is that agricultural policy would be 'shielded' from the process of enlargement. This would be in the interest of both the Community and – one may add – Andriessen's home country of the Netherlands.

One advantage of Andriessen's proposal was that it was not particularly susceptible to the criticism that the EC is excluding the rest of Europe from its unification process thereby creating a first and a second class of Europeans. Andriessen pointed out that treaties on affiliate membership should make clear the perspective of possible accession. Moreover, the membership candidates would be offered some sort of influence in crucial and politically salient areas like monetary affairs and foreign policy, although it was not clear whether Andriessen thought in terms of co-decision.

The logical implication of Andriessen's suggestions was that the EEA circle ought to be supplemented by other circles in a new multifaceted pattern of Pan-European cooperation. Later in 1991 Andriessen once again made a controversial statement arguing that 'deepening must take into consideration the perspectives for enlargement and study must focus on both elements simultaneously' (*Agence Europe*, 4 August 1991). He also warned against creating new structures that might soon become unusable.

At first, the rest of the Commission did not show much sympathy for affiliate membership along the lines suggested by Andriessen. Instead the accent was on the need for a reform in the EC institutions and procedures in the light of comprehensive enlargement. Henning Christophersen argued that a transformation of the Community system would be necessary if the Community was enlarged to 18, 20 or 24 member states. If that happened 'a radical overhaul of all procedures would be necessary' (Christophersen, 1991). The same message was conveyed by Leon Brittan, the British Commissioner for Competition, in a speech to the Central Chamber of Commerce of Finland in September 1991. Enlargement would in Brittan's view force the Community to 'adapt and strengthen its distinctive institutions if it was to retain its dynamism as a much larger organization' (Brittan, 1991).

Jacques Delors also argued in favour of a transformation of the EC's institutional set-up. In January 1992, he told French television that in a Community of 24 or 35 member states, there would be a need for a Community president. Such a president would be responsible to the Council and the European Parliament. He or she should be able to appoint his own ministers, and a majority should be able to dismiss him (quoted in *Dagens Nyheter*, 7 January 1992). The Commission held its first preliminary debate on enlargement policy in November 1991 in the wake of the finalization of the EEA talks (*Financial Times*, 25 November 1991). The majority in the Commission rejected the idea of admitting all applicant countries simultaneously. There were federalists who advocated this 'big bang' strategy because it would in their view force the EC into radical institutional reform. But most Commissioners considered that the applicant countries' interests and problems were too diverse to be dealt with simultaneously. The preferred strategy was therefore to organize the applicants into different groups and admit them in successive rounds. There were mixed reactions to Andriessen's idea for a European political area to be set up alongside the EEA's economic area. Some commissioners felt that such a political area would whet Central European States' appetite for full EC membership at an inopportune moment.

Given the sensitivity of the issue in some member states, the Commission report on the challenge of enlargement presented to the European Council in Lisbon trod carefully; compared to the preliminary report, it is rather bland and uncontroversial. But it contains one important analytical point: it points out that in a wider Union, the principle of subsidiarity will have to be applied more strictly. The Union's legislative programme will thus have to be smaller and less detailed; there will have to be a redistribution of competence between levels of government and finally there will have to be a clearer distinction between decision-making competence and executive competence ('Europe and the Challenge of Enlargement', *EC Bulletin* 3/92).

Among federalists in the European Parliament, the emphasis was also on deepening of integration. In the months following the Swedish application for EC membership, the influential daily bulletin *Agence Europe*, whose editor is known to be close to the federalists in the EP, ran several editorials which underlined that priority must be given to deepening (*Agence Europe*, 9–10 September 1991; 16–17 September 1991). After the Maastricht Summit, *Agence Europe* ran another series of editorials on enlargement. Once again the editor warned against over-hasty enlargement. Priority had to be given to deepening of integration because the rest of Europe looked to the EC for guidance and because a strong European Union could help the world attain a better balance. The bulletin was particularly sceptical with regard to admission of the non-EFTA countries, for which the response was – in its view – not necessarily enlargement. Instead *Agence Europe* expressed cautious support for the Mitterrand idea of a European confederation with a federal Union as its core. In this connection, the editor mentioned the possibility of creating several substructures ('sub-assemblies') within the wider confederation (*Agence Europe*, 12 February 1992; 13 February 1992).

The preference for continued deepening of integration was shared by Klaus Hänsch, an influential German Social-Democrat MEP, who argued that 'it is neither possible nor essential that all European states, or states linked to Europe, should soon unite in a Federal State of Europe'. Hänsch agreed with the Commission's majority view that enlargement would have to be accompanied by deepening. He even went as far as suggesting that a new intergovernmental conference should be convened with a view to deepening democracy in the EC before concluding entry negotiations with Sweden and Austria. Hänsch also argued that enlargement should not be open-ended and that the future pan-European organization could not be a classical confederation (as suggested by French President Mitterrand) but would have to be a grouping of functional confederations with the Community as the central core and motor. Such a system of confederal cooperation should, according to Hänsch, in particular cover areas like security, environment and economic policy. Candidates for this kind of cooperation would be the former Soviet republics, Turkey and non-European Mediterranean countries (*Agence Europe*, 17 September 1991).

Hänsch's view is reflected in a report from the EP on the shaping of the Union, its strategy of enlargement and the formulation of a global perspective on European cooperation presented in May 1992 and adopted by a majority on 20 January 1993 (EP documents A3-189/92). In the report, Hänsch presents a global vision of how integration and enlargement could and indeed should be combined. Sketching out a new common European order, the report argues that all European states which possess *fully developed* (my emphasis) democratic and legal institutions, which guarantee human rights, have market economic structures and are willing and able to assume the obligations of membership, including the EMU and the political union, can become members of the Union. One notices the new formulation that democratic and legal institutions should be fully developed, undoubtedly added with a view to applicants like Turkey, a country having been subjected to severe and repeated criticism from the EP. Enlargements should be accompanied by new daring steps towards the creation of a Union with federal features and based on respect for the principle of subsidiarity. The report further argues that 'it is neither possible nor necessary that all European states or states which feel European or states attached to Europe should in the future be merged in a Union'. Instead the report argues first that the potential of Article 238 in the Treaty of Rome which provides for forms of association has not yet been exhausted and that the Union ought to contemplate new forms of association such as participation of some associated states in political areas of the Union (like CFSP and internal and legal affairs); association which aims at a gradual accession to the Union and new multilateral forms of regional cooperation and a regional political dialogue between the Union and groups of associated states with a view to fostering closer cooperation among the associated states and preventing nationalist tendencies.

Furthermore, it is argued that the Union should continue its policy of keeping specific programmes like SPES, ERASMUS and PETRA open for the participation of all European countries. The report also repeats Hänsch's earlier plea for a new confederal order in the wider Europe consisting of a number of functional confederations dealing with specific tasks. In a more recent article, Hänsch pursues this line of thought stressing that there is a need for two types of new structures: new forms of permanent association, which because they are meant to be permanent must include a political dimension, and new forms of functional bodies along the lines of EUREKA (Hänsch, 1993).

There have been other calls for more 'untidy' variable geometry solutions. Heinz Kramer, an analyst from the influential Stiftung Wissenchaft und Politik in Germany, which has close links to the German Chancellor's office, argued in favour of a mixed strategy distancing himself both from the tight and highly integrated European Union of 12 and the 'Greater EC', encompassing all European CSCE members. He argued that, on the one hand, the exclusive 'Union of 12' would be unable to achieve a tightly integrated political community and a powerful EMU in the foreseeable future. On the other hand, the 'greater EC' would in his view be unable to move beyond the integration level of the Single European Market. And this greater Europe would probably be too loose a structure to be able to promote stability in Eastern Europe. The compromise proposed by Kramer was to work towards a 'European system of varying integrated circles or areas'. The idea was to build on the example of differentiation within the EMU, extending it to the political area.

Kramer put his finger on a sore spot in the EC's present enlargement strategy: neither economically nor politically does the present division between EC members and non-members correspond to the patterns of convergence and divergence in interests and values, nor to the patterns of economic interaction. Some of the present EC members are further away from the EMU core than some EFTA economies. Similarly, some of the non-Union members in Europe are at least as committed to the notion of a common European defence policy as are some of the members, and in some cases these countries are of greater geo-strategic importance to the Community than some of the present members.

The evolving debate about Union responses to enlargement and the future European architecture thus seems to centre around a vision of a decentralized federal Union as the core of the new Europe but with new and more flexible structures supplementing the Union. One hears

voices suggesting new forms of partial membership as well as suggestions for a network of functional confederations to be set up together
with the Central and Eastern Europeans. But despite these new suggestions, the emphasis is clearly on institutional reforms as a corollary to
geographical expansion.

9 Towards a continental Union?: enlargement and integration

The size of the problem

The European Union is expanding with important consequences for both outsiders and for the shape of the Union itself. Any assessment of the future size of the Union will of course inevitably be speculative. Not only does the extent of enlargement depend on internal political and economic developments in the Union. One recalls how French agricultural interests managed to delay Iberian accession for several years. We should also not lose sight of the volatile public opinion in the applicant and candidate countries which will after all have a decisive impact on the fate of the enlargement process.

By 1993, around eight countries were knocking on the doors of the European Community. We do not yet know for certain how many EFTA governments will be able to convince their electorate of the need to become members of the EC. In most EFTA countries negative attitudes to EC membership are coming more to the fore, a trend that may be reinforced if the integration process continues to lose momentum. Yet, in all EFTA countries the major part of the political elite is in favour of EC membership and in most EFTA countries the popular opposition is not so strong as to make the outcome of the enlargement debate a foregone conclusion. The trend is thus relatively clear: in the 1990s several EFTA countries will probably join the European Union.

In the medium term, focus will shift to Turkey, Malta and Cyprus and the Central and Eastern Europeans. Of these Turkey deserves particular attention, not only because of the country's size and political

147

importance but also because in the debate on enlargement it has somewhat unjustly tended to be overshadowed by the Central and Eastern European countries (cf. Redmond, 1992). Turkey has had an association agreement with the EC since 1964 (Kramer, 1988). Much to its regret, the EC at the time inserted a clause promising eventual membership, a step taken to balance the promise to Greece. After years of foot-dragging from the EC, Turkey then applied for membership in 1987. In its 1989 opinion on Turkish membership (Com (89) 2290 final), the Commission expressed serious reservations about Turkish membership of the EC. But in principle, Turkey remained a candidate for membership – unlike Morocco which also applied in 1987 but was not taken seriously. The Commission opinion argued that Turkish membership was not possible in the short term mainly owing to economic factors. Despite the impressive level of economic growth in Turkey, there was a big gap between the economic level in the EC and in Turkey. Around 50 per cent of the Turkish workforce is still employed in agriculture. Besides, industrial development has been achieved in part by means of a high level of external protection. The Commission thus feared that Turkey would be unable to fulfil its obligations as an EC member. More important perhaps was the fact that as a member Turkey would put enormous pressure on the structural funds and the CAP.

The Commission proposed instead to intensify EC–Turkish cooperation *inter alia* through the adoption of the so-called Fourth Financial Protocol. The Commission also called for the completion of the EC–Turkish Customs Union by 1996. Symbolically, this was an important step because it placed Turkey higher in the EC hierarchy of external relations than the Central and Eastern European countries. The proposals were, however, rather empty gestures since Greece was adamant in opposing both. The opinion furthermore criticized Turkey for its less-than-perfect human rights record. It was widely felt not only in Turkey that apart from these official objections to Turkish membership, the Community was very hesitant to admit a Muslim country as a member and that in fact the cultural factor was the greatest obstacle to membership.

At the beginning of the 1990s, the Union's relationship to Turkey constituted one of its most troublesome third-country relationships. The new post-cold war security situation facing the EC had made Turkey a more valuable partner for the EC. On the new 'arc of crisis', stretching from Eastern Europe and the Western part of the SNG to the Middle East and North Africa, Turkey took up a key position.[1] The problem was that the EC had little concrete to offer and whatever it did decide to offer was normally vetoed by Greece. The Commission in its report on enlargement to the Lisbon Summit drew attention to the neglect of Turkey, recommending an extension of the political dialogue (*EC Bulletin* 3/92, p. 17). The Lisbon European Council followed the suggestion and decided to introduce a political dialogue with Turkey at the highest level. The EC–Turkish Association Council held in November 1992 under UK Presidency put into effect the decision to introduce a high-level political dialogue deciding *inter alia* to hold meetings as necessary between the president and prime minister of Turkey and the presidents of the European Council and the European Commission. Earlier in 1992 the Community had tried in various ways to circumvent the Greek veto against further financial assistance to Turkey. Thus, in January 1992 Vice-President Bangemann of the Commission and the Turkish Deputy Prime Minister Inonu had signed a programme which foresaw Turkish involvement in trans-European networks in the field of transport, telecommunication and energy; joint EC–Turkish initiatives to assist the CIS and Turkish participation in horizontal sections of the Renovated Mediterranean Programme. To this should be added the fact that in 1992 Turkey obtained status as an associated member of the WEU and concluded an economic agreement with EFTA.

In economic terms the EC gestures did not amount to much. The tenuous links to Turkey should be measured against the rising importance of the region on Europe's south-eastern flank and Turkey's new won confidence as a potential leader of a large Turkish-speaking community in south-western Asia: 45 million Muslims in the six Muslim republics of the former Soviet Union are looking to Ankara for guidance (*The Economist*, 14 December 1991). Their alternative point of reference is Iran. Hardly surprising then that the Turkish government has begun if not turning its back on the Community then at least turning its attention to the opportunities towards the north-east. Significantly, it does so with the blessing of the United States, whose strategic interests have shifted from Europe towards the Middle East, the Gulf and Asia and who regards Iran as a potential source of instability in the region. As the founder of the Black Sea Economic Cooperation Zone, Turkey has become the centre of an economic community at the fringe of Europe. The zone brings together the Balkan and Caucasian countries in the west and east, Russia in the north and Turkey in the south. On top of this, Turkey plays a prominent role in the Islamic community for economic cooperation, of which Iran, Pakistan,

Azerbaijan, Turkmenistan and Uzbekistan are also members (*Frankfurter Algemeine*, 3 April 1992; *Die Zeit*, 3 April 1992). Turkey's economic offensive towards the east and north is backed up with a determined effort to exert cultural leadership in the region. A programme called 'Eurasia-TV' is transmitted in Turkish language as far as Central Asia via satellite (*Frankfurter Algemeine*, 14 May 1992).

A further aspect of the Turkish problem is the Turkish frustration at the West's failure to credit Turkey for its support of the West in the Gulf War. This is part of the reason why there has been a certain diversification of Turkey's external links in recent years and an upgrading of relations with its north-eastern and southern neighbours. But the Turkish political elite remains officially committed to the goal of membership of the European Union. Turkey has undertaken to realize the Customs Union by 1995, although this will be painful for the Turkish economy (Tashan, 1992). And despite some Turkish irritation at the constant criticism levelled at Turkey by the EP, the Council of Europe and some member states of the European Union on account of the human rights situation in Turkey, there is evidence that Turkey has in fact in a number of cases responded to EC criticism or anticipated EC reactions in recent years by making improvements in human rights legislation, etc. To take but two examples, on 22 January 1987, a few months prior to the Turkish application for membership, the Turkish government granted its citizens the right of individual application to the European Human Rights Commission; and in 1990, the Turkish government eventually bowed to pressure from the EP, which in 1988 had endorsed the Walter Report, and removed several articles restricting political activities from the penal code (Muftuler, 1992). Although the Turkish political elite thus remains in essence pro-European, public opinion in Turkey is much more volatile reacting strongly to Western criticism of Turkey and not least to Western impotence in the face of Croat–Serbian aggression against Muslims in the former Yugoslavia.

For the European Union, the Turkish problem is somewhat similar to the German problem. Like Germany, Turkey has for decades been forced by the cold war to conduct a one-option foreign policy; now the iron curtain has gone and the (cultural) family can reunify. For the European Union, the Turkish problem is in essence a question of being able to offer the country an attractive future as an integrated part of the Western organizations to prevent it from going East – and doing it alone. The European Commission in its report to the Lisbon Summit on enlargement does not mention membership but speaks of the need to 'take all appropriate steps to anchor Turkey firmly within the future architecture of Europe' (*Europe and the Challenge of Enlargement*, op. cit., p. 17). This indicates that the Commission would prefer Turkey to be linked to the Union through some kind of variable geometry arrangement. The European Council in Lisbon was more forthcoming referring in its statements on Turkey to the Association Treaty of 1964 which talks about membership. But it is certainly open to question whether the Union, beset by its internal problems and Germany's future in Europe, has done enough to keep Turkey from drifting slowly towards the East.

Cyprus and Malta applied for membership of the Union in 1990. The Commission submitted its opinions on these countries in June 1993 (Com (93) 312 final and Com (93) 313 final). As for Cyprus, the Commission concludes that the country is eligible for membership and that negotiations on accession can start as soon as there are more certain prospects for solving the Cyprian problem. In this respect, the Commission is quite optimistic, referring to the recent progress achieved by the UN. With regard to Malta, the Commission opinion concludes that the country is in principle eligible for membership of the European Union and that accession negotiations may start as soon as circumstances permit it. The opinion emphasizes the need for a global restructuring of the Maltese economy, which *inter alia* applies a protectionist external trade policy. It recommended initiating a dialogue with the Maltese government and laying down a timetable for the implementation of the necessary reforms. The Commission also mentions Maltese neutrality as a possible problem. Having gone through the opinions on Cyprus and Malta, one is left with the impression that the Commission does not expect the two countries to become members before 1996. Quite apart from the problems already mentioned as 'micro-states', the two countries pose institutional problems for the Union which are not expected to be solved until the next Intergovernmental Conference.

The Central and Eastern European countries (CEECs), most of which have association agreements ('Europe agreements') concluded in 1991, have not yet submitted formal applications for membership. Yet most of them have repeatedly declared their intention to apply. Their motives are both economic and political. Membership of the European Union is seen as a return to normalcy. In 1928 Western Europe accounted for 70.5 per cent of Hungary's exports (Skak, 1993).

151

Full membership is also seen as a crucial element in the modernization of the CEEC economies. The export dependence on the Union is now for some CEECs on a par with the typical EFTA economy. While EEA membership may provide much the same market access as full membership, the CEECs consider that only full membership will reassure foreign investors that Central and Eastern Europe is a safe place to put their money. Political motives are equally important. The goal of membership of the European Union has an important symbolic value as an expression of the European identity of these countries. Since the abortive coup in Moscow in August 1991, security considerations have added to the urgency of closer links with the Union.

At the European Council in Copenhagen in June 1993, the Union declared that the European associates could become full members as soon as they fulfilled the necessary economic and political requirements. But clearly the Union prefers to admit at least some of these countries *en bloc*. The reason is partly that placing applicants in groups is administratively more expedient. But the Commission and a number of member states are also thinking in terms of creating the 'critical mass' necessary to force through centralizing reforms of the Union's institutions. Yet, the CEECs are not always willing to play according to the rules set by Brussels. Some instead prefer to pursue a unilateralist strategy. Among the frontrunners in the Visegrad grouping (Poland, Hungary, the Czech Republic, Slovakia), Hungary has been especially eager to distinguish itself from the others and notably from Poland. As early as 1990 Josef Antall, the Hungarian Prime Minister, expressed his wish that Hungary become a member between 1992 and 1995 (*Agence Europe*, 18 April 1990). However, having received a cool response from Germany, which wants the Visegrad countries to cooperate and join the Union *en bloc*, Hungary scaled down its ambitions, mentioning 1997–8 as a more realistic date of entry (*Le Monde*, 21 May 1991). Poland, the Czech Republic and Slovakia have so far been more modest in their European policy, typically mentioning the year 2000 as a deadline for entry into the Union. Interestingly, the man behind Slovakia's independence, former Prime Minister Carnogursky, spoke of using a separate access to the EC as a means of eventually achieving a dissolution of the Czechoslovak federation, explicitly referring to the Maastricht Treaty and its principle of subsidiarity. Yet, the EC was not quite as enthusiastic about Slovak (or Czech) secession. The Polish policy towards the European Union is reminiscent of that of other states sharing common borders with Germany. There is thus a certain element of containment policy in the Polish thinking on this issue. It is as yet unclear to what extent the Polish policy towards the Union will be affected by the change of regime in 1993, but it would be reasonable to expect a certain toughening of the Polish negotiating position *vis-à-vis* the European Union. It would in any case be wrong to portray all CEECs as ardent supporters of the Union. The Czech government, while supporting the process of the European Union, has gradually moved towards a 'Thatcherite' vision of European cooperation criticizing ambitious plans for supranational regulation. In all the CEEC countries, one notices a greater pragmatism in the debate about Union membership as the realities of the internal market become better known. There has also been a certain diffusion across Europe of the Danish and British message on the deficiencies of the Maastricht Treaty.

Bulgaria, Romania, Slovenia and Albania are also realistic candidates for membership in the foreseeable future. An open question is whether some of these countries, most likely Bulgaria and Romania, could be admitted along with the Visegrad countries. This will depend not only on economic-political conditions in these countries but also and perhaps to a greater extent on internal balance of power considerations in the Union. The Union for its part, recalling the unfortunate case of Turkey, has been wary of setting specific dates. One European Commissioner has, however, stated that accession negotiations with the first CEECs could start in the second half of the 1990s (Skak, 1991, p. 24). This is probably too optimistic an assessment. The timetable of enlargement for the CEECs is in any case impossible to predict as it will depend on volatile economic and political variables in the Union. The internal political development in the CEECs will also be an important factor.

Hard facts suggest that politicians in the CEEC countries may be over-optimistic in their expectations. Although the democratic revolutions in Eastern Europe and the collapse of the cold war order have changed the parameters of the enlargement process, removing a number of political barriers to entry into the Union, the economic level of development in the CEEC countries and the physical-administrative infrastructure are still far short of allowing membership. Baldwin *et al.* (1992, p. 109), perhaps erring on the side of caution, estimate that it will take several decades before full membership for these countries is realistic, partly because the CEECs are poor with per capita incomes around two-thirds of Portugal's at the end of the 1980s; and partly, probably more importantly, because membership for the CEECs would place enormous strain on the Union's redistributive policies. They

153

calculate that Czechoslovakia, Poland and Hungary alone would require a combined annual net inflow of about Ecu 8 billion and Bulgaria and Rumania another Ecu 5 billion. This leads them to conclude that a variant of the EEA may be useful as an intermediate arrangement for the CEECs.

Such a scenario would seem to suggest that contrary to what many observers have argued, the Union may well get a relatively long breathing space after the EFTA enlargement round before having to embark on the next expansion. This view lends support to the advocates of new forms of partial membership. Still, caution is warranted. The case of the Iberian applicants shows that economics seldom gets the final word in EC politics. The Iberian economies also represented a threat to sectoral interests in the member states, but powerful political arguments in favour of enlargement were able to overcome such concerns. Similarly, an acute security crisis in the eastern part of Europe involving Russia and/or Ukraine may speed up the accession of the CEECs.

A serious threat to the stability of the democratic regimes in the CEECs might also prompt a reappraisal of the Union's enlargement policy. Yet the case of the Iberian enlargement is different from the CEEC case in at least two respects. First, in the 1980s Germany was still able to act as Europe's generous paymaster which meant that the distributive problems of enlargement were manageable. This will probably not be the case for the rest of this decade. Second, the scale of the adaptive problems is likely to be somewhat bigger in the case of the CEECs not only economically but also politically. The Union may at some point have to consider very carefully whether the cause of democracy in Europe as a whole is best served by admitting unstable and threatened democratic regimes as full members of the Union or by keeping them at arms's length while bringing various kinds of pressure to bear on those regimes. The answer depends upon the Union's *ex-ante* stability as well as upon its ability to encapsulate and influence weak democratic regimes within the Union. The possibility of 'negative ideological spillover' from unstable democracies should certainly be taken seriously.

A reasonable prognosis would seem to be that during the next two decades the European Union will grow from the present 12 members to between 16 and 24 members. We leave out states bordering on regional big powers like Russia and Turkey, that is the former Yugoslavia, Ukraine, Moldova, Belorussia, the Baltic Republics and perhaps Albania (a cultural frontier state), assuming that for security reasons and as a means of sidestepping the issue of admission of big states the Union will prefer to set up special association arrangements with these frontier states. The more precise timetable of enlargement is anybody's guess. Much will depend on domestic political developments in the member states of the Union as well as on the economic state of the Union. It is possible that the Union will try to divide the CEEC enlargement into two rounds, the first one involving only Poland, Hungary and the Czech and Slovak Republics. Assuming that Switzerland is eventually 'turned', this would make for a membership of between 21 and 23 at the start of the new millennium depending on whether Cyprus and Malta are admitted during the coming decade. But in view of the very considerable popular resistance to membership in many of the candidate countries, this is clearly an optimistic prognosis. An open question is to what extent a rejection of membership in several EFTA referendums would have a domino effect not only in other EFTA countries but also in Central and Eastern Europe.

Enlargement and integration

The prospect of a wider Union to be created through a succession of enlargement rounds obviously raises a number of intriguing questions to do with the relationship between geographical expansion and the evolution of the EC system. Some of these questions relate to sectoral policies; others to institutions and procedures. Here we shall concentrate on the institutional issues.

At the extreme, there are two possible consequences of geographical expansion: decrease and increase in integration. The intuitive answer seems to be that increases in size will lead to a decrease in the level of integration. Common sense suggests that as an organization increases its membership, it becomes more heterogeneous and less cohesive, especially if one is talking about the adhesion of many new members. There is a threshold somewhere or what could be called an optimal size for organizations. Although all organizations will probably face problems if they grow fast in terms of membership, the problem is likely to be particularly acute for an evolving organization with an ambition to become more closely integrated. Integration of course has various aspects and dimensions. Frei (1984) mentions three dimensions: institutional, normative and transactional. It would seem that normative integration poses the biggest problems for an organization expanding its membership. Adaptation to a set of formal procedures is easier than assimilation to new norms and values. The old members of an organization have gone through a process of socialization which in the nature of things sets them apart from new members, although in our case the new members have a long history of rather close interaction with the Union which may reduce the problem of normative assimilation.

At the same time, both abstract reasoning and empirical evidence suggest that there are ways of avoiding negative effects on the integration system at least in the short term. We can point to at least four 'protective strategies':

    (a) a take-it-or-leave-it position *vis-à-vis* applicants;
    (b) the formation of subsystems;
    (c) incremental enlargement (or associate membership);
    (d) variable geometry.

A take-it-or-leave-it negotiating position is helpful in maintaining internal cohesion in the Union since it ensures that a number of fundamental aspects of the integration system will not be reassessed or renegotiated as a result of the adhesion of members. This reflects the general point that the weaker and more heterogeneous an organization is, the more inflexible its external negotiating position tends to be because it runs the risk of seeing its internal divisions exploited by the opponent. This is the logic behind the Union's current position of requiring acceptance of *l'acquis* from new adherents. The notion of *l'acquis communautaire* was first mentioned in the context of the first enlargement. France was worried that the adhesion of the United Kingdom with its different values and strong presence in other parts of the world would threaten the Community. France only changed position after having made it a condition of entry that the United Kingdom should totally accept the decisions made by the Community prior to the UK adhesion. The negotiations would therefore in principle only discuss transitional measures and terms of adaptation (Michalski and Wallace, 1992, p. 20). The principle of acceptance of *l'acquis* remained the Community's precondition in the second and third enlargement rounds as well as in the EEA negotiations.

Subsystems may be different in nature and have different functions but some subsystems clearly help the integration system maintain its cohesion in the face of geographical enlargement. Differentiation by means of the formation of several tiers in the integration process is likely to have a disciplining effect in that it excludes and marginalizes certain states from the core of the system, at the same time implicitly offering rewards for compliance with the norms of the core structure.

Philippe de Schoutheete uses the term 'subsystem' as an umbrella concept encompassing various kinds of differentiated participation in integration (de Schoutheete, 1990). He thus regards variable geometry as an aspect of a broader phenomenon. The *directoire* aimed at giving the regional big powers a special role is one type of subsystem. 'Variable geometry' is another type of subsystem. It has a specific meaning in de Schoutheete's terminology, referring to transitory differentiation that allows a smaller group to move forward in a specific field when all member states are not able to follow them. Finally, subsystems may also have a more defensive function. They may 'preserve certain positions acquired prior to the joint effort' (ibid., 1990, p. 107). The second and third types of subsystem are both of relevance to the debate about enlargement and integration. Both may help the system preserve its cohesion in the face of an adhesion of a number of new members which do not (yet) share the norms of the integration system.

It seems evident that some of the problems that led to subsystem formation or reactivation of dormant subsystems in the past are similar to those raised by major enlargements. One of the main causes of the reactivation of the WEU in 1984 was the growing distance between the nucleus of the European part of NATO and some fringe countries which attacked official NATO policy. In other words, the problem was one of weakening political cohesion. A somewhat similar problem will arise in the case of the accession to the Community of countries with a neutral tradition like Sweden, Finland and Austria even if neutrality has to varying degrees been redefined in all three countries.

As William Wallace has pointed out, it is important to distinguish between differentiation as a transitory and informal arrangement and differentiation as a permanent and formalized arrangement (Wallace, 1985). Differentiation is functional from a systemic point of view if defined as a transitory arrangement. If on the other hand it takes the form of permanent and formalized arrangements affecting a wide range of policy areas, it may weaken the overall cohesion of the system. The Franco–German axis is an example of a stable subsystem. As such it may be argued that it is disfunctional to the stability of the integration system. But the Franco–German axis could also be regarded as a hegemonic structure exerting informal leadership in an integration system with weak formal leadership structures. The Commission president plays a certain leadership role in a number of policy areas but is hampered by a lack of legitimacy. The Presidency also plays a leadership role, notably in the political area, but lacks continuity. There is thus a 'leadership vacuum' in the present Union, all the more lamentable given the huge problems facing Europe. The Franco–German subsystem fills this vacuum. But it is clearly a second best. There is a certain tension between the growing need for effective European leadership and the fact that the available (informal) leadership lacks democratic legitimacy. At some point this imbalance may pave the way for the creation of a genuine, perhaps elected, European Presidency.

The strategy of incremental enlargement implies deferring enlargement by dividing it into stages, typically starting integration in the less controversial sectors. The rationale behind this strategy is to give the supporters of deepening sufficient time to prepare the system for comprehensive enlargement, while at the same time setting up valuable links with the applicant. A strategy resembling incremental enlargement would consist in offering applicant states a more permanent associate membership which confers a number of tangible benefits on candidate countries without burdening the Union's decision-making apparatus with new participants. We could call this 'a strategy of associate membership'. Although the concrete modalities can be quite varied, this strategy will typically imply the creation of a hegemonic relationship between the integration system and the country in question since associate membership will only serve to protect the integration system if organized in such a way that the new 'half-members' will not take part in the system's decision-making procedures (cf. Pedersen, 1993a).

One may draw a parallel with Puerto Rico's relationship with the United States. Under the Federal Relations Act, the USA–Puerto Rican association means a common market and a common monetary system. Although subject to federal laws, the Puerto Ricans do not pay federal taxes, do not vote in federal elections. (They do, however, participate in the American parties' presidential conventions!) They have no representation in Congress (Duchacek, 1970, pp. 184ff.). One of the distinguishing features of the Puerto Rican–US relationship is the extraterritorial impact of US rules. Interestingly, this is also a feature in the EC's policy towards its European periphery.

Finally, one may use variable geometry as a means of combining deepening with widening. The recent history of the EC is ripe with examples of the Community's aptitude for finding flexible solutions to the problem of diversity (Wallace, 1985). The Maastricht Treaty provides several examples of this kind of *ad hoc* differentiation. One type of variable geometry consists in *ex ante* opting out. In this case, a country places itself outside a field of cooperation from the outset (Wijkman, 1993, p. 153). The United Kingdom position on the social protocol is an example of this. Another type of variable geometry consists in *ex-post* opting out. In this case a country commits itself to a new type of cooperation, while reserving its right to decide whether and when to adhere to the more binding part of this cooperation. The Danish and UK opt outs on the EMU are cases in point. The Danish relationship with the European Union agreed at the Edinburgh Summit also constitutes a case of *ex-post* opting out. In the Edinburgh agreement, Denmark subscribes to the goal of the European Union accepting that its special arrangement does not prejudice the goals of the Union. Yet, Denmark has been given a transitional period of at least three years until the next intergovernmental conference on the further evolution of the Union. Denmark has been granted a '*Denkpause*'. Whether Denmark's transitional period can be extended beyond 1996 is unclear but must be regarded as doubtful.

It is interesting to consider whether extensive use of differentiation will transform the system. Where is the threshold beyond which differentiation can no longer be encapsulated but begins to effect the integration system as such? Two problems deserve mention in this connection. First, some of the older members may start demanding arrangements similar to those offered to the country in question. Second, as more states acquire a special status, variable geometry arrangements will tend to weaken the system's decision making. The reason is that the range of common policies will become narrower, thereby making it more difficult to put together package deals.

All in all, it would therefore seem that the assumption that an increase in size will weaken the cohesion of an integration system is too rash. However, the propositions made above are based on several assumptions: first of all, system consolidation through subsystem formation will only be possible if the system has a stable and highly integrated core at the time of enlargement. Similarly, if the *ex-ante* cohesion is weak, it may prove difficult to uphold the take-it-or-leave-it posture. A time dimension must also be added. While new members of an organization must quite naturally abide by the existing rules as defined by the old members, once members they will come to influence the future of the organization. Thus, the cohesive effect of take-it-or-leave-it positions is a short-term effect. An additional consideration relates to the effect of new adherents on the behaviour of old members of the organization. Assuming that we are talking about a relatively heterogeneous organization, an increase in the number of actors is likely to have both a primary and a secondary effect. The primary effect could be defined as the effect of the behaviour of the new members themselves on the integration system. The secondary effect could be defined as the effect of new members on the behaviour of old members. One might imagine that minorities in the organization which have hitherto suppressed their dissent because they were in a minority of one will be more disposed to manifest their dissent if joined by other dissidents. This logic may be relevant to the enlargement of the Union. By way of illustration, it has been shown that in the UN General Assembly Denmark has generally voted with the EPC grouping in cases where it had differing views, except for cases where other members supported the Danish view. In other words, one disintegrative effect of enlargement may be to weaken the pressure of conformity in a number of areas.

A final consideration is rather simple but could be important. This is the fact that as the number of members of the integration system grows, this will cause a decline in the relative influence of each member. Hosli (1992, p. 13) shows how for example the three big members have seen their share of the total vote decline from 23.5 per cent in the period from 1958–73 to 13.2 per cent after the latest enlargement in 1986. Correspondingly, their share in a blocking minority dropped from 66.7 to 43.5 per cent. Thus, a steady increase in the size of an integration system requires a steady increase in the mutual solidarity or 'we-feeling' to use Deutsch's expression. Otherwise, geographical expansion is a recipe for disintegration whether in the form of a system collapse or a managed build-down. Recent trends in European integration do not suggest a continuing growth in cultural integration. On the contrary, it seems that new states will join the Union at a time of growing self-assertion on the part of regions and member states.

One may, however, also point to important integrative effects of an increase in the number of members. Lindberg and Scheingold made the classical distinction between the scope and the institutional capacity of an integration system (Lindberg and Scheingold, 1970). Expansion in scope refers to expansion in the number of issue areas subject to formal Union competence. Institutional capacity refers to the decision-making structure and the decision-making rules and norms of the system. Now, it seems quite clear that geographical expansion will *ceteris paribus* lead to increases in the scope of integration. New member states bring with them particular concerns, which can often only be accommodated through setting up new common policies or through expanding existing policies. The adhesion of the United Kingdom and Ireland played a role in the setting up of the regional fund, and the fact that the United Kingdom had extensive ties to colonies in Africa and the Caribbean led to an expansion in EC aid policy towards the Third World through the creation of the Lomé cooperation. The adhesion of Greece, Spain and Portugal was of course accompanied by a dramatic expansion in regional distribution policies in the EC. There appears to be at least one policy area which always expands in scope as a result of enlargement and that is external relations (see also below).

It is much more questionable if geographical expansion also leads to growth in the institutional capacity of an integration system. Lindberg and Scheingold argued that enlargement typically has wide-ranging implications for an integration system. They described it as one form of system transformation, unfortunately with no case material on which to base their arguments (their book was published in 1970 before the first enlargement). System transformation is defined as 'an extension to specific or general obligations that are beyond the bounds of the original treaty commitments, either geographically or functionally. It typically entails a major change in the scope of the Community or in its institutions that often requires an entirely new constitutive bargaining process among the member states, entailing substantial goal redefinition among national political actors.' The authors thus argued that British accession would amount to a system transformation in the EC (ibid., p. 137).

Lindberg and Scheingold seem to suggest that enlargement has implications for both the functional scope and the institutional development of the integration system, arguing that enlargement will force institutional and procedural changes upon the existing system. This proposition is supported and elaborated upon by Keohane and Hoffmann in a more recent contribution. They point out correctly that the historical experience with enlargement suggests that, contrary to prevailing expectations, enlargement may contribute to the strengthening of Community institutions (Keohane and Hoffmann, 1990, pp. 289ff.). Greek and Iberian accession was preceded by the French-inspired 'Report on the European Institutions' (the so-called 'Wise Men's Report'). And there was a clear policy link between the Iberian enlargement and the provisions for majority voting in the SEA (Wallace, 1989).

Keohane and Hoffmann put it this way 'expansion of the Community led to anticipation of institutional stalemate, and – since the key actors sought policy changes – created incentives for formal institutional change (Keohane and Hoffmann, 1990, p. 290). The authors regard this as a new kind of spillover which they call 'institutional spillover'. However, it would seem that there are two different ways in which enlargement may lead to growth in institutional capacity: first of all, there is clearly a functional logic which has to do with optimal size. But there is also likely to be a logic which could be called 'political linkage expansion'. What we are referring to is the possibility that the enlargement issue may be linked to institutional deepening of integration by means of a kind of constitutional package deal. Until the adoption of the SEA, this linkage was informal. It has now become institutionalized, since the European Parliament has obtained a right of veto over enlargements (Ehlermann, 1990). We would therefore expect the linkages between enlargement and system transformation to become more pronounced in the 1990s. It is important to stress that whereas the functional factor is related to the size of integration, that is to the number of new adherents, the political linkage factor is not related to the size of enlargement. Thus, the political linkages between enlargement and the constitutional development of the Union can in principle play a role at any level of enlargement.

In this connection it is also worth considering whether increases in size may lead to further increases in size. If that is the case the enlargement process is likely to accelerate in the years ahead and by implication the centralizing effect of large-scale enlargement can be expected to be powerful in the European Union in the next decades. Is there such a thing as a *multiplicateur d'élargissement?* Philippe Schmitter (1969) has argued that increases in the scope and capacity of a regional integration system have external effects which 'feed back' on the system and tend to reinforce it. Here one must distinguish between different groups of third countries. Third countries in the system's local periphery are particularly exposed to the effects of internal developments in the integration system. Geographical expansion of the integration system also has external effects and it may safely be argued that the external economic effects of enlargement are mainly felt by the local periphery. For the local periphery, enlargement of an integration system raises the costs of non-membership. The dynamic dimension is of course crucial. It is only once an integration system has become the dominant economic and political factor in a region that the *multiplicateur d'élargissement* acquires a major importance.

In the foregoing, it has been argued that not only can the integration level achieved so far be maintained in the face of enlargement by means of various protective strategies, it is even possible that geographical enlargement could actually stimulate a further deepening of integration. However, as already indicated, enlargement is also likely to have certain disintegrative effects on the integration system. In fact, one of the most severe threats to integration posed by enlargement could well be a premature politicization of the question of *finalité* or a politicization of that issue in a context of growing problems in European integration.

There appear to be three possible constitutional effects of large-scale enlargement. We can thus sketch out three scenarios for a wider Union:

First, as argued above, enlargement may, once it reaches a threshold level, lead to a significant further centralization of the Union's institutional system as a means of ensuring that the Union remains capable of making decisions and acting cohesively not least *vis-à-vis* the rest of the world. Both an inherent logic of efficiency and political linkages between geographical enlargement and constitutional change may facilitate such a development. An additional factor which might help neutralize the disintegrative effects of enlargement would be severe external threats since such factors are known to be particularly effective in drawing states in a region together. Given Europe's inherent diversity, further centralization would probably only be feasible if accompanied by a stricter application of subsidiarity (see below). This scenario presupposes that enlargement is accompanied by system transformation and by implication that piecemeal incrementalist enlargement gives way to large-scale enlargement 'rounds' (*federalization*).

Second, enlargement may lead to growing diversity and the introduction of a variable geometry Europe with integration in different speeds inside the Union and new permanent forms of partial membership for some applicants. What we call 'variable geometry' Europe borders on what Philippe Schmitter calls 'condominio' in his stimulating contribution on the dependent variable in European integration (Schmitter, 1991). He defines the condominio as 'a set of previously independent national states that agree to remove all barriers to the exchange of goods, services, capital and persons and to establish functionally specific authorities to regulate the conditions for these exchanges without, however, agreeing to govern their impact through a territorial redistribution of benefits' (Schmitter, op. cit., p. 8). As Schmitter points out 'one of the hidden virtues of the condominial outcome is that it could exploit the "vice" of European eccentricity. So far the EC has expanded in membership by requiring all new entrants to accept the full acquis communautaire … the recent events in Eastern Europe … will place quite a strain on that concentric design.' Rather than a center-periphery Europe with a smack of domination, the variable geometry or condominio Europe would essentially create a non-hierarchical network-Europe composed of different subsets of European states. As Schmitter points out, one might have a European environmental agency stretching from 'Brest-to-Brest-Litovsk' or further and perhaps a European Central Bank with a more compact group of 10, a European energy network with an intermediate number, etc. A Europe of variable geometry or condominia Europe would be complex but also quite flexible. It could prove the only viable option if the European electorates were to resist federalization. The risk is that this model might cause the integration process to stagnate as the area of common commitments shrinks and it becomes more difficult to negotiate broad package deals (*Europe of variable geometry/condominio*).

Third, enlargement, unless accompanied by institutional reform or some new mechanism of flexibility, might at some point create efficiency and legitimacy problems in the Union on a scale that could force Europe's political leaders to 'build-down' the integration system and opt for a truly confederal model of integration. Thus, enlargement could in this scenario create severe problems of governance and implementation, which would confront decision makers with a stark choice between further centralization or abandonment of the current model of integration. After all, the popular acceptance of further transfers of sovereignty depends on the perceived quality of the Union's policy output (cf. below). If that quality is reduced, one has either to reduce the scope of integration or centralize the common institutions. Likewise, the attempt to create a functioning democracy in a continental-size polity with a weak common political culture will prove exceedingly difficult. In essence, democracy means a willingness to be voted down on issues of importance. Supranational majority rule is only viable if nation states and citizens of nation states agree to be voted down on matters of importance. But nation states and citizens of nation states will only agree to be voted down by other states with whom they feel a reasonably strong cultural and ideological affinity. Does a wider Union meet that test? One doubts it. This does not mean that supranational integration on a continental scale is impossible. But it does mean that a long period of time is needed for the creation of the 'we-feeling' necessary to make supranational democracy workable. Supranational democracy along the lines sketched out in the Maastricht Treaty can hardly be introduced in a continental-size Union with a great cultural diversity without this producing dangerous tensions that might in a worst case analysis foster strong currents of neo-nationalism (*confederalization*).

Although different and conflicting trends can be identified, it has been argued here that some kind of centralizing system transformation is the most likely scenario, at least in the short term. The main reason is that federalist forces in the Union are powerful and able to establish political linkages between institutional reform and enlargement and that these forces now have effective procedural weapons at their disposal enabling them to apply such linkages with success. From a purely technical point of view, the admission of three or four new states of limited size would not seem to be a persuasive argument for system transformation. In theoretical terms, we expect the institutional spillover dynamic to be rather weak. But enlargement policy will be – and already is – an integral part of the constitutional debate about the Community's long-term goal. And in the medium and longer term the pattern of interests and preferences in the Union may become more diverse, structural problems of size may become more difficult to solve and federalist linkage politics more difficult to apply. Hence the calls for an early overhaul of the EU's institutional system. What kinds of demands for institutional changes in the EC system can be envisaged as a consequence of enlargement?

Enlargement and institutional reform

In order to maintain efficiency, there will first of all be demands for changes in the decision-making procedures. With, say, 20 member states the requirements of efficiency will add to the pressure for a more generalized use of various forms of majority voting in the EC Council of Ministers. In its preliminary report on the challenge of enlargement, the Commission was outspoken, almost brutal, in describing the need for a reduction in the use of unanimity. It essentially presented the choice as one between reducing unanimity to a minimum and alternatively preserving a qualified majority for major issues and introducing simple majority voting for 'routine' business (*A Strategy for Enlargement*, Brussels, 14 November 1991). There are of course other possibilities.

The president of the CDU group in the Bundestag has thus presented a proposal for radical reforms of the European institutions. The current system of qualified majority would be replaced by a system of double majority voting. According to this model, to be adopted a proposal would have to muster a majority of both states and population in the Union. Unanimity would be eliminated and replaced by a four-fifths majority (*Agence Europe*, 27 August 1993). Another less radical option would be to redefine what constitutes a blocking minority.

It is doubtful whether majority voting will be introduced in foreign-policy cooperation as a consequence of enlargement (cf. Pedersen, 1993a). Given the jealousy with which some member states protect their autonomy in this area, one can hardly expect sweeping changes in this direction. Some incremental changes may occur by means of a 'sectoral' approach to majority voting. However, the barrier between intergovernmentalism and supranationalism is not easy to cross in the foreign-policy field – not to mention security and defence. A more likely development therefore is that the number of areas in which majority voting applies will be extended to new economic and social areas, but that this will be accompanied by 'subsystem' or '*directoire*' solutions in the security and defence fields along the lines of the existing WEU–Union pattern.

With 20 or 25 member states, the Council of Ministers will be unable to continue its current 'diplomatic' working style with presentations of national positions. With 20 member states a normal round of opening statements would last almost three and a half hours, assuming that each state representative speaks for 10 minutes. Several avenues of reform can be envisaged: one would lead to a more 'parliamentarian' working style, which could provide ammunition for those wanting to transform the Council into a senate. Another option would be significantly to strengthen the administrative structure of the Council as a corollary to enlargement. Yet the biggest problem which will arise is that since most of the expected new member states are small or medium size, the big member states will see their relative influence diminish unless the cards are distributed in a new way. Hosli (1992) has shown how, with the adhesion of the EFTA countries, the larger and middle-sized member states will lose voting power, whereas the smallest members stand to gain. She uses the Banzhaf power index, which defines voting power as the number of winning coalitions in which a member's defection from the coalition would make it lose, divided by the total number of critical defections for all members. Already today the big member states are underrepresented in the institutional power structure. The five big member states together have a population of 290 million people but only control 48 votes in the Council. The seven 'smaller' members with a combined population of 54 million control 28 votes. The combined opposition of two big states such as France and Germany is no longer sufficient to veto a proposal. The big member states can be expected to call for changes making it more difficult for the smaller states to obtain blocking minorities, calls that have in fact already been made. It must be added though that the small members rarely form a common front against the big.

A total of 23 votes (out of 76) are required to make a proposal fall under the present system. Blocking minorities can be composed of four middle-sized countries (for example Belgium (5), Greece (5), the Netherlands (5) and Portugal (5) with a small state, say, Denmark (3). A 'southern' constellation can be formed for example by France (10), Spain (8) and Greece (5) (Hosli, op. cit., p. 12). One of the reasons why leading southern members like Spain call for institutional reforms is that they fear losing this blocking majority as a consequence of enlargement. Were this to happen, it could theoretically lead to big changes in the CAP and in regional policy to the disadvantage of the south in the Union. A blocking 'northern coalition' can also be formed under the present system. It could consist of for example the United Kingdom (10), the Netherlands (5), Belgium (5) and Denmark (3). Assuming that the EFTA adherents are given the same number of votes as they have in the Comité Européen de Normalisation (CEN), the EFTA enlargement round will lead to a significant strengthening of the northern block in the Council and thus in Union politics as a whole, since the Council is the most important decision-making body (Hosli, 1992).

Fiddling with the principle of overrepresentation of small states is in any case not going to be easy. Denmark for one is opposed to any such moves. But even some of the most ardent supporters of federalism, the Benelux countries, are somewhat miffed and criticized the idea in a memorandum published in the summer of 1992. But the negotiating position of the small states is rather weak. The issue of enlargement may break up traditional alignments in the Community's constitutional debate. Thus, it seems likely that the United Kingdom will side with France and Germany when it comes to decisions on institutional adaptations to enlargement. Even so, a redistribution of votes in the Council will probably be regarded as too controversial as recognized by the EP (EP document A3-189/92, p. 17). The most likely outcome of the debate is therefore a redefinition of what constitutes a qualified majority and/or a blocking minority.

The structure and composition of the Parliament will also come under pressure as a result of geographical enlargement. At present there are 518 seats in the EP. New member states will lead to an increase in the number of seats. But since nobody wants a 'Soviet-style' assembly, there is a natural upper limit to the number of seats. Incidentally, this threshold is defined somewhat differently by Brussels and Strasbourg. The new EP building in Brussels has room for 750, while the competing project in Strasbourg will apparently be able to house around 1,000 parliamentarians. At the same time, some big member states led by Germany are pushing for a more proportional representation, arguing that this is necessary in order to strengthen the legitimacy of the new and more powerful supranational Parliament. The influencial German analyst Wolfgang Wessels has calculated that with a relationship between population and parliamentary seats similar to that of the United States, an EC of 20 member states might well have 750 seats (Wessels, 1990; see overleaf). Wessels recommends a more strict proportionality in the distribution of seats in the European Parliament but recognizes that the proportionality principle may have to be modified in the case of the smallest member states. His proposal for a redistribution of seats in the EP is shown in Table 9.1.

One notes how enlargement will in time lead to a reduction in the representation of the small states. Thus the Nordic countries and Ireland must foresee a reduction of their already limited representation in the EP. If accompanied by a further transfer of legislative powers to the EP this could provoke quite strong reactions from the small members. One way of countering such resistance would be to set up a genuine senate in the Union in which each member state would have equal representation. The German CDU has thus suggested the creation of a senate consisting of representatives of the national parliaments (*Agence Europe*, 27 August 1993). The evolution of the EP in a wider Union will not only affect the inter-state balance but also the inter-party balance. The Northern enlargement will tend somewhat to weaken the Christian Democratic EPP, although the Austrian ÖVP would provide some compensation. The admission of the British Conservatives to the EPP in 1991 could in part be seen as a skilful move by the EPP designed to make the EPP a more attractive partner for the non-religious right-wing parties in the future member states (*Financial Times*, 15 April 1991).

Table 9.1 Distribution of seats in the European Parliament in an EC with 20 member states

Country	Representation
Germany	119
United Kingdom	88
Italy	89
France	86
Spain	62
The Netherlands	27
Belgium	20
Greece	21
Portugal	21
Denmark	13
Ireland	11
Luxembourg	7
Sweden	18
Austria	17
Switzerland	15
Finland	13
Norway	12
Poland	61
Czechoslovakia	29
Hungary	21
Total	750

Enlargement will more generally imply a risk of inflated and by implication more inefficient common institutions. If one continues the present practice of member state representation according to which each member state is entitled to at least one member in each institution, membership of several bodies will be inflated with unfortunate consequences for efficiency.

It is probably unrealistic to envisage radical changes in the size of the most important policy-making bodies like the European Council or the Council. But the Parliament will, as we have seen, at some point have to consider limiting its size. And other bodies may be more amenable to reform than the Council of Ministers and the European Council. In principle, one can envisage at least three approaches to limiting the size of Union institutions (Baldwin *et al.*, 1992, pp. 95ff.). First, one can adopt the method of 'districting' known from the United States and from the reform of the German Central Bank Council following the German unification. Districting consists in dividing the Union into sub-regional districts along population lines. The big states would thus constitute one district, whereas the smaller states would be asked to join together in districts, each of which would have one representative in the central body. Districting might appeal to the Benelux countries and could be an acceptable option for the Nordics since it would legitimize the formation of a Nordic bloc within the Union.

Tony Verheijen of the European Institute of Public Administration has suggested an ingenious combination of majority voting and districting (Verheijen, 1992). The model consists in dividing the Union into five permanent 'regions' each consisting of a number of member states; a Mediterranean region, a north-west European region, a Central European region, a Balkan region and a Scandinavian region. The Union would have an 'Executive Council' which would consist of one representative for each region. The decision-making procedure suggested is that inside each region decisions should be taken by a qualified majority, whereas in the Executive Council, which will consist of one representative from each region, consensus should be reached. This idea is intriguing because it represents an attempt to create procedures that take into account the sub-regional heterogeneity of a continental Union. The main weakness of the model is that it would be exceedingly difficult to reach agreement on where to draw the lines between the 'macro regions'. Furthermore, in practice the model could lead to the dominance of one big state within certain (sub)regions.

Second, one might opt for an approach which could be called 'alternation of voting membership'. The method implies that the Union is once again divided into groups according to size of population. By way of illustration, Baldwin shows how an expanded Union with 17 members might be divided into four groups. The first group, consisting of the five big countries, would be permanent voting members of the central body in question. Group two with two seats would consist of four medium-size countries which would each be voting members only every second year. In group three, three countries would share one seat with each state thus voting every third year and group four, consisting of the five smallest states, would only be voting members every fifth year.

Third, one might opt for a more radical 'deepening' approach by simply 'denationalizing' Union institutions. Denationalizing implies that a person is elected on the basis of professionalism rather than on the basis of nationality. In the case of the Commission, this solution would be quite logical since Commission officials are in any case not expected to represent national interests. No doubt, some institutions would be regarded as 'untouchables' for reasons of national feeling. The main candidates for radical reform along the lines suggested above are executive or in other ways 'technical' bodies. Baldwin primarily has in mind a European Central Bank. The Commission could be another candidate.

Like the Parliament, the Commission will face the problem of inflated size. The current norm is that each member state has the right to at least one commissioner. With 20 member states this implies a Commission of at least 20 members, assuming that the big members will accept the same representation as the small. In a Commission that size it will be difficult to find meaningful portfolios for all commissioners, a problem which is already evident today. A reduction in the size of the Commission is therefore on the cards. The German CDU has proposed that the number of commissioners be reduced to 10 and that the president of the Commission be given the right to appoint commissioners upon suggestions from member states and also to reshuffle the members if necessary (but under the control of the European Council and the EP) (*Agence Europe*, 27 August 1993).

The (six-monthly) rotating Presidency which serves as the Union's main spokesman in the field of foreign and security policy will similarly come under pressure as the Union grows wider. With 20 members, an incumbent Presidency would have to wait 10 years before assuming the Presidency again. During this period, it would in most cases lose the necessary insight and experience. The problem would be particularly acute for the small member states or new member states with limited foreign-policy experience. As the Union acquires new and more important foreign-policy tasks extending into the security area proper, the leadership problem will become more acute. There will be a need for greater competence and greater continuity in the Union's external representation. How can the Union gain respect and establish lasting ties to, say, American leaders if a new personality turns up in Washington every six months? The problem is of course not new. In the 1970s Henry Kissinger was known to be somewhat annoyed at having to discuss 'Europe's' problems with the foreign minister of Denmark. An extension of the Presidency period to one year has been proposed. But any extension of the Presidency would make the problem of rotation even bigger. One can envisage several alternative arrangements. A rather modest reform would consist in creating a troika-Presidency based on the present system of troika-representation in external relations. The drawback is that it would give the Union a rather weak international profile. It might also meet with opposition from big states, which regard the Presidency as an opportunity to leave a decisive imprint on the evolution of the Union. A second and more radical reform would consist in introducing a distinction between big and small member states. Only the five big member states would hold full Presidencies under this system, whereas the smaller members would occupy vice-presidencies. This would allow an extension of the Presidency period from six months to one year. A third solution would be to apply the method of districting mentioned above. A fourth solution would be to limit the foreign-policy tasks of the Council to laying down guidelines and at the same time to increase the foreign-policy competences of the Commission as suggested by the European Parliament (EP document A3-189/92). A fifth model has been suggested by the German CDU (*Agence Europe*, 27 August 1993). The CDU proposes to extend the Presidency to one year. It should alternate between big and small member states but rotation by alphabetical order would be replaced by the election of the presiding country by a majority of member states. Finally, one could adopt the federalist approach suggested by the Benelux governments, who in their common memorandum of 17 June 1992 argue that 'in a larger Community it will become ever more imperative to establish a true Presidency, possibly elected' (quoted in *Le Monde Diplomatique*, June 1993).

The technical efficiency problem is compounded by a problem of ideological–political cohesion. Would France, say, agree to be represented by Finland or Poland in negotiations with third countries? This is certainly questionable. As a result of enlargement, we shall therefore probably see an accentuation of the current trend towards a *directoire* pattern in European foreign policy and security cooperation reflected in a system of concentric circles around a *directoire* of big European countries. Already today the WEU is portrayed – and widely accepted – as the 'executor' not only of EC policy but also in some cases of wider CSCE–European interests. There is a striking parallel between this evolving *directoire* model in European foreign policy and the way the UN Security Council currently acts as *de facto* (hegemonic) leader in the international community. As is well known, the Security Council has both permanent and non-permanent members. To be binding upon all member states, a decision in the Security Council must be based on the unanimous consent of the five permanent members to which any four votes from among the ten non-permanent members must be added. Are we moving towards a similar system in the EC with the big

European states essentially calling the tune in most of Europe? Will this be acceptable to the smaller states?

The management capacity of the executive is another aspect of system transformation which is likely to be discussed in the context of enlargement. There is no point in hiding the severe challenges posed by large-scale enlargement of the Union. One problem relates to the differing administrative cultures in a wider Union and the difficulties involved in assimilating administrators from Central and Eastern and perhaps Southern Europe. Another problem is that the Union may find itself confronted with a growing implementation problem in a continental-size Union. This would seem to support the conclusion drawn in the Commission report on enlargement that the Union must of necessity apply the principle of subsidiarity more strictly and in a more decentralizing fashion, as the Union expands geographically. The Commission would have to concentrate on essential common tasks. A move towards more 'executive federalism' would, on the other hand, hardly be wise. The implementation problems pointed to earlier suggest that, on the contrary, there will be a need for a stronger supervisory role for the Commission in a wider Union.

Finally, it is possible that one will see changes in linguistic working methods in a wider Union. At present, there are nine working languages in the EC which is a great burden for the administration. Would this continue in an EC of 20 members or more? Or would there be a reduction in the number of working languages? One option would be to apply the distinction between official languages and working languages in the EC. All national languages would then be granted the status of official EC languages, but only English, French and German would be working languages. Such a change could have negative effects on political participation in the Union. This relates to the general problem of reconciling a living democracy with the pressure of internationalization, a problem which becomes acute in a continental-size Union.

The geopolitics of the Union

As soon as we are talking about the accession of more than one new state or the accession of a big country, enlargement also affects the geopolitical balance of power in the region – unless of course we are talking about a fully developed federation, in which case territorial politics would be less relevant. The size of the applicant makes a difference. The adhesion of Ukraine or Turkey might upset the whole European balance of power, whereas the adhesion of, say, Austria would be to a lesser degree a high-politics issue in the Union. Thus, there were two levels in the debate about British EC membership in the early 1960s. At the first level, the debate was explicit and dealt with 'adaptive' issues. At the second level, the debate was tacit and dealt with what we may call 'systemic issues'. The explicit discussion was about the adaptation of the United Kingdom to the CAP and the EC's Common Commercial Policy. But there was also a hidden agenda, on which politico–military issues like the EC's future relationship with the United States and the consequences of British entry for the balance of power within the Community figured prominently (Lindberg and Scheingold, 1970, pp. 232ff.; Davidson, 1969, pp. 128ff.).

The existing inter-state balance will be profoundly affected by the enlargement envisaged in the next decades and so will the Union's coalition politics. If economic and cultural factors predominate, Germany looks set to become the winner and France (and Spain) the loser(s) *par excellence* in the enlargement game. The United Kingdom with its traditionally close ties to Scandinavia and peripheral states like Turkey appears to be in an intermediate position. This poses a number of questions which can only be dealt with briefly in this context: will for instance the Franco–German relationship continue as before, in a situation where Germany is less dependent on France in European coalition politics? The debate about *Einbindung* is in dire need of a time dimension. In the medium to longer term, the Union which is meant to 'tie down' Germany will come to include the traditional German sphere of influence in North-Central Europe. One suspects that confronted with the prospect of a loss of status and influence in the European institutions, France may feel tempted to fall back on old-style nationalist balance-of-power politics (cf. Stares, 1992).

A second trend will be the new coalitions which may come into being as a result of enlargement. The challenge of enlargement may well, as we have seen, serve to weld new links between the United Kingdom and France and Germany. This could have important indirect effects on integration, for example by marginalizing Denmark and other Nordic countries of a more sceptical bent. A last trend would seem to be a weakening of the position of the Southern European member states notably Spain, which finds itself far away from the expanding frontier of the Union. How will a Spain which feels on the defensive in a Union with a new Northern bias react towards the CEEC applicants? It may try to block or delay the Eastern enlargement, or it may apply very tough linkage politics, which could easily create a 'Spanish problem' equivalent to the British budgetary problem of the 1970s and 1980s. But Spain may also look for second best and make the accession of the Visegrad countries dependent on a simultaneous accession of Cyprus, Malta and 'latin' Romania. It should be apparent that quite apart from the institutional haggles, the process of enlargement may place new strains on political cohesion in the Union. Enlargement politics is high politics in two respects: it concerns the future direction of formal integration in Europe, but it also, and not least, concerns the struggle for leadership in the new Europe.

A wider Union in a world of blocs

Geographical enlargement of the Union will effect the external relations of the Union in various ways (cf. Pedersen, 1993a). Some of these effects will be undirected and structural. Others will be politically determined. First of all, enlargements have repercussions for third countries. Often one will experience 'band-wagoning' effects, when certain third countries demand readjustments as a result of the entry on the scene of a new and enlarged international grouping. For non-members in the region, the incentive to seek membership will grow as the costs of remaining outside rise. As argued elsewhere one may talk of enlargements having a 'multiplier effect'. This multiplier effect becomes more powerful as the regional entity grows in size, since this implies that the alternatives to membership become less and less attractive. Wijkman (1993, p. 156) makes a similar point when he argues that 'once started, preferential trading areas tend to grow. If a nucleus of countries creates a preferential trading area in a region, it is likely to attract additional members ... Thus small beginnings can lead further than grand designs.' What we are dealing with here is a variation on the theme of spillover. The expansive logic of enlargement is reminiscent of Philippe Schmitter's externalization thesis because it relates to the external environment of the integration system, but it differs from it in that it is related to the size of an integration system basically arguing that growth in size may lead to further growth in size.

This side effect of enlargement was clearly visible after the first EC enlargement (Etienne, 1980, p. 297). It was also apparent after the

Mediterranean enlargement, when the EC entered into negotiations with the North African Maghreb countries on improvements in trade conditions and assistance and Morocco applied for EC membership (Tsoukalis, 1981). And it will become apparent in Central Europe once Austria joins the Union and in the Baltic states as a result of the adhesion of the Nordic EFTANs. These additional adjustments in external relations need not be caused by third-country pressure. They may also be caused by pressure from the new member states. Both the Free Trade Agreements with the remaining EFTA countries negotiated in 1972, and the up-grading of the EC's relations with Latin America in the 1980s resulted from pressure from new entrants to the Community (Pedersen, 1986).

Enlargement also raises a delicate problem of economic redistribution which is likely to spill over into external economic relations. Enlargement involves shifts in the balance of burdens and benefits between member states, both through the market and through budgetary adjustments. The consequences are most severe if one is dealing with low-growth adherents and if accession takes place at a time of recession in the Union. As Christian Deubner has argued in the context of the Iberian enlargement, new member states with weak economies basically have only two options if they go for export-led growth: they can maintain a wage level that is substantially below that of the rest of the Union, but this would mean the creation of an intolerable gap in incomes and welfare within the Union. This policy would therefore in time provoke demands for equalizing redistribution measures over the Union budget. Alternatively, they can press for higher EC import tariffs and for lower import quotas to keep the lower-cost Third World imports out of EC markets to make room for their own (Deubner, 1980).

The latter option may, as has been the case in the past, be resisted by globally oriented export economies like Germany. But it should be kept in mind that as the Community system expands towards the east and north, an ever greater part of wealth creation will take place inside the Union's borders even for a big economy like Germany. Intra-European trade will increase as trade barriers are removed and production factors can move freely. And the new member states will in some cases lower the EC's dependence on imports from the rest of the world. All in all, this will tend to lower the cost of a protectionist posture and make life more difficult for the free-trade lobby in Europe. At the same time, the temptation to solve the adjustment costs of enlargement through a more protectionist external trade policy will put additional pressure on outsiders to join the integration system. This protectionist trend in Europe should be seen in the context of regionalist trends in both North America and Asia. NAFTA is not yet a common market but some have ambitions in that direction. Geographically, it may at some point be extended southwards. At least, this seems to be the USA's intention: witness the 'Enterprise for the Americas' initiative which could be seen as a first step in the direction of a Western hemisphere free-trade area. Externalization effects of NAFTA will in any case be hard to avoid. Chile and Mexico have since January 1992 had a free-trade agreement. Mexico is negotiating with several Central American countries and Colombia and Venezuela on a similar agreement. Argentina, Brazil, Paraguay and Uruguay are setting up a common market, Mercosul. At present, it seems as if Mexico and Argentina–Brazil are locked into confrontation, but it is at least theoreticaly possible that economic interest will at some point prevail over political assertion and the two Latin American liberalization schemes become fused.

In Asia cooperation initiatives have so far been more common than genuine economic integration. But this may be changing. In January 1992, the ASEAN summit decided to set up AFTA, the ASEAN free-trade arrangement, which is clearly modelled on EFTA. The agreement will remove internal tariffs within a period of 15 years. It covers industrial goods, processed agricultural goods and capital products. Agricultural produce in the strict sense is not covered by AFTA. From a European point of view the crucial question is, of course, whether Japan and China will be involved in Asian regionalization initiatives. This is clearly a possibility, although in the short term it will probably be a question of rather modest forms of cooperation and not outright integration. Thus a further evolution of the East Asian Economic Caucus (EAEC) seems likely. EAEC consists of Brunei, China, Hong Kong, Indonesia, Japan, South Korea, Malaysia, the Philippines, Singapore, Taiwan and Thailand.

All in all, there are clear signs of a tripolar division of the world into trade blocs centring around the EEA, NAFTA and South-east Asia. Lloyd (1992) has tried to test the proposition of regionalization and concludes that there is a trend towards regionalized trade since trade in Western Europe and Asia has increasingly become intra-regional trade. In a longer-term perspective Europe appears to be the most dynamic of these blocs in the one important sense that its bloc formation is more structured than that of Asia and its enlargement prospects more promising than those of NAFTA. One can foresee a double externalization effect of wider European integration. It accelerates the process of bloc enlargement by raising the costs for outsiders of remaining non-members. And it provokes retaliatory measures from other trade blocs, which incidentally also produce externalization effects. One thus detects a self-reinforcing tendency towards regionalization of the world economy. Two political factors reinforce the economic trend and exacerbate the problem of controlling regionalization. First of all, the leading power in Europe, Germany, is absorbed with domestic economic problems and may in the near future feel tempted to lend some support to the protectionists in the Union. Second, and probably more importantly, the US–European relationship is entering more troubled waters as a result of the collapse of bipolarity. Since Europe is no longer dependent upon the United States to protect it against the East, there will not be the same political will in Europe to constrain economic rivalry as used to be the case. Some may protest that the Gulf War proved Europe's continuing dependence on the United States for protection in the new era, but while this is certainly true in the short term, European politicians are going through a learning process. What is more, energy and raw-material dependence may well decrease significantly in the future if the European Union succeeds in building an economic partnership with Russia.

Obviously, the nexus between enlargement and protectionism in the European Union is a problem for the medium and longer term since it is first and foremost the adhesion of the Central and Eastern European countries which will prompt structural adjustments in other parts of the Union. One should also not overlook the possibility of new global countermeasures against regionalization such as systematic surveillance of regional free-trade arrangements.

It should be added that in the short term, enlargement of the Union is more likely to have positive effects for the outside world (Wijkman, 1993, p. 154). The adhesion of the EFTA countries will add to the strength of the free-trading coalition in the Union (basically the United Kingdom, Germany, the Netherlands and Denmark) and push the Union in the direction of a more liberal stance in international trade policy. Given the special '*tiermondiste*' tradition in the Third World policy of the EFTANs, EFTA adhesion is also likely to influence the Union's policy on development assistance. In this connection, one can foresee a serious clash between the Central and Eastern Europeans who will be anxious to protect possible gains in market shares in areas of importance for Third World producers and the former EFTA countries who will not necessarily be prepared to sacrifice Third World survival on the altar of East European welfare politics.

Enlargement will also add to the Union's status and influence as an international actor. While enlargement may in some cases weaken the decision-making capacity of the Union, as was the case in the 1980s with Greece, it will also lead to an expansion in the foreign-policy network of the Union. Each new member brings with it new diplomatic resources which will add to the international presence and actor capability of the Union (cf. Pedersen *et al.*, 1993b). In the case of the EFTA accession, this will strengthen the Union's Third World network as well as its links to the Central and Eastern European sub-region. Austrian adhesion will build up additional pressure for an early Hungarian adhesion to the Union and in any case will create a need for adjustments in the Union's agreements with Hungary. The adhesion of the Nordic EFTANs will speed up cooperation between the Union and the Baltic states since the Nordic countries have concluded free-trade agreements with the Baltic states and will do their utmost to prevent the erection of high economic and political barriers between the Union and these states. The Nordic EFTA countries, notably Sweden, have also made clear their intention to push the Union in the direction of a more activist policy with regard to the relationship between Russia and the small Baltic states. If Norway becomes a member of the Union, this will give the Union a common border with Russia in the North where the Union as a whole might be involved in joint projects with Russia dealing with *inter alia* the protection of the environment and resource policy. These advantage in terms of growth in the scope of the CFSP should be measured against the more uncertain and mainly negative effects on institutional capacity and cohesion (see above).

The effect of EFTA enlargement on Union policies in the field of security politics is more uncertain. Much depends on how one assesses the problem of neutrality and how the European security situation develops. As we have seen, all neutral applicants have at the declaratory level tried to redefine their policy of neutrality. They have also in practice demonstrated a clear willingness to take an active part in European conflict solution. Within the new Western community of values, the neutral EFTANs are far from being odd men out. Yet, neutrality is to some extent also a code word for a specific foreign-policy tradition. There are ideological differences between the majority of the small neutral EFTA states with their strong social democratic and/or pacifist traditions and the European big powers which often have different traditions. Although double standards have been applied in a number of cases, it remains a fact that several EFTA neutrals have for decades been conducting a 'social democratic foreign policy' at variance with NATO policy in some areas. While the cold war is a thing of the past (although new East–West divides may emerge), social democracy will not disappear quite so easily. One wonders therefore whether it is really in the interest of the European Union to insist that new members participate fully in the CFSP, keeping in mind neutral EFTANs like Sweden and Austria. Might not the adhesion of these countries to the WEU or a future European defence Union jeopardize the compromise worked out between NATO and the WEU and Union according to which the WEU is closely linked to NATO. And perhaps more importantly: how would the adhesion of these countries affect the Union's policy towards out-of-area conflicts in which specific European interests were threatened? On this interpretation, it is possible that the European Union will at the end of the day conclude that it is in its best interest to grant Sweden, Austria and Finland a 'Danish status' on the margins of the CFSP.

Much will also depend on the nature of the security threats facing the Union. Though to some extent security policy in the new Europe is about creating a new collective peace order, several of the current security threats to the Union have a distinct geographical bias, which could at some point place considerable strain on EU cohesion. A general shift of focus in European security policy towards the South could be expected to create tensions in an enlarged Union. It is not difficult to imagine how, for example, the prospect of massive illegal immigration from Northern Africa could elicit quite different policy responses from Paris, Madrid and Rome on the one hand, and Stockholm, Oslo and Vienna on the other.

Note

1. The expression has been coined by Curt Gasteyger.

References

Allen, Hilary (1979), *Norway and Europe in the 1970s.* Oslo: Universitets-forlaget.

Andriessen, Frans (1991), *Towards a Community of Twenty Four.* Speech by Vice-President Andriessen to the 69th Plenary Assembly of Eurochambers, Brussels, 19 April 1991.

Antola, Esko (1990), 'Finnish Perspectives on EC–EFTA Relations'. In Finn Laursen (ed.), *EFTA and the EC: Implications of 1992.* Maastricht: EIPA.

Antola, Esko (1991), 'Finland'. In Helen Wallace (ed.), *The Wider Western Europe.* London: Pinter.

Arnold, Hans (1989), 'Austria and the European Community'. *Aussen-politik*, IV/1989.

Axelrod, Robert (1984), *The Evolution of Cooperation.* New York: Basic Books.

Baldwin, Richard *et al.* (1992), *Is Bigger Better? The Economics of Enlargement.* London: Centre for Economic Policy Research.

Bergquist, Mats (1969), 'Sweden and the European Economic Community'. *Cooperation & Conflict*, vol. IV.

Bergquist, Mats (1970), *Sverige och EEC.* Stockholm: PA Norstedt & Söners Förlag.

Bildt, Carl (1993), *Address to 'La Fondation Paul-Henri Spaak'*, Palais des Academies, Brussels, 16 September 1993.

Biroli, C. Pirzio (1988), 'Balancing Burdens and Benefits'. In J. Jamar and H. Wallace (eds), *EEC – EFTA. More than Just Good Friends?* Bruges: College of Europe.

Bonjour, Edgar (1970), *Geschichte der Schweizerischen Neutralität.* Helbingen: Lichtenhahn.

Brittan, Leon (1991), *Finland and the European Community: Perspectives after 1992.* Speech by Sir Leon Brittan to the Central Chamber of Commerce of Finland, Helsinki, 30 September 1991.

Camps, Miriam (1964), *Britain and the European Community.* London: Oxford University Press.

Carlsnæs, Walter (1993), *Are the EFTA Neutrals Qua Neutrals Comparable?* Paper presented to the Planning Session on 'The EFTA Neutrals and the EC: Foreign Policy Implications of Membership', ECPR Joint Sessions of Workshops, Leiden, 2–8 April 1993.

Carlsson, Marianne (1991), *Att Välja Väg: Finlands roll i Europa.* Helsinki: Söderströms.

Charlton, Michael (1983), *The Price of Victory.* London: BBC.

Christoffersen, Henning (1991), *Speech at the World Economic Forum,* Prague, 21–2 November 1991.

Church, Clive (1993), *The Changing Domestic Dimensions of Swiss Neutrality.* Paper presented to the 21st Joint Sessions of Workshops, Leyden University, April 2–8, 1993.

Clerq, de Willy (1988), Report. In J. Jamar and H. Wallace (eds), *EEC – EFTA. More than Just Good Friends?* Bruges: College of Europe.

Davidson, Ian (1969), *Britain and the Making of Europe.* London: Macdonald.

Delors, Jacques (1989), 'Declarations sur les Orientations de la Commission des Communautés européennes'. *Agence Europe,* Documents, January 26.

Delors, Jacques (1990), 'Presentation of the Community's Programme for 1990'. *Bulletin of the European Community.* Supplement 1/1990, pp. 6–16.

Deubner, Christian (1980), 'The Southern Enlargement of the European Community'. *Journal of Common Market Studies.* Vol. XVIII, no. 3.

Deutsch, Karl W. (1957), *Political Community in the North Atlantic Area.* Princeton: Princeton University Press.

Dinkelspiel, Ulf (1992), *Information to Parliament concerning Sweden and the European Community,* Stockholm, 8 October 1992.

Dinkelspiel, Ulf (1993), *Statement by Ulf Dinkelspiel, Minister for European Affairs and Foreign Trade at the opening of Sweden's accession negotiations,* Brussels, 1 February 1993.

Duchacek, Ivo (1970), *Comparative Federalism.* New York: Holt, Rinehart and Winston.

EFTA from Yesterday to Tomorrow (1987). Geneva: EFTA Secretariat.

Ehlermann, Claus-Dieter (1990), 'The Institutional Development of the EC under the Single European Act'. *Aussenpolitik*, II/1990.

Eide, Espen Barth (1990), 'Europadebatten i Arbejderpartiet'. *International Politikk*, N. 3, 1990.

Etienne, Henri (1980), 'Community Integration: The External Environment'. *Journal of Common Market*, vol. XVIII, no. 4, June.

Fagerberg, Jan (1991), 'The Process of Economic Integration in Europe. Consequences of EFTA Countries and Firms'. *Cooperation and Conflict*, 4/1991, pp. 197–215.

Fischer, Roger and Scott Brown (1988), *Getting Together. How to Build a Relationship that Gets to Yes.* Boston: Houghton.

Fox, Anette Baker (1959), *The Power of Small States*, Chicago, University of Chicago Press.

Fox, Anette Baker (1964), *The Politics of Attraction.* New York.

Frei, Daniel (1967), *Neutralität – Ideal oder Kalkül?*, Frauenfeld & Stuttgart: Verlag Huber.

Frei, Daniel (1984), 'Integrationsprozesse'. In Werner Weidenfeld (Hrsg.), *Die Identität Europas.* Munich: Carl Hanser Verlag.

Gilpin, Robert (1987), *The Political Economy of Internal Relations.* Princeton: Princeton University Press.

Godal, Bjørn Tore (1993), *Statement at the Ministerial Meeting opening the Negotiations on the Accession of Norway to the European Communities*, Luxembourg, 5 April 1993.

Griffiths, Richard T. (1992), *The EEC and EFTA: The Formative Years, 1956–1963.* Unpublished draft paper.

Groom, A.J.R. and P. Taylor (eds) (1990), *Frameworks for International Cooperation.* London: Pinter.

Habeeb, William Mark (1987), *Power and Tactics in International Relations.* The Johns Hopkins University Press.

Hager, Wolfgang (1983), 'Little Europe, Wider Europe and Western Economic Cooperation'. In L. Tsoukalis (ed.), *The European Community. Past, Present and Future.* Oxford: Basil Blackwell.

Hakovirta, Harto (1988), *East–West Conflict and European Neutrality.* Oxford: Oxford University Press.

Hamilton, Carl B. (ed.) (1987), *Europa och Sverige.* Stockholm: SNS Förlag.

Hänsch, Klaus (1993), 'Vertiefung der Gemeinschaft und gesamteuropäische Identität. Ein System konföderaler Zusammenarbeit in Europa'. *Europa Archiv*, N. 13/14. 25 July.

Harrison, R.J. (1990). 'Neo-Functionalism'. In A.J.R. Groom and P. Taylor (eds), *Frameworks for International Cooperation*. London: Pinter.

Haskel, Barbara G. (1976), *The Scandinavian Option*. Oslo: Universitetsforlaget.

Hayes, Eric (1990), 'The Internal Market and EFTA as viewed from Brussels'. In Finn Laursen (ed.), *EFTA and the EC: Implications of 1992*. Maastricht: EIPA.

Hine, R.C. (1985), *The Political Economy of European Trade*. New York: Harvester Wheatsheaf.

Hosli, Madeleine (1992), *Voting Power in the EC Council of Ministers after an Adhesion of EFTA States: An Analysis Based on the Banzhaf Power Index*. Paper presented to the ISA Convention in Atlanta, GA. 31 March–4 April 1992.

Hubel, Helmut (1993), 'Finnland nach dem Ost–West-Konflikt. Vom Randstaat zum Stabilisierungsfaktor'. *Europa Archiv*, N. 15, 10 August.

Jacobsen, Max (1982), *Den Finländska Paradoxen*. Stockholm: P.A. Norstedt & Söners Förlag.

Jamar, J. and H. Wallace (1988), *EEC – EFTA. More than Just Good Friends?* Bruges: College of Europe.

Jenkins, Roy (1987), *European Diary*. London: Collins.

Kelstrup, Morten (ed.) (1992), *European Integration and Denmark's Participation*. Copenhagen: Copenhagen Political Studies Press.

Kelstrup, Morten (1990), 'Politologisk integrationsteori og den ny dynamik i Vest- og Østeuropa' (Political Science Theory on Integration and the New Dynamics in Western and Eastern Europe). In Morten Kelstrup (ed.), *Tendenser i Politologien* (Trends in Political Science) III. Copenhagen: Politiske Studier.

Keohane, Robert H. and Stanley Hoffmann (1990), 'Conclusions: Community Politics and Institutional change'. In William Wallace (ed.), *The Dynamics of European Integration*. London: Pinter.

Keohane, Robert H. and Joseph S. Nye (1989), *Power and Interdependence*. 2nd Edition. Glenview: Scott & Foresman.

Kivinen, Olli (1993), 'Finland: Coming in from the Cold'. *European Brief*, vol. 1, N. 1.

Koivisto, Mauno (1992), *Finland och Morgondagens Europa*. Tiden Förlag.

Koller, Arnold (1993), 'Die Schweiz und Europa. Eine integrationspolitische Standortbestimmung'. *Europa Archiv*, 13/14, 25 July.

Kramer, Heinz (1988), *Die Europäische Gemeinschaft und die Türkei*. Baden-Baden: Nomos.

Kramer, Heinz (1992), 'The EC and the Stabilisation of Eastern Europe'. *Aussenpolitik*, 1/1992.

Kremenyuk, Victor (ed.) (1991), *International Negotiation: Analysis, Approaches, Issues*. San Francisco: Jossey-Bass.

Krenzler, Horst (1993), 'Der Europäische Wirtschaftsraum als Teil einer gesamteuropäischen Architektur'. *Integration*, 2/92.

Kriesi, Hans-Peter *et al.* (1993), *Analyse de la Votation du 6 Septembre 1992*. Gfs Institut de Recherche, University of Geneva.

Landau, Alice (1993), *The Swiss Neutrality: Burgeoning Policy or Obstinate Continuity*. Paper presented to the ECPR Joint Sessions of Workshops, University of Leyden, April 1993.

Lange, Herman de (1988), 'Taking Stock of the EC–EFTA Dialogue'. In J. Jamar and Helen Wallace (eds), *EEC–EFTA. More than Just Good Friends?* Bruges: College of Europe.

Laursen, Finn (1990), 'The Community's Policy Towards EFTA: Regime Formation in the European Economic Space (EES)'. *Journal of Common Market Studies*, vol. XXVIII, no. 4, June 1990.

Laursen, Finn (1991), 'Comparative Regional Economic Integration: The European and Other Processes'. *International Review of Administrative Sciences*, vol. 57, pp. 515–26.

Laursen, Finn (1991–2), 'The EC and Its European Neighbours: Special Partnerships or Widened Memberships?', *International Journal*, vol. 47, no. 1 (Winter), pp. 29–63.

Leskela, Jukka and Seija Parviainen (1990), *EFTA Countries' Foreign Direct Investment*. Occasional Paper no. 34. Geneva: EFTA Secretariat.

Lindberg, Leon and Stuart Scheingold (1970), *Europe's Would-Be Polity*. New York: Prentice-Hall.

Lloyd, Peter J. (1992), 'Regionalization and World Trade'. *OECD Economic Studies*, no. 18, Spring 1992.

Lucas, Pierre (1990), 'Switzerland and the New EC–EFTA Dialogue: Comments on the National Report'. In Finn Laursen (ed.), *EFTA and the EC: Implications of 1992*. Maastricht: European Institute of Public Administration.

Luif, Paul (1988), *Neutrale in der EG?* Vienna: Wilhelm Braunmüller.

Luif, Paul (1991), 'Austria'. In Helen Wallace (ed.), *The Wider Western Europe*. London: Pinter.

Maclay, Michael (1992), *The Community beyond Maastricht*. London: Royal Institute of International Affairs.

Martens, Hans (1979), 'Danmarks Ja, Norges Nej. EF–folkeafstemningerne i 1972'. Copenhagen: *DUPI Skrift*, no. 6.

Meier, Alfred (1991), 'Schweizerische Optionen im Europäischen Integrationsprozess'. In *Herausvorderung Europa. Vereinigung für freies Unternehmentum.* Schaffhausen.

Michalski, Anna, Sarah Collinson and Hugh Miall (1993), *A Wider European Union? Integration and Cooperation in the New Europe.* London: RIIA Discussion Papers 48.

Michalski, Anna and Helen Wallace (1992), *The European Community: The Challenge of Enlargement.* London: Royal Institute of International Affairs.

Miljan, Toivo (1977), *The Reluctant Europeans.* London: C. Hurst.

Milward, Alan S. (1992), *The European Rescue of the Nation-State.* London: Routledge.

Mock, Alois (1990), 'Austria in a Changing Europe'. *The World Today,* March.

Mock, Alois (1993a), 'Austria. Ready and Waiting'. *European Brief,* vol. 1, no. 1.

Mock, Alois (1993b), Statement by the Austrian Federal Minister for Foreign Affairs Dr Aois Mock at the Ministerial Meeting opening the Conference on the Accession of Austria to the European Union, Brussels, 1 February 1993.

Moravcsik, Andrew (1991), 'Negotiating the Single European Act'. *International Organization,* 45/1, Winter.

Morin, Edgar (1987), *Penser L'Europe,* Paris: Gallimard.

Mouritzen, Hans (1988), *Finlandization: Towards a General Theory of Adaptive Politics.* Aldershot: Avebury.

Muftuler, Meltem (1992), *The Impact of External Factors on Internal Transformation: Turkey's Structural Adjustment Process and the European Community.* Paper presented to the Pan-European Conference on International Relations, Heidelberg, September.

Nedergaard, Peter (1991), 'Conceptualizing the EC Trade Policy: An Eclectic Framework'. *Business and Economic Studies on European Integration,* Copenhagen: Institute of International Economics, WP 16–91.

Nordlöf-Lagerkranz, Ulla (1990), *Svensk Neutralitet, Europa och EG.* Stockholm: Utrikespolitiska Institutet/MH Publishing.

Norge ved et Veivalg (Norway at the Cross-Roads) (1992), Europautredningen. Hovedrapport. Oslo: Utrikesdepartementet, November.

Odell, John S. (1982), *US International Monetary Policy. Markets, Power and Ideas as Sources of Change.* Princeton N.J.: Princeton University Press.

Pedersen, Thomas (1986), 'EF og Latinamerika'. Dansk Udenrigs-politisk Årbog 1985. Copenhagen: DJØF.

Pedersen, Thomas (1988), *The Wider Western Europe: EC Policy towards the EFTA Countries.* London: RIIA Discussion Paper, no. 10.

Pedersen, Thomas (1990), 'Problem of Enlargement: Political Integration in a Pan-European EC'. *Cooperation & Conflict,* XXV.

Pedersen, Thomas (1991a), 'Community Attitudes and Interests'. In Helen Wallace (ed.), *The Wider Western Europe.* London: Pinter.

Pedersen, Thomas (1991b), 'EC–EFTA Relations: An Historical Outline'. In Helen Wallace (ed.), *The Wider Western Europe.* London: Pinter.

Pedersen, Thomas (1991c), 'På vej mod EF–Unionen'. In *Norden i det nye Europa* (The Nordic region in the New Europe). Report from the Nordic Foreign Policy Institutes. Copenhagen, Stockholm, Oslo, Helsinki, Reykjavik.

Pedersen, Thomas (1992a), 'EFTA–Staaten und Europäischer Wirtschaftsraum'. *Jahrbuch der Europäischen Integration 1991/92.* Bonn: Europa Union Verlag.

Pedersen, Thomas (1992b), 'Maastricht traktaten i føderalistisk belysning (the Maastricht Treaty in a Federalist Interpretation). In Jon Bingen (ed.), *Europa etter Maastricht.* Oslo: Cappelen.

Pedersen, Thomas (1992c), 'Political Change in the European Community. The Single European Act as a Case of System Transformation'. *Cooperation & Conflict,* 1/1992.

Pedersen, Thomas (1993a), 'The Common Foreign and Security Policy (CFSP) and the Challenge of Enlargement'. In Ole Nørgaard, Thomas Pedersen and Nikolaj Petersen (eds), *The European Community in World Politics.* London: Pinter.

Pedersen, Thomas, Ole Nørgaard and Nikolaj Petersen (1993b), *The European Community in World Politics.* London: Pinter.

Pentland, Charles (1973), *International Theory and European Integration.* London: Faber and Faber.

Perez, P. (1988), 'Report'. In J. Jamar and H. Wallace (eds), *EEC–EFTA, More than Just Good Friends?* Bruges: College of Europe.

Petersen, Nikolaj (1991), *Tysklands enhed. Europas sikkerhed.* Copenhagen: SNU.

Redmond, John (1992), *The European Community and the Mediterranean Applicants.* Paper presented to the Pan-European Conference on International Relations. Heidelberg, September.

Regelsberger, Elfriede and Geoffrey Edwards (eds) (1990), *Europe's Global Links.* London: Pinter.

Riker, William H. (1964), *Federalism. Origin. Operation. Significance.* Boston: Little Brown & Company.

Ross, John F.L. (1991), 'Sweden, the European Community and the Politics of Economic Realism'. *Cooperation and Conflict,* 3/1991, pp. 117–28.

Rothstein, Robert (1979), *Global Bargaining: UNCTAD and the Quest for a New International Economic Order.* Princeton: Princeton University Press.

Salolainen, Pertti (1993), *Statement at the Ministerial Meeting Opening the Conference on the Accession of Austria, Sweden and Finland.* Brussels, 1 February 1993.

Sandholz, Wayne and John Zysman (1989), '1992: Recasting the European Bargain'. *World Politics,* vol. XLII, no. 1.

Schelling, Thomas (1963), *The Strategy of Conflict.* New York: Oxford University Press.

Schmieding, Holger (1989), 'A Concept of Pan-European Economic Integration'. *European Affairs,* 2/89.

Schmitter, Philippe C. (1969), 'Three Neo-Functionalist Hypotheses about International Integration'. *International Organization,* no. 23, pp. 161–6.

Schmitter, Philippe C. (1991), *The European Community as an Emergent and Novel Form of Political Domination.* Paper presented at the Center for Advanced Study in the Social Sciences of the Juan March Institute, Madrid, 16 May 1991.

Schneider, Heinrich (1990), *Alleingang nach Brüssel.* Bonn: Europa Union Verlag.

Schou, Tove-Lise (1980), *Norge og EF. En undersøgelse af ydre og indre faktorers påvirkning af de norske partiers stillingtagen til spørgsmålet om Norges forhold til EF 1961–72.* Copenhagen: Politiske Studier.

Schoutheete, Philippe de (1990), 'The European Community and Its Sub-Systems'. In William Wallace (ed.), *The Dynamics of European Integration.* London: Pinter.

Schwok, Rene (1989), 'Switzerland and the Price of the Single European Market'. In Kari Möttöla and Heikki Patomäki (eds), *Facing the Change in Europe. EFTA Countries' Integration Strategies.* Helsinki: Finnish Institute of International Affairs.

Schwok, Rene (1992), *European Integration and Swiss Identities.* Paper presented to the British International Studies Association (BISA), 15 December 1992.

Skak, Mette (1991), *East Europe, the Soviet Union and Europeanisation.* Paper for the 1991 Annual APSA Meeting, Washington DC, 29 August –1 September.

Skak, Mette (1993), 'The EC Policy of the Visegrad Countries'. In Ole Nørgaard, Thomas Pedersen and Nikolaj Petersen (eds), *The European Community in World Politics*. London: Pinter.

Stares, Paul B. (ed.) (1992), *The New Germany and the New Europe*. Washington DC: The Brookings Institution.

Stoltenberg, Thorvald (1992), *Utenrikspolitisk redegørelse for Stortinget* (Foreign Policy Statement before the Storting), 10 February, UD Information.

Story, Jonathan (1993), *The New Europe*. Oxford: Basil Blackwell.

Stålvant, Carl-Einar (1990), 'Rather a Market than a Home, but Preferably a Home Market'. In Finn Laursen (ed.), *EFTA and the EC: Implications of 1992*. Maastricht: European Institute of Public Administration.

Sucharipa, Ernst (1993), 'Von der Neutralität zur europäischen Sicherheitsidentität: Österreich und die Europäische Union'. *Integration*, 3/1993.

Sundelius, Bengt (1989), *The Committed Neutral*. Boulder: Westview Press.

Sundelius, Bengt (1990), 'Neutralitet och konfliktfylld interdependens'. In Ulla Nordlöf-Lagerkranz (ed.), *Svensk Neutralitet, Europa och EG*. Stockholm: Utrikespolitiska Institutet/MH Publishing.

Sæter, Martin (1990), 'Norway'. In Finn Laursen (ed.), *EFTA and the EC: Implications of 1992*. Maastricht: European Institute of Public Administration.

Sæter, Martin and Olav F. Knudsen (1991), 'Norway'. In Helen Wallace (ed.), *The Wider Western Europe*. London: Pinter.

Tashan, Seyfi (1992), *Turkey and the European Community*. Speech to the Second Annual Conference of Journalists, Istanbul, 20–21 November.

Taylor, Michael (1987), *The Possibility of Cooperation*. Cambridge: Cambridge University Press.

Thune, Christian (1987), 'Denmark, Europe and the Creation of EFTA.' In *EFTA from Yesterday to Tomorrow*. Geneva: EFTA.

Törnudd, Klaus (1969), 'Finland and Economic Integration in Europe'. *Cooperation and Conflict*, vol. IV.

Tranholm-Mikkelsen, Jeppe (1990), *Neo-Functionalism: Obstinate or Obsolete? A Reappraisal in the Light of the New Dynamism of the EC*. Millennium.

Tsoukalis, Loukas (1981), *The European Community and Its Mediterranean Enlargement*. Oxford: Oxford University Press.

Turner, Barry and G. Nordquist (1982), *The Other European Community*. London: Weidenfeld & Nicolson.

Ugglas, Margareta von (1992), *Sweden at the Heart of Europe*. Address by the Swedish Minister for Foreign Affairs at Chatham House, 26 November.

Underdal, Arild (1973), 'Multinational Negotiating Parties: The Case of the European Community'. *Cooperation & Conflict*, vol. VIII.

Verheijen, Tony (1992), *Towards a United States of Europe: Possible Scenarios for incorporating Central and Eastern Europe in the EC*. Maastricht: European Institute of Public Administration.

Vibe, Johan (1992), 'Norden – et samarbejde nedefra? (The Nordic Region – a Collaboration from Below). In Iver B. Neumann (ed.), *Hva skjedde med Norden?* Oslo: Cappelen/Europaprogrammet.

Wallace, Helen (1989), *Widening and Deepening: The European Community and the New European Agenda*. London: RIIA Discussion Paper no. 23.

Wallace, Helen (1991a), *The Wider Western Europe*. London: Pinter.

Wallace, Helen (1991b), 'Vers un espace économique européen'. *Revue du Marché Commun et de l'Union européenne*. no. 351, pp. 694–703.

Wallace, Helen and Wolfgang Wessels (1989), *Towards a New Partnership: The EC and EFTA in the Wider Western Europe*. EFTA Occasional Paper no. 28. Geneva: EFTA Secretariat.

Wallace, William (1985), 'Relaunching the Western European Union: Variable Geometry, Institutional Duplication or Policy Drift?'. In P. Tsakaloyannis (ed.), *The Reactivation of the WEU*. Maastricht: European Institute of Public Administration.

Wallace, William (1989), *The Transformation of Western Europe*. London: Pinter.

Walton, Richard and Robert Mckersie (1965), *A Behavioral Theory of Labor Negotiations*. Ithaca: Cornell University Press.

Webb, Carole (1983), 'Theoretical Perspectives and Problems'. In Helen Wallace, William Wallace and Carole Webb (eds), *Policy-Making in the European Community*. London: John Wiley and Sons.

Weber, Shlomo and Hans Wiesmeth (1992), 'Issue Linkage in the European Community'. *Journal of Common Market Studies*, vol. XXIX, no. 3.

Wessels, Wolfgang (1990), 'Institutionelle Strategien für die Politische Union: Eine Neuaflage der EEA?' *Integration*, 13/4/1990.

Wijkman, Per (1990), 'Patterns of Production and Trade'. In William Wallace (ed.), *The Dynamics of European Integration*. London: Pinter.

Wijkman, Per (1993), 'The Existing Bloc Expanded? The European Community, EFTA and Eastern Europe'. In C. Fred Bergsten and Marcus Noland (eds), *Pacific Dynamism and the International Economic*

System. Washington DC: Institute for International Economics.

Woschnagg, G. (1988), 'Balancing Burdens and Benefits: EFTA's View'. In J. Jamar and H. Wallace (eds), *EEC–EFTA. More than Just Good Friends?* Bruges: College of Europe.

Wæver, Ole *et al.* (1993), *Identity, Migration and the new Security Agenda in Europe.* London: Pinter.

Zartman, William I. (1988), 'Common Elements in the Analysis of the Negotiation Process'. *Negotiation Journal,* January.

Newspapers and periodicals

Aftenposten
Agence Europe
Dagbladet (Oslo)
Dagens Nyheter
Die Zeit
EC-Bulletin
Economist
EFTA Annual Reports
EFTA Bulletin
EFTA Information
EFTA News
EFTA Trade
Financial Times
Frankfurter Allgemeine
Göteborg Posten
Guardian
Hufvudstadsbladet
Independent
Information (DK)
Le Monde
Le Monde Diplomatique
Neue Zürcher Zeitung
OECD Economic Outlook
OECD Historical Statistics
Politiken (DK)
Reuters
Trend (Austria)
Wall Street Journal

Appendix

Table A.1 EFTA: Country indicators

	Austria	Finland	Norway	Sweden	Switzerland	EFTA 5 Total/ Average
1. Population	7,555,338	4,910,619	4,091,132	8,360,178	6,365,960	31,283,227
2. Surface area (km²)	83,853	338,127	323,895	449,964	41,293	1,237,132
3. Average life span (years)	75.44	74.67	76.6	77.1	77.3	76.2
4. GDP US$ million (1990)	157,378	137,251	105,703	228,110	224,845	853,287
5. GDP per capita per year (1990) in $000	20.830	27.950	25.837	27.285	35.319	27.444
6. Unemployment rate (1993)	4.8%	16.6%	5.7%	7.3%	4.6%	7.8%
7. Inflation (1992)	4.0%	2.9%	2.3%	2.3%	4.0%	3.1%
8. Annual growth rate (1992)	1.5%	-3.5%	3.3%	-1.7%	-0.6%	-0.2%
9. Employed in agriculture (1992)	7.6%	8.4%	5.4%	3.2%	N.A.	6.15%

Sources: 1-5 *UN Statistical Yearbook*, 38th edition, UN, New York, 1993.
6-8 *OECD Economic Outlook* 53, June 1993. OECD, Paris.
9. *ILO Year Book of Labour Statstics* 1992, ILO.

Table A.2 EC trade with EFTA

EFTA countries	EU imports Ecu million 1992	% of total import	Rank*	EU exports Ecu million 1992	% of total exports	Rank**
Austria	23,075	4.7	5	29,670	6.8	3
Finland	10,854	2.2	8	7,508	1.7	14
Norway	17,199	3.5	6	9,852	2.3	8
Sweden	24,611	5.0	4	21,393	4.9	4
Switzerland	34,933	7.2	3	38,601	8.9	2
Total	110,672	22.6		107,024	24.6	

*Ranked in order of importance as exporters to EU.
**Ranked in order of importance as markets for EU export.
Source: Eurostat, Udenrigshandel og Betalingsbalancer, 1993.

Index